MAKING SENSE OF
EVERY CHILD MATTERS

Multi-professional practice guidance

Edited by Richard Barker

This edition published in Great Britain in 2009 by

The Policy Press
University of Bristol
Fourth Floor
Beacon House
Queen's Road
Bristol BS8 1QU
UK

Tel +44 (0)117 331 4054
Fax +44 (0)117 331 4093
e-mail tpp-info@bristol.ac.uk
www.policypress.org.uk

North American office:
The Policy Press
c/o International Specialized Books Services (ISBS)
920 NE 58th Avenue, Suite 300
Portland,
OR 97213-3786, USA
Tel +1 503 287 3093 • Fax +1 503 280 8832
e-mail info@isbs.com

British Library Cataloguing in Publication Data
A catalogue record for this book is available from the British Library.

Library of Congress Cataloging-in-Publication Data
A catalog record for this book has been requested.

ISBN 978 1 84742 011 4 paperback

Cover design by IN-Text Design, Bristol.
Front cover: thanks to Edward Brewer (aged 9) and Alice Brewer (aged 6).
Printed and bound in Great Britain by MPG Books, Bodmin.

Contents

List of tables and figures   iv

List of acronyms   v

Notes on contributors   viii

Introduction: making sense of Every Child Matters   I
Richard Barker

one   Beginning to understand Every Child Matters   5
           Richard Barker

two   Interprofessional working and the children's workforce   29
           Pamela Graham and Alison I. Machin

three   Education and Every Child Matters   45
           Pat Broadhead and Douglas Martin

four   Early years, childcare and Every Child Matters   59
           Joan Santer and Lindey Cookson

five   Sure Start Children's Centres and Every Child Matters   79
           Sue Barker

six   Nursing and Every Child Matters   95
           Steve Campbell and Judith Hunter

seven   Maternity care and Every Child Matters   III
           Fiona Hutchinson

eight   Playwork and Every Child Matters   129
           Lesli Godfrey

nine   Social work and Every Child Matters   147
           Richard Barker and Sue Barker

ten   Child and adolescent mental health services and Every Child Matters   169
           Allan Brownrigg

eleven   Every Child Matters: current possibilities, future opportunities and   187
           challenges
           Richard Barker

List of tables and figures

Figures

1.1	ECM and the CAF continuum	14
2.1	Multi-professional working: traditional model	33
2.2	Multi-professional working: integrated model	33
2.3	Towards integrated working	34
2.4	ECM and integrated services	35
2.5	ECM and integrated services: integrated working at the core	36
5.1	Harrow Council Wheel of partners and services	92
9.1	Framework for the Assessment of Children in Need	155
11.1	Integrating children's services	195

Tables

2.1	ECM levels of integration: influences on interprofessional working	37
2.2	Collaboration and integration: a case example	39
2.3	Strengths, challenges, opportunities, risks and expectations that professionals might face in working interprofessionally	41
4.1	Recent developments in early years and childcare policy and legislation	62
9.1	ICS functions that replace child protection register functions	157
10.1	Examples of professionals working within a tiered approach to CAMHS	171

List of acronyms

ACPC	Area Child Protection Committee
APA	annual performance assessment
BASW	British Association of Social Workers
CA	common assessment
CAF	Common Assessment Framework
Cafcass	Children's and Family Court Advisory and Support Service
CAMHS	child and adolescent mental health services
CBT	cognitive behavioural therapy
CGWT	Children Care Group Workforce Teams
CHPP	Child Health Promotion Programme
CPD	continuing professional development
CSCI	Commission for Social Care Inspection
CWDC	Children's Workforce Development Council
CYPP	Children and Young People's Plans
CYPS	children's and young people's services
DCMS	Department for Culture, Media and Sport
DCS	Director of Children's Services
DCSF	Department for Children, Schools and Families
DES	Department of Education and Science
DfES	Department for Education and Skills
DHSS	Department of Health and Social Security
DoH	Department of Health
EBP	evidence-based practice
ECM	Every Child Matters
EIP	evidence-informed practice
EPO	emergency protection order
EPPE	Effective Provision of Preschool Education
ERA	1988 Education Reform Act
EWO	education welfare officer
EYDCP	Early Years Development and Childcare Partnership
EYP	early years professional
FCA	family court adviser
GDP	gross domestic product
GNC	General Nursing Council
GSCC	General Social Care Council
GTC	General Teaching Council for England
HAS	Health Advisory Service
ICS	Integrated Children's System
IFSW	International Federation of Social Workers
ILP	individual learning plan
IQF	Integrated Qualifications Framework

JAR	joint area review
LEA	local education authority
LM	Lead Member for Children's Services
LP	lead professional
LSA	Local Supervising Authority
LSCB	Local Safeguarding Children Board
MHF	Mental Health Foundation
MSW	maternity support worker
NCH	National Children's Home
NESS	National Evaluation of Sure Start
NFER	National Foundation for Educational Research
NHS	National Health Service
NICE	National Institute for Clinical Excellence
NISW	National Institute of Social Work
NMC	Nursing and Midwifery Council
NNP	neonatal nurse practitioner
NOS	National Occupational Standards
NPQICL	National Professional Qualification in Integrated Centre Leadership
NQF	National Qualifications Framework
NQSW	newly qualified social worker
NQT	newly qualified teacher
NRwS	New Relationship with Schools
NSF	National Service Framework
NSPCC	National Society for the Prevention of Cruelty to Children
NVQ	National Vocational Qualifications
OCD	obsessive compulsive disorder
ODPM	Office of the Deputy Prime Minister
Ofsted	Office for Standards in Education/Office for Standards in Education, Children's Services and Skills
ONS	Office for National Statistics
PCT	Primary Care Trusts
PGCE	Postgraduate Certificate in Education
PMHW	primary mental health workers
PVI	private, voluntary and independent
QCA	Qualifications and Curriculum Authority
QTS	qualified teacher status
RCM	Royal College of Midwifery
RCN	Royal College of Nursing
RCPCH	Royal College of Pediatrics and Child Health
RCT	randomised controlled trial
SAT	standard assessment task
SCIE	Social Care Institute for Excellence
SCITT	school-centred initial teacher training

SfH	Skills for Health
SHA	Strategic Health Authority
SSC	Sector Skills Council
SSLP	Sure Start Local Programmes
TfC	Together for Children
UN	United Nations
UNCRC	UN Convention of the Rights of the Child
UNICEF	United Nations Children's Fund
WHO	World Health Organization

Notes on contributors

Richard Barker is Professor of Child Welfare at Northumbria University. He is a registered social worker and qualified teacher with wide experience of social work, research and consultancy with services for children and families in the UK and overseas. His research interests include child welfare issues, services for children, lone fathers, and globalisation and its relationships to children's services.

Sue Barker is a registered social worker with a career of more than 40 years in children's social care as a practitioner and strategic manager. She is a previous regional programme lead with Together for Children, responsible for supporting and challenging local authorities in the development of their Sure Start Children's Centres and working closely with Government Offices and local authorities. Her recent and current practice involves working at assistant director level, steering the recovery of children's social care services.

Pat Broadhead is Professor of Playful Learning at Leeds Metropolitan University. She began her career as a nursery nurse, going on to qualify as a teacher and to work in early years and primary settings. Her main research interests are around open-ended play in educational settings, and she has also researched the development of the children's workforce.

Allan Brownrigg is Senior Lecturer in Child Welfare at Northumbria University with qualifications in social work, systemic practice and cognitive therapy. His practice has centred on mental health, working with children and young people in family settings, and his research interests are in self-injury, suicidal ideation and resilience. More recently, Allan has practised as a cognitive behavioural psychotherapist specialising in the treatment of trauma.

Steve Campbell has a joint appointment as a professor of nursing at Northumbria University and with a local hospital trust. He is a qualified children's nurse with experience in acute paediatrics, and has also worked as one of the few male health visitors in the UK. He was head of a university department of children's nursing, and is a previous chair of the Association of British Paediatric Nurses. In recent years, his joint appointment has kept him close to the application of theory and policy to practice. He is shortly to become a dean of the School of Health at the University of New England, Australia.

Lindey Cookson is Senior Lecturer for Care and Education (Early Years) at Northumbria University, and Lead Assessor for the early years professional provision. She began her career as a nursery nurse, before moving into lecturing after graduating from Newcastle University. She then worked for a local authority Early Years Development and Childcare Partnership, leading on workforce development for the early years and childcare sector, which encouraged further her particular interests in early years policy and the children's workforce agenda.

Lesli Godfrey started her playwork career aged 18, as a holiday playscheme worker, and since then has continued working for children in a range of settings. She now works as the National Programme Manager for Playwork Education, Training and Qualifications with SkillsActive, the sector skills council for active leisure and learning, where she co-ordinates the development of qualifications for playwork.

Pamela Graham is Director for the Children's Agenda in the School of Health, Community and Education Studies at Northumbria University. Before coming to the university to lecture in early childhood studies, she worked as an early childhood practitioner and as a community worker in a range of settings: as manager of a multi-agency family support centre, in training and staff development for a social services department and as a lecturer at Newcastle University. Her main research interests are parenting and childhood.

Judith Hunter MBE is a qualified children's nurse who has worked in acute paediatrics in the UK and the Netherlands and who has extensive experience of linking policy with practice. She has been a hospital head of children's nursing and is currently working in an acute NHS hospital as a clinical director in trauma and orthopaedics.

Fiona Hutchinson is Senior Lecturer in Nursing and Midwifery at Northumbria University, where she teaches on courses ranging from pre-registration through to masters level. Her nursing background is in neonatal intensive care and she is course leader for the Neonatal Nurse Practitioner course. She has an interest in the concept of evidence-based practice, and her research and professional interests are practice development.

Alison I. Machin is Director of Interprofessional Education (IPE) in the School of Health, Community and Education Studies at Northumbria University. Her key area of responsibility is the strategic development, leadership and management of interprofessional learning and teaching activity in the school. Her research interests include pedagogic research into IPE, the development and maintenance of professional identity in an increasingly integrated public sector and managing collaborative workforce change.

Douglas Martin is currently a full-time PhD Centennial student at Leeds Metropolitan University researching extended services and Every Child Matters (ECM). He is a previous lead officer on ECM developments for Leeds City Council, and also supported the development of ECM nationally via secondment to the DCSF.

Joan Santer is Senior Lecturer in Childhood Studies at Northumbria University. She has worked in teaching and nursery settings, as an adviser in early years for a local authority and as a lecturer at Newcastle University where she developed and was director of the Early Childhood Studies degree. She has worked as a consultant in Europe and Africa, and has undertaken research for the Nuffield Foundation, the Home Office and for the Play Council who recently published her literature review *Free play in early childhood*.

Contributors have written in a personal capacity and the views expressed do not necessarily reflect those of their employing agencies.

Introduction: making sense of Every Child Matters

Richard Barker

The purpose of this book is to consider the implications of the Every Child Matters (ECM) agenda for changes to children's services in the 21st century, and the consequent possibilities and difficulties related to the development of what has been termed the 'new children's workforce'. This will be done with particular reference to issues viewed in the light of the relevant different professionals' viewpoints and practices.

This book contains a wide range of contributions from experts in the main disciplines and professions that form the 'new children's workforce' and who are thus key to achieving the ECM programme objectives for children. These chapters, which focus on and analyse ECM from a particular professional or work perspective, have been written so they can stand alone in their own right, while forming part of a coherent overview of the book's topics.

The premises that this book is based on include that:

1. The work of individuals and agencies should primarily be to improve the position of children not improve the position of individuals and agencies.
2. It is important for those who work with and for children and their families to understand their own role, and the roles of others with whom they should be co-operating to provide the best services possible.
3. Multi-professional work with children should be based on accepting and, indeed, celebrating the different contributions made by the individual professions and agencies, not seeking to change them so that each is offering something similar.
4. The social and policy context of children's services influences individual work and vice versa.

At a time of change, such as that currently experienced by children's services members, it is both more difficult and more important to achieve the above. The introductory chapter looks at the ECM agenda and related developments to set the context for the different contributors that follow. The breadth of the agenda regarding services for children and young people is enormous. This book is primarily focused on services for and with children; while they are touched on in places youth services and youth offending issues are not a central focus of any of the chapters.

In Chapter One, the editor looks at the background to the Every Child Matters agenda, and the range of initiatives and developments that are contained within it and relate to it. Key developments are introduced and described to set the overall context for subsequent chapters.

In Chapter Two, Pamela Graham and Alison Machin look at issues relating to ECM and the challenges and possibilities for professionals and agencies to work together. They suggest that to be successful ECM demands a move from traditional and integrated methods of multi-professional working towards new ways of interprofessional working, and consider the problems and possibilities involved.

The chapters that follow, until the final chapter, move from the more universal to the more selective services for children – the fact that not everyone will agree with the choice within this ordering in itself illustrates the different views of, and the complexity within and between, services and professions. Each chapter provides a brief recent history and description of the current position with regard to the ECM agenda and to work and professional issues in respect of the area under consideration. Having regard to what the specialist authors feel is most significant for their areas, each chapter reflects on the tasks undertaken by workers in the specialism/area they are considering, and a description of the professional area in relation to structure, roles, current training processes and current trends. Following this each chapter looks at the contributions of the profession to achieving the ECM themes, including significance issues with respect to skills and knowledge and particular challenges for the profession. The role of the profession in contributing to the assessment of children's needs and multi-disciplinary working is considered, and chapters conclude with a discussion of areas of significance for development and future trends.

Thus in Chapter Three Pat Broadhead and Doug Martin look at the ways in which the education system and those who work within and with it have responded to and shaped the ECM agenda. They suggest that many schools have focused on the cognitive at the expense of the affective, to the detriment, at times, of children being able to 'enjoy' as well as 'achieve', with negative impacts on their childhoods.

In Chapter Four Joan Santer and Lindey Cookson consider early years and childcare. Having located this in its historical and policy context, they describe and reflect on the current position. Issues highlighted include the possible negative impacts on children of an 'outcome driven' early years foundation stage, and the uncertain impact of the newly introduced early years professionals.

In Chapter Five Sue Barker looks at the history and context of Sure Start Children's Centres. She suggests that they are central to the holistic delivery of the Every Child Matters agenda, while coping with the demands of challenging rapid development. Policy and practice issues faced by Sure Start Children's Centres include the tensions between delivering universal and targeted services, striking a balance within the range of services for children and parents offered, and achieving effective teamwork within centres while at the same time enabling them to have strong, open links with their local communities.

In Chapter Six Steve Campbell and Judith Hunter look at the contributions of nursing to the ECM agenda and consider some of the implications of the agenda for nursing. They note the challenge to overcome the fragmentation between different elements of nursing itself and between hospital and primary care, and suggest ways in which nursing needs to develop at qualifying and post-qualifying levels to best contribute to children's services.

In Chapter Seven Fiona Hutchinson focuses on the contribution of maternity services to the ECM agenda. She describes the range of services available in hospitals and communities, and looks at how the challenges of improving outcomes for disadvantaged families, optimising the skill mix of the workforce, and providing a choice of safe, flexible care for women might be addressed.

In Chapter Eight Lesli Godfrey considers playwork for school-age children and its response to ECM, placing the current profile of playwork in its historical context. She explores the challenges of playwork being increasingly located in settings and environments that do not chime with the professionally desired principle of 'freely chosen, personally directed, intrinsically motivated play', suggesting, nevertheless, that there are positive opportunities for playwork and for children.

In Chapter Nine the editor and Sue Barker look at social work's contribution to ECM. Topics explored include the specialist nature and role of the social work task, the ways in which social work can contribute to the five ECM outcomes, and the genericism versus specialism debate within social work.

In Chapter Ten Allan Brownrigg considers and describes ECM and child and adolescent mental health services, including a discussion about evidence-based practice. He suggests that there are problems in relation to the need for and availability of CAMHS, and that children at risk of developing mental disorders may often go unrecognised. He concludes with an outline of areas that need improvement.

The book concludes with an overview of some of the main issues for current and future development and consideration in relation to children's services and ECM.

There are some areas of overlap between chapters, which reflects the areas of overlap of services to children and young people. There are also some areas of difference between chapters, which reflects the diversity in different elements of children's services.

Although each chapter can largely stand alone in its own right, to appreciate the range of services to children that ECM is seeking to influence and to respond to, a fuller picture will be gained by the reader consulting more than any one chapter.

ONE

Beginning to understand Every Child Matters

Richard Barker

'Every Child Matters' has featured in the title of a number of government publications and is best now understood as the overarching name for an approach towards children, their families and significant others. Every Child Matters (ECM) was introduced as a Green Paper – a consultation relating to possible government legislation (DfES, 2003). The following year the government produced *Every Child Matters: Next steps* and passed the 2004 Children Act, thus 'providing the legislative spine for developing more effective and accessible services focused around the needs of children, young people and families' (DfES, 2004a).

Following this, *Every Child Matters: Change for children* (DfES, 2004b) was published in 2004. This document seeks to be an integrated and government-originated approach aimed to improve the well-being of children and young people from birth to age 19.

> The government's aim is for every child, whatever their background or their circumstances, to have the support they need to:
>
> • Be healthy
> • Stay safe
> • Enjoy and achieve
> • Make a positive contribution
> • Achieve economic well-being
>
> This means that the organisations involved with providing services to children – from hospitals and schools, to police and voluntary groups – will be teaming up in new ways, sharing information and working together, to protect children and young people from harm and help them achieve what they want in life. (DfES, 2004b)

Reforming services to children and families, so that they support the five outcomes more effectively, with a stronger focus on early identification and prevention, requires and has required action at national and local levels. The ambitious aim is that a clear, supportive national framework needs to be put in place to underpin this vision. To this end, the Department for Children, Schools and Families

(DCSF) Children's Workforce Unit (previously at the Department for Education and Skills) is developing:

- the Children's Workforce Strategy (DfES, 2005), which sets out action to be taken nationally and locally to ensure that there are the skills, ways of working and capacity in the children's workforce to deliver change for children;
- practical guidance on multi-agency working;
- the Common Assessment Framework (DfES, 2004c);
- a common core of skills and knowledge for the children's workforce;
- a 'climbing frame' of qualifications building on the common core, to ease progression and support retention of staff;
- a better infrastructure for employer-led reform through the emerging Children, Young People and Families Workforce Development Council, which will be part of the Social Care, Children and Young People's Sector Skills Council.

The context for children in the UK

While at times there are contradictory attitudes towards children, as will be discussed elsewhere in this book, over the past decade there have been some improvements in their positions, and it has been an explicit policy of the Labour government to seek to reduce child poverty in Britain substantially. Since 1997 the proportion of children living in poverty has declined, and the proportion of GDP spent on benefits for children has increased from 1.38% to 2.04% (1997–2003); however, in 2005 there were still 3.3 million children living in poverty (compared with 4.4 million in 1997). Although child poverty in Western Europe is not as grave as elsewhere in the world, children in the UK are, relatively speaking, worse off: 23% of UK children are officially living in poverty; compared with 18% for original EU members and 5% for Denmark (UNICEF, 2005). Within the UK there are also clear class differences in relation to experiences associated with 'life chances', for example 15% of children of 'unskilled workers' go to university, compared with 79% of children of 'professionals', and there are also other structural and related factors that affect life chances particularly gender, minority ethnic status, disabilities and episodes within public care. In relation to child well-being, in 2007 the UK was evaluated as being at the bottom of a league table of 21 industrialised countries across the six categories of material well-being, family and peer relationships, health and safety, behaviour and risks, and children's own sense of well-being (the Netherlands and Sweden were placed first and second) (UNICEF, 2007). Increasingly, there have been concerns about a range of other issues and children (Hendrick, 2003; 2005), including an increase in the rates of childhood obesity (House of Commons, 2007), an increase in the extent and negative impact of alcohol consumption amongst children (NHS, 2007), the sexualisation of childhood (DoH, 2007), and the continuing targeting of children as commercial consumers (Schor, 2004).

The 1989 Children Act

The main legislation regulating the area covered by the ECM strategy prior to and at the time of its launch was the 1989 Children Act (DoH, 1989). To an extent, the Act partly echoed some of the principles of the United Nations Convention on the Rights of the Child 1989 (UN, 1989), which was ratified by the UK government in 1991.

The convention gives children and young people over 40 substantive rights. These include the right to:

- special protection measures and assistance;
- access services such as education and health care;
- develop their personalities, abilities and talents to the fullest potential;
- grow up in an environment of happiness, love and understanding;
- be informed about and participate in achieving their rights in an accessible and active manner.

The Act looked forward to a position in which children were seen to have rights, with parents having responsibilities towards them, rather than parents having rights and children being passive recipients of their care and control. In so doing, the 1989 Children Act (legislation that went through parliament with all-party support) had a number of key principles including:

- children tend to do best if brought up in families;
- parental responsibility towards children is more important than parental rights over children;
- partnership (although not defined in the legislation) should be the basis for working with children and families;
- the welfare of the child is paramount in decision making;
- the law and the courts should only intervene and make an order if it is better to do so than not do so;
- a minimum of delay in court proceedings;
- courts should use the results of a 'welfare checklist', part of which is designed to ascertain children's views when making judgments;
- a strong emphasis on planning what outcomes are necessary and how they are to be achieved for the particular child or children.

While the 1989 Children Act has been seen as partly successful in improving the position of children in society, there is a view that it has never been underpinned by sufficient resources for the services that deal with children to enable all its aims to be achieved, for example, continuing delays in court proceedings have undermined the meeting of children's and families needs in many cases. As will be seen later, the 2004 Children Act has further developed legislation in respect of children, particularly in respect of their protection – the safeguarding of their welfare.

The 1989 Children Act defines children as being those under the age of 18, as does the UN Convention on the Rights of the Child (UN, 1989), to which the UK is a signatory. This sets out the rights of children and the obligations of government in relation to areas including the right to civil liberties, life, health, social care, education and freedom from abuse. Nevertheless, in the UK (as in other countries) the formal and informal rights of children vary and at times may appear contradictory or at times confusing. In England the 1985 House of Lords case *Gillick v West Norfolk and Wisbech Area Health Authority* established that children under the age of 16 could, subject to their level of understanding, consent to medical treatment without the involvement of their parents. In contrast, the 2007 Animal Welfare Act makes it illegal for children under 16 to buy a pet. While children of seven can open bank accounts, those under 18 still do not have the right to vote in elections and, at the time of writing, the government have announced that they plan to raise the age at which children can leave education or training to 18. Different value positions that reflect the, at times, contradictory stances and policies that relate to children and the state are considered in the concluding chapter of this book.

These and other factors will have impacts on and be reflected in the ECM agenda and related developments. Before looking at this in more detail, it is helpful to consider the background to ECM.

Background to Every Child Matters

There is a long history in the UK for changes to services to children to be triggered in part by responses to the death of a child. Thus, the death of O'Neill (Monckton, 1945) led directly to the 1946 Children Act and the subsequent local authority Children's Departments. Throughout the last three decades of the 20th century there were a number of inquiries into child deaths that subsequently influenced policies and practices in respect of services to children (Parton, 1985), among them Maria Colwell (DHSS, 1974) and Jasmine Beckford (Blom-Cooper, 1985). Related to these, although not always directly, state intervention regarding children increased at times (for example as highlighted by the events in Cleveland (Butler-Sloss, 1988; Campbell, 1988) or decreased (for example following the so-called refocusing approach in the 1990s when services and professionals were encouraged to take a 'lighter touch' in relation to allegations of abuse [DoH, 1995]).

catalyst

The immediate catalyst of the introduction of ECM was the response to the death of Victoria Climbié in 2000 (Laming, 2003), although changes in services were being planned in any event so it is not entirely accurate to say that her death 'caused' the ECM programme.

Victoria Adjo Climbié was born in the Ivory Coast in 1991, the fifth of seven children. She died in London on 25 February 2000 as a result of horrific abuse caused by her great aunt and her great aunt's boyfriend. During the time she lived in the UK Victoria was seen, for health and welfare reasons, by a wide range of representatives from different social services departments, health services and hospitals, as well as the police, but all failed to intervene appropriately in order to protect her. The subsequent inquiry, established to inquire into the circumstances surrounding her death, concluded that:

> Not one of the agencies empowered by Parliament to protect children in positions similar to Victoria's − funded from the public purse − emerge from this Inquiry with much credit. The suffering and death of Victoria was a gross failure of the system and was inexcusable. It is clear to me that the agencies with responsibility for Victoria gave a low priority to the task of protecting children. They were under-funded, inadequately staffed and poorly led. Even so, there was plenty of evidence to show that scarce resources were not being put to good use. (Laming, 2003, s 1.18)

[handwritten margin note: negs of multi-agency approach as no-one communicated]

The report made 108 recommendations for changes to services to children at a national and local level, and within and between the different agencies and professions. While some were not translated into subsequent action, many were and have been influential in the development of the ECM.

ECM was published as a Green Paper (DfES, 2003) alongside the Laming Report (Laming, 2003). It was suggested by the government that ECM built on their existing plans to strengthen preventative services by focusing on four key themes:

1. increasing the focus on supporting families and carers − the most critical influence on children's lives;
2. ensuring necessary intervention takes place before children reach crisis point and protecting children from falling through the net;
3. addressing the underlying problems identified in the report into the death of Victoria Climbié − weak accountability and poor integration;
4. ensuring that the people working with children are valued, rewarded and trained. (DfES, 2003)

[handwritten margin note: research based policy making]

The Green Paper prompted a widespread debate about services for children, young people and families. There was subsequent wide consultation with people working in children's services, and with parents, children and young people, following which the government published *Every Child Matters: Next steps* (DfES, 2004a) and passed the 2004 Children Act.

As a result of political devolution, there is a range of different policy, legal and guidance documents that relate to the changing context in which services to children are delivered in the in the four countries of the UK. The ECM agenda relates specifically to England alone, while other initiatives relate to two or more of the four countries. Although the ECM programme is centrally initiated from government, a key premise is that local needs should be met via 'what works best' locally. There is not therefore a 'one size fits all' approach, which means that different areas will be developing differently depending on local needs and local influences, such as the varying impact and power of individuals and agencies in different areas. Therefore, the changes are subject to 'bottom-up' as well as 'top-down' influences. To help understand this context, the following outlines some of the main trends and changes that are part of, or influence, the ECM programme.

Sector Skills Councils

Sector Skills Councils (SSCs) replaced National Training Organisations in March 2002 and are key organisations with regard to ECM and workforce issues. SSCs are employer-led bodies with responsibility for identifying and tackling issues of skills, productivity and employability for the private, public and voluntary sectors they represent.

The key aims of SSCs are to:

- reduce skills gaps and shortages;
- improve productivity, business and public service performance;
- increase opportunities to boost the skills and productivity of the children's workforce, including action on equal opportunities;
- improve learning supply, including apprenticeships, higher education and national occupational standards.

The 'children's workforce' is spread across a range of sector skills councils. Although it is not an SSC, there is one key government funded body which is highly influential for children's services and the ECM agenda, and that is the Children, Young People and Families Workforce Development Council.

Children, Young People and Families Workforce Development Council

The Children, Young People and Families Workforce Development Council (more commonly known as the CWDC) aims 'to improve the lives of children and young people'. It aims to do this by ensuring that the people working with children have improved training, qualifications, support and advice, with the child being at the centre of services.

The CWDC is one of five bodies forming the UK Skills for Care and Development Sector Skills Council. It co-ordinates the Children's Workforce Network and acts as a 'critical friend' of government and is charged with improving and co-ordinating the training and qualifications systems of those working with children. It seeks to do this by the stated aims of:

- the creation of new training opportunities, career development and flexible career pathways between sectors, as defined by the Children's Workforce Strategy;
- ensuring that all workers have appropriate skills and qualifications and working to increase recruitment into the children's workforce and improve the retention of high-quality employees;
- helping the workforce to deliver joined-up services and improved communication across the sectors.

However, the CWDC is not looking to develop a 'one size fits all' profession for working with children and in its aims specifically states that it 'continues to recognise the unique qualities and contributions of individual professions' in working with children.

Common Core of Skills and Knowledge for the children's workforce

Another way in which the ECM agenda and the moves towards more joined-up working is being carried forward is via the development of the Common Core of Skills and Knowledge, comprising six areas that are seen to be common to all people working with children, whether they be paid or volunteers. The intention of the Common Core is to set out areas which are important for promoting the welfare of children in either single discipline or multi-disciplinary working.

The basic skills and knowledge seen to be essential for the children's workforce are:

- effective communication and engagement with children, young people and families
- child and young person development
- safeguarding and promoting the welfare of the child
- supporting transitions
- multi-agency working
- sharing information

It is intended that a basic level of competence in these six areas will be a future prerequisite for working with children and young people and that the Common Core Curriculum, which will cover these areas, will provide a foundation on which employers and training and educational providers can base future training.

An integrated qualifications framework

Currently under development is an integrated qualifications framework (DfES, 2006a) that aims to establish comparative qualifications and facilitate easier and freer vertical and horizontal progression within the children's workforce sector.

It is proposed that there should be a mixture of generic and specialist modules, covering higher education and professional routes. Generic modules will aim to cover the areas of work identified as being key in the Common Core of Skills and Knowledge. Specialist modules are likely to provide specialist routes for learning in:

- early years
- playwork
- school workforce
- youthwork
- justice
- healthcare workforce
- social care and social work

Obviously some of these areas, such as playwork, are more focused than others, for example, the school workforce or the healthcare workforce, and this will have implications for the nature and scope of the specialist modules within each route. Additionally, to prepare professionals effectively it will surely be necessary to cater for specialisms within these specialist routes. Again, this will be an easier task for the more focused areas than for the others. Thus, while it will be relatively easy for playwork to accommodate the inclusion of specialisms such as play therapy and therapeutic play within its specialist route, it will be much harder for all the specialisms involved in the school workforce and the healthcare workforce to be accommodated within their respective routes.

Ten Year Child Care Strategy

In 2004 the government established what is commonly known as the Ten Year Child Care Strategy, entitled *Choice for parents, the best start for children* (HM Treasury et al, 2004). This strategy has four key themes:

1. **Choice and flexibility**: parents are to have greater choice about balancing work and family life.
2. **Availability**: for all families with children aged up to 14 who need it, an affordable, flexible, high-quality childcare place that meets their circumstances.
3. **Quality**: high-quality provision, with a highly skilled childcare and early years workforce among the best in the world.
4. **Affordability**: families should be able to afford flexible, high-quality childcare that is appropriate for their needs.

Although the key driver for this strategy appears to be increasing parents', particularly mothers', participation in the paid labour market, the strategy is also clearly looking to improve childcare services for children (and their parents) as an integral part of the ECM agenda

Joined-up and multi-agency working

Legislation seeks to embed shared outcomes for children across government departments – at a national and a local level in England there has been shared and at times confused responsibility for children. A number of government departments have shared responsibility for children, including the Department for Education and Skills (DfES), the Department of Health (DoH), the Home Office, the Department for Culture, Media and Sport (DCMS), and the Office of the Deputy Prime Minister (ODPM). Since the creation of the Department for Children, Schools and Families (DCSF) in 2007 there appear to have been greater moves towards co-ordination of services for children led by that department and this has been underlined in the 2007 National Children's Plan (discussed later in this chapter).

There is a general steer which suggests that services for children can only be improved by better and more effective joined-up working and multi-agency and interprofessional working for both universal and targeted, specialist services for children.

crucial

The Common Assessment Framework

The Common Assessment Framework (CAF) is a shared assessment tool for use by agencies working with children and their families in England. The stated aim is that it has been designed to help practitioners develop a shared understanding of a child's needs, and aims 'to avoid children having to tell and retell their story', by using a relatively simple approach to assessing whether children need services (DfES, 2006c).

> The use of the CAF relates to children 2nd, 3rd and 4th levels or tiers of need as outlined in the guidance materials. The hierarchy of needs is as follows:
>
> **LEVEL 1:** Children and young people who make good overall progress in all areas of development; broadly, these children receive appropriate universal services.
>
> **LEVEL 2:** Children and young people whose needs require some extra support from a targeted service.
>
> **LEVEL 3:** Children and young people whose needs are more complex and require integrated support from targeted services.
>
> **LEVEL 4:** Children and young people who have complex and enduring needs that require integrated support from statutory or specialist services.

Figure 1.1: ECM and the CAF continuum

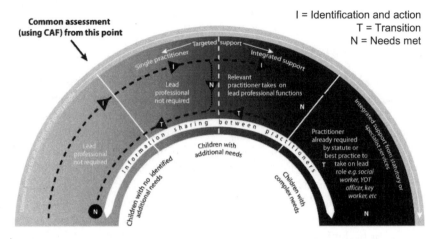

Source: DfES, 2006d

A diagrammatic example of the CAF as used in the ECM training materials (DfES, 2006d) is illustrated in Figure 1.1. It can be seen that the CAF is designed to be a proactive tool for use in 'non-high-risk' situations, so, where there is a concern that a child be at risk of harm, practitioners are instructed *not* to follow the CAF guidelines but to follow Local Safeguarding Children Board procedures. (In these situations the Assessment Framework guidance for assessing children in need [DoH et al, 2000], also discussed in Chapter Nine, and the Working Together guidance [HM Government, 2006] would be the basis for these procedures.)

Thus, the CAF should be used when it is seen that a child will not be able to make progress towards one or more of the five ECM outcomes without additional services (which in fact may prove to be a very general trigger).

It is suggested that the CAF is a purely voluntary procedure and therefore can only be completed with the consent of the child or parents, and after a pre-assessment checklist has been completed. It is intended that the CAF should be a speedy assessment to be completed in ten days.

The three broad assessment areas of the CAF are:

1. How well the child is developing including health and progress in learning;
2. How well the parents are able to support their child's development and respond appropriately to any needs;
3. The impact of wider family and environmental elements on the child's development and on the capacity of the parents.

Professionals are assisted in this process by government guidance which provides 'a general description of signs to look for in each of these three areas'.

The assessment is completed by:

- agreeing a general conclusion with the child or parent;
- identifying solutions with relevant actions required – if necessary and appropriate based on the assessment;
- agreeing who will do what and when progress will be reviewed.

Where necessary, more detailed assessment of children's needs can then be undertaken as shown in Chapter Nine, Figure 9.1 (DoH et al, 2000).

The lead professional role

Alongside the CAF, the ECM agenda has also introduced the role of the 'lead professional' with regard to working with children – a person to act as a single point of contact for the child and family; to enhance planned and effective intervention, and to reduce overlap and inconsistency of interventions for the range of professionals and agencies who may be involved in the child's life (DCSF, 2007a). It is envisaged that lead professionals will be drawn from those involved in delivering early intervention to the child and that the role will (or should) vary according to the needs of the child:

> For example, the lead professional for a child who requires regular physiotherapy, has speech delay and feeding difficulties, will be very different to the lead professional required for a child and their family whose primary support needs are to improve the mother's self-esteem, help the parents develop effective behaviour management skills, and provide additional support to the child in school to support their behaviour and learning. (DfES, 2006)

> An evaluation of one pilot of the CAF and the lead professional role indicates that this is seen as positive and welcome, despite teething troubles, such as some lack of clarity about how lead professionals could ensure agencies of which they were not members followed agreed plans. (City of Derby, 2006c)

More recent anecdotal evidence suggests, perhaps not unexpectedly, that there have continued to be some problems with regard to the ongoing implementation of the CAF and lead professional (LP) roles – including a lack of an agreed common knowledge between different professionals, confusion at times regarding who is the LP, and a reluctance of some professionals to share confidential information with other professionals.

The appointment of a Children's Commissioner for England

As part of the implementation of the ECM agenda, the post of Children's Commissioner for England was established under the 2004 Children Act following the other three countries of the UK where there were already Children's Commissioners. The first appointment to the post, Al Aynsley-Green, took up his post on 1 July 2005. In his website he has defined the role thus:

> The Children's Commissioner's function is to promote awareness of views, needs, rights and interests of children and young people, so as to raise their profile and improve their lives and well-being. This includes encouraging people working with children and with responsibility for children, in the public and private sectors, to take account of children and young people's views and interests. The Commissioner will advise government on the views, needs and interests of children. The Commissioner must have regard to the United Nations Convention on the Rights of the Child when determining what constitutes the interests of children and young people. The Commissioner also has a UK wide role to play in non-devolved matters. The Commissioner can consider or research any matter relating to the interests of children, including the operation of complaints procedures. (Children's Commissioner, 2007)

Shows country variation of national policy.

While it is too early to determine how the role will develop in practice, concerns have been expressed because the English Commissioner has a more limited remit than his three UK counterparts – his role is to promote the views and interests of children and young people, rather than to safeguard their rights. The role is also seen to be less formally independent of government, as the other three commissioners are seen to have more powers to initiate inquiries. There is also a concern that the English Commissioner could undermine the autonomy and authority of his counterparts in Scotland, Wales and Northern Ireland as he has responsibility for all non-devolved powers across the whole of the UK (such as criminal justice, social security and refugee issues). However, it appears that some of these fears may be unfounded in that the English Commissioner has thus far taken a robust approach to defend the rights of children, for example, warning the government that 'plans to X-ray the teeth of unaccompanied child asylum seekers to assess their age (and hence their eligibility for asylum) contravene medical ethics and may constitute assault' (*The Guardian*, 2007).

Database of children and an information sharing index

Changes in the 2004 Children Act under section 12 established a new power for local authorities and their partners in that it requires them to create and keep a database for children in their areas, giving them a duty to co-operate to improve children's well-being as part of their duty to safeguard children and promote their welfare. It was intended that from 1 October 2008 (now postponed to at least 1 January 2009 to allow 'further testing' [DCSF, 2008]) that a data base called ContactPoint be introduced that holds information on 11 million children in England and Wales including name, address, date of birth, gender, a unique identifying number for each child, names and details of those with parental responsibility/daily care, services provided for the child, and any 'causes for concern'. It is perceived that the database will remove the need for a separate list of children about whom there are 'child protection concerns'. A range of over 330,000 professionals, including head teachers, social workers and hospital consultants will have access ContactPoint to check such matters as whether a child has been the subject of a previous formal assessment and, if so, who is the lead professional.

A database of all children goes to the heart of the tension between the rights of the State and the rights of parents in relation to children, and the proposed introduction of such a database has attracted some controversy. It has been strongly argued that it is a potential breach of privacy and civil liberties, for example. It is also feared by some that there are information security issues, and that too many people will have access to children's details. Critics have also questioned whether the database will be effective and efficient. In its defence, it has been suggested that child abuse tragedies have often been caused by a lack of integrated, relevant information about children, and that a database will be a powerful tool in tacking this problem, particularly in a globalised world where there are increased numbers of refugee and asylum seeking children coming into and living in the UK. Views of children questioned about the introduction of ContactPoint ranged from 'this is a waste of time' to 'well done for making this up – and keep us safe' (Ofsted, 2007).

Integration of inspection frameworks

ECM and the 2004 Children Act both are based on the assumption that the greater integration of inspection mechanisms for services to children will be essential in improving the planning, accountability and performance of the services. Largely this is being done by joint area reviews (JARs) of children's services within specific local areas every three years. JARs have been taking place since 2005, replacing a number of different inspection programmes. Initially the Office for Standards in Teacher Education (Ofsted) and the Commission for Social Care Inspection (CSCI) conduct the reviews, partly basing their analysis on the annual performance assessments (APAs) produced by local authority Children and Young People's Services each year. They look at how well services are working together to improve the well-being of children, and how far services are becoming integrated and better than 'the sum of their parts'. As part of this process the views of young people themselves are sought.

It has recently been decided that JARS will be replaced by CAAs (Common Area Assessments) from 2009 (Community Care, 2008). These CAAs will look at how local public bodies are meeting local needs, and their potential to improve outcomes for local people. Detailed inspections will only be triggered by evidence of poor/declining services, risks to users, or major information gaps. The exception to the scaling down of detailed inspections is LSCBs, which will each be inspected once every three years from 2009.

The extent to which a range of different inspection mechanisms are being brought together under the ECM agenda can be gauged by the fact that the legislation relating to joint inspection in the 2004 Children Act is directed towards the Chief Inspector of Schools, the Adult Learning Inspectorate, the Commission for Healthcare Audit and Inspection, the Audit Commission for Local Authorities and the NHS in England and Wales, the Chief Inspector of Constabulary, and the Chief Inspectors of the Probation Service, the Prison Service and the Court Administration.

To streamline this inspection regime, the 2006 Education and Inspection Act included measures to create the Office for Standards in Education, Children's Services and Skills (rather confusingly still called Ofsted). In relation to children's services, from 1 April 2007 Ofsted has responsibility for:

- the registration and inspection of childcare;
- inspection of state schools (but not all independent schools);
- the registration and inspection of arrangements for the care and support of children and young people;
- JARs and APAs of local children's and young people's services;
- inspection of teacher training;
- the inspection of the Children and Family Court Advisory and Support Service (Cafcass).

It is planned that, as well as inspecting these different elements, the integration within the new Ofsted makes possible inspections on the basis of 'themes' across different elements of children's services more easily than was possible under the previous inspection regime. An example of this cited is the education of children in care.

Director of Children's Services

Until recently every local authority in England had a Director of Education responsible for the authority's functions in schools and related services to children and young people, and a Director of Social Services responsible for the authority's social services to children and adults. This has been changed as a result of the 2004 Children Act, which requires every top-tier or unitary local authority in England to appoint a Director of Children's Services (DCS) and to designate a Lead Member (councillor) for Children's Services (LM) by 2008.

The DCS is professionally accountable for the delivery of local authorities' education and social services functions for children, and any health functions for children delegated to the authority by an NHS body. The intention of the legislation is that these posts will have a key role in creating wider partnerships between services for children and therefore improve and 'transform' services. The LM will exercise local political accountability for the same range of services as the director and, presumably based on findings in the Laming Report (Laming,

2003), is expected to take a role in safeguarding. However, the legislation is keen to stress that there is not a single uniform approach in relation to the nature of the role of the DCS or the services they will lead and develop. Rather, it is suggested that 'local challenges and circumstances ... and organisational and staff changes' should influence the structures created and the appointments made.

The changes that have taken place so far in relation to these arrangements indicate that Directors of Children's Services are being drawn more from education rather than social services backgrounds. While the impact of this is yet to be determined, there are concerns about this trend in some quarters, as discussed in Chapter Nine.

Annual local Children and Young People's Plans

Following the 2004 Children Act regulations have required each local authority and their partners to have a Children and Young People's Plan (CYPP) to produce 'a powerful force in driving forward better local integration of children's services and the development of local partnership arrangements'. This process is intended to build on the principle of more integrated services for children and young people, and its introduction replaces the previous requirements for agencies to produce seven statutory and twelve non-statutory plans related to children and young people. Increasingly, authorities are producing plans online, which set out their targets for the next few years with regard to integrated and multi-disciplinary services for children and families.

The National Foundation for Educational Research (NFER) analysed 75 of these plans in 2006, and found that:

- The importance of developing local partnerships and responding to local needs is recognised across the plans.
- There is a marked diversity in the coverage of the different themes across the plans.
- The ECM outcomes framework is used in a variety of ways, suggesting that local authorities work with it as a conceptual tool rather than adhering to it as a blueprint formula.
- Many local authorities produced additional material written specifically for children and young people, reflecting an intention to be accessible and to engage young people.
- There is scope for future guidance on identification and allocation of resources, performance management arrangements and commissioning strategies. (Lord et al, 2006)

The research found over 90 different types of targets were listed, the key groups of children most focused on being children with disabilities and learning difficulties, young offenders, minority ethnic children, and children in care. In relation to the latter group, a Green Paper, *Care Matters* (DfES, 2006b) was launched, aiming to ensure earlier intervention and more support for families in which children are at risk of coming into care, and to improve the performance of local authorities in relation to children in care and in their transition to adulthood. Following consultations, further government action in this area of services is proposed.

Children's Trusts

Children's Trusts are structures which seek to bring together all services for children and young people in an area, underpinned by the 2004 Children Act duty to co-operate in order to focus on improving outcomes for all children and young people. Their stated aim is to support those who work every day with children, young people and their families to deliver better outcomes, with children and young people experiencing more integrated and responsive services, and specialist support embedded in and accessed through universal services.

It is intended that people will work in effective multi-disciplinary teams, be trained jointly to tackle cultural and professional divides, use a lead professional model where many disciplines are involved and be co-located, often in Extended Schools or Children's Centres. Children's Trusts will be supported by integrated processes. Some processes, like the CAF, will be centrally driven, whereas others will be specified at a local level. While integrated delivery can be fostered in many ways, and at many levels, making sure the system is meeting the right needs for the right children and young people overall requires effective integrated strategies, including:

- a joint needs assessment
- shared decisions on priorities
- identification of all available resources
- joint plans to deploy them

The ambitious goal is that joint commissioning, underpinned by pooled resources, will ensure that those best able to provide the right packages of services can do so.

All of this requires arrangements for governance that ensure everyone 'shares the vision' and give each the 'confidence to relinquish day-to-day control of decisions and resources' while maintaining the necessary high-level accountability for meeting their statutory duties in a new way.

Across the whole system there are some proposed unifying features (such as a stated aim to listen to the views of children and young people) that might help to link the various elements, although this may prove to be more rhetoric than reality. Whether lack of vision, lack of skills and other resources, or organisational and professional 'turf wars' will have an impact on achieving the ambitious targets of Children's Trusts will become more apparent as they develop.

Local Safeguarding Children Boards

As noted above, the launch of the ECM agenda was linked to the report on the death of Victoria Climbié, a child protection failure. Since then, there has been the development of the concept of 'safeguarding children' as a wider aspect of child protection. The following are official definitions of child protection and safeguarding children, based on the most recent statutory guidance.

> **Child protection** is the process of protecting individual children identified as either suffering, or at risk of suffering, significant harm as a result of abuse or neglect.
>
> **Safeguarding and promoting the welfare of children** is the process of protecting children from abuse or neglect, preventing impairment of their health and development, and ensuring they are growing up in circumstances consistent with the provision of safe and effective care that enables children to have optimum life chances and enter adulthood successfully. (HM Government, 2006, p 28)

To promote and regulate child protection and safeguarding children, the 2004 Children Act established statutory Local Safeguarding Children Boards, which replaced the previous non-statutory Area Child Protection Committees (ACPCs). Their role is to promote the effective collaborative working of key agencies to safeguard and promote the welfare of children. Members include local authorities, health bodies, the police, other criminal justice agencies and voluntary organisation representatives. The local authority is responsible for the appointment of the chair of the board and government guidance suggests that the chair and other board members should have sufficient authority to 'get things done' rather than being organisations which are just 'talking shops'.

Sure Start, Children's Centres and Extended Schools

Although its origins preceded the ECM agenda, the Sure Start programme for children has subsequently become an integral, key part of achieving the ECM outcomes. Sure Start was loosely based on the Head Start programme, which was a programme based in the USA that aimed at improving the development and education of pre-school children in the most disadvantaged areas. Between 1999 and 2004 over 500 Sure Start programmes in England, aimed largely at pre-school children, were given the objectives of 'improving social and emotional development; improving health; improving children's ability to learn; strengthening families and communities' (NESS, 2005, s 1.14).

Sure Start programmes have generally been viewed as successful, although there are indications that the most disadvantaged groups have had difficulties in accessing them, and there are also seen to be tensions between:

- selectivity versus universality;
- locally expressed need versus centrally directed need;
- the needs and rights of children versus the needs and rights of parents;
- evidence-based versus entitlement-based services.

While the Sure Start programme has continued, its work in achieving the ECM aims is being supplemented by the development of Sure Start Centres into Children's Centres and the broadening of school's roles into Extended Schools.

The development of Extended Schools to support implementation of the ECM outcomes was announced in the Extended Schools Prospectus of 2006. Extended Schools will offer core services between 8.00am and 6.00pm including childcare, breakfast clubs, homework clubs, and parenting support and family learning programmes. They are also, perhaps ambitiously, seen to be a 'service hubs' to facilitate easy referral on to a range of more specialist services such as speech therapy, CAMHS, sexual health services etc.

There may also be tensions for Extended Schools in relation to:

- balancing providing universal versus selective services;
- involving the most disadvantaged members (both adults and children) of the community; and
- meeting the Extended Schools agenda targets alongside meeting the more competitive, neo-market services and pupil achievement targets that have been imposed on all schools in the recent past.

The National Service Framework for Children

Covering both England and Wales the NHS has produced a number of National Service Frameworks (NSFs), which are long-term strategies for improving specific areas of care. Their stated aims are to set national standards and to identify key interventions for a defined service or care group, to put in place strategies to support implementation, and to establish ways to ensure progress within an agreed time scale.

The NSF for Children (DoH, 2004a) was published with the explicit aim of setting standards 'for children's health and social services, and the interface of those services with education', and is a ten-year programme intended to stimulate long-term and sustained improvement in children's health.

As well as the ECM agenda, a number of other drivers were cited as being fundamental to its design and launch including:

- the Department of Health's plans to improve children's health services following the failings associated with children's heart surgery at the Bristol Royal Infirmary (DoH, 2001);
- the government's proposal to have a comprehensive Child and Adolescent Mental Health Service by December 2006;

- the appointment in England in 2003 of the first 'Children's Minister';
- the NHS Improvement Plan (DoH, 2004b) – the government 's plan for the modernisation of the health service;
- the Treasury Child Poverty Review of 2004 (HM Treasury, 2004), which examined the changes necessary to halve child poverty in the UK by 2010 and eradicate it by 2020.

The NSF for Children comprises three sections:

Section One: the so-called Core Standards document – sets out five standards which aim to help the NHS and relevant partner agencies, including local authority services, to achieve high-quality universal service provision for children and their parents/carers. These standards include promoting health and well-being; supporting parents and carers; safeguarding children; and having child and family-centred health services.

Section Two: standards six to ten – addresses targeted services for children and young people and their parents/carers, including children ill in the community and in hospital, disabled children, and child and adolescent mental health issues.

Section Three: standard 11 – contains a range of targets relating to the particular needs and choices of women and their babies before or during pregnancy, throughout birth, and for the first three months of parenthood.

The National Children's Plan

In December 2007 the launch of the first ever National Children's Plan brought together many of the ECM initiatives so far described and made new proposals to cover the next ten years (DCSF, 2007b). Five principles underpin the plan:

1. Government does not bring up children – parents do – so government needs to do more to back parents and families;
2. All children have the potential to succeed and should go as far as their talents can take them;
3. Children and young people need to enjoy their childhood as well as grow up prepared for adult life;
4. Services need to be shaped by and responsive to children, young people and families, not designed around professional boundaries; and
5. It is always better to prevent failure than tackle a crisis later. (DCSF, 2007b, p 5)

A number of initiatives were launched in relation to children's well-being, including appointing two expert 'parenting advisers' in each local authority and at least two outreach workers in Sure Start Children's Centres in the most disadvantaged areas, as well as increased funding for short break provision for disabled children. Workforce reforms included making teaching a masters-led profession and guaranteeing induction support for newly qualified social workers. Children's play was prioritised, with £225 million being made available to local authorities over three years for the regeneration of 3,500 playgrounds, including making them disability friendly, and for the creation of 30 adventure playgrounds nationally. The intention to publish a national play strategy by summer 2008 was also announced.

The plan highlighted new initiatives in relation to education, including new partnership arrangements between schools and parents, arranging a smoother transition from play-based learning in early years into primary school, and pre-secondary school contact with families by staff members. The participation age for children in education, employment or training will rise to 18 by 2015. Additional support or funding was promised for children with Special Educational Needs and children with dyslexia, and £26.5 million for new alternative provision for excluded pupils. Investment in youth services was increased by at least £160 million.

With regard to promoting health and well-being, new strategies for child health, obesity action and elements of safeguarding children were proposed, and reviews or consultations announced in relation to CAMHS, children and new technology, the impact of commercial activity on childhood, and issues such as children's behaviour, the primary curriculum and special educational needs provision.

The National Children's Plan also stated the intention to review the consistency of Children's Trust arrangements nationally; to publish a children's workforce action plan, and to develop strong school-level indicators for all ECM outcomes.

Key 'ambitions' for children's lives that flow from the plan are suggested:

- At age 5, 90% of children will be developing well across all areas of the early years foundation stages.
- At age 11, 95% of children will have reached expected levels in literacy and numeracy.
- At age 19, 90% will have achieved the equivalent of five good GCSEs.
- At age 19, the majority of children will be ready for higher education with at least 6 out of 10 children achieving the equivalent of A-levels.
- Child poverty will be halved by 2010 and eradicated by 2020.
- There will be clear improvements in child health, with the proportion of overweight children reduced to 2000 levels.
- The number of first time young offenders will be reduced so that by 2020 the number receiving a conviction, reprimand or final warning for a recordable offence has fallen by a quarter. (ECM, 2008)

The plan seeks to put the needs of children and families, rather than services and professionals, first and, to do so, providing universal services within a preventative system. It thus sees early years and schools as being the base for early intervention and prevention within communities.

Reaction to the Children's Plan has ranged from enthusiastic approval to criticism that it is a rehash of previous policies and strategies which also extended the role of the state too far into the lives of children and families. It is clear, however, that unless or until there is a change of government in the UK it will be a key document in relation to the shape and delivery of children's services.

Conclusion

This chapter has discussed the range of different initiatives, strategies, policies and pieces of legislation that interact with the ECM agenda. As illustrated later in this book, there are also many different ways in which the rights and responsibilities of parents and children are 'seen' by society, and these can have highly influential impacts at micro and macro levels. It is also clear that there are key challenges facing the different elements of the children's workforce if the ECM targets for children are to be achieved.

It is also important to emphasise that the whole area of children's services is one which for the past decade and beyond has been characterised by rapid change, and this pace of change is unlikely to ease in the future, not least because change is necessary to meet the challenges of improving services to and for children and families.

References

Blom-Cooper, L. (1985) *A child in trust – Report of the Panel of Inquiry into the Circumstances Surrounding the Death of Jasmine Beckford*, London: London Borough of Brent.

Butler-Sloss, E. (1988) *Child abuse in Cleveland*, London: HMSO

Campbell, B. (1988) *Unofficial secrets: Child sexual abuse – the Cleveland case,* London: Virago.

Children's Commissioner (2007) 'More info about the Children's Commissioner', www.11million.org.uk/commissioner.

City of Derby (2006) *Report of the evaluation of Lead Professional Trailblazer in the Osmaston/Allerton Children Centre Area*, Derby: City Of Derby.

Community Care (2008) *Ministers in drive to reduce burden on children's and adults' services with limited visits*, 5 August 2008.

DCSF (Department for Children, Schools and Families) (2007a) 'What is a lead professional?' www.everychildmatters.gov.uk/deliveringservices/leadprofessional/

DCSF (2007b) *The National Children's Plan – Building brighter futures*, London: DCSF.

[handwritten margin note: link to Ball. Modern society constantly changing.]

DCSF (2008) Letter from Kevin Brennan, MP, to Chair of House of Commons Children, Schools and Families Select Committee, London; DCSF

DfES (Department for Education and Skills) (2003) *Every Child Matters – the Green Paper*, London: DfES.

DfES (2004a) *Every Child Matters – Next steps*, London: DfES.

DfES (2004b) *Every Child Matters – Change for children*, London: DfES.

DfES (2004c) *Common Assessment Framework – A consultation*, London: DfES.

DfES (2005) *Children's Workforce Strategy – A strategy to build a world class workforce for children and young people*, London: DfES.

DfES (2006a) *The Children's Workforce Strategy – Building an integrated qualifications framework*, London: DfES.

DfES (2006b) *Care Matters*, London: DfES.

DfES (2006c) *The Common Assessment Framework for Children and Young People*, London: DfES.

DfES (2006d) *The Common Assessment Framework for Children and Young People – integrated working training materials*, London: DfES.

DHSS (Department of Health and Social Security) (1972) *Report of the Committee of Inquiry into the Care and Supervision Provided in Relation to Maria Colwell*, London: DHSS.

DoH (Department of Health) (1989) *The Children Act 1989*, London: HMSO.

DoH (1995) *Child Protection – Messages from Research*, London: HMSO.

DoH (2001) *The Inquiry into the Management of the Care of Children Receiving Complex Heart Surgery at the Bristol Royal Infirmary 1984-1995*, Cm 5207, London: HMSO.

DoH (2004a) *The National Service Framework for Children, Parents and Midwifery Services*, London: HMSO.

DoH (2004b) *The National Health Service Improvement Plan*, Cm 6268, London: HMSO.

DoH (2007) *Sex, drugs, alcohol and young people*, London: DoH.

DoH, DfEE and the Home Office (2000) *Framework for the Assessment of Children in Need and their families*, London: DoH Publications.

ECM (Every Child Matters) (2008) 'The Children's Plan', available at www.everychildmatters.gov.uk/strategy/childrensplan/.

Gillick v West Norfolk and Wisbech AHA [1985] 3 All ER 402.

The Guardian (2007) 'Watchdog opposes plan to x-ray child asylum seekers', 3Nov, p 11.

HM Government (2006) *Working Together to Safeguard Children*, London: TSO.

HM Treasury (2004) *Child Poverty Review*, London: HMSO.

HM Treasury, DfES, Department for Work and Pensions (DWP) and Department for Trade and Industry (DTI) (2004) *Choice for parents, the best start for children: A ten year strategy for childcare*, London: Stationery Office.

Hendrick, H. (2003) *Child welfare: Historical dimensions, contemporary debate*, Bristol: The Policy Press.

Hendrick, H. (ed.) (2005) *Child welfare and social policy: An essential reader*, Bristol: The Policy Press.

House of Commons, Committee of Public Accounts (2007) *Tackling child obesity – First Steps*, HC 157, London: Stationery Office.

Lord, P., Wilkin, A. and Kinder, K. (2006) *Analysis of Children and Young People's Plans, 2006*, London: National Foundation for Educational Research.

Laming, H. (2003) *The Victoria Climbié Inquiry*, London: HMSO.

Monckton, W.T. (1945) *Boarding out of Dennis and Terence O'Neill at Bank Farm, Minsterley and the steps taken to supervise their welfare*, London: Home Office.

NESS (National Evaluation of Sure Start) (2005) *Variation in Sure Start local programme effectiveness*, London: HMSO.

NHS (National Health Service) (2007) *Statistics on alcohol: England 2007*, London: NHS/The Information Centre.

Ofsted (Office for Standards in Education) (2007) *Making ContactPoint Work*, London: Ofsted.

Parton, N. (1985) *The Politics of Child Abuse*, London: Macmillan.

Schor, J.B. (2004) *Born to buy: The commercialised child and the new consumer culture*, New York, NY: Scribner.

UN (United Nations) (1989) *UN Convention on the Rights of the Child*, New York: UN (also accessed at www.everychildmatters.gov.uk/uncrc/).

UNICEF (2005) *Child poverty in rich countries, 2005*, Florence: UNICEF Innocenti Research Centre.

UNICEF (2007) *Child poverty in perspective – An overview of child well-being in rich countries*, Florence: UNICEF Innocenti Research Centre.

TWO

Interprofessional working and the children's workforce

Pamela Graham and Alison I. Machin

Introduction

This chapter will focus on interprofessional working and information sharing and will consider some of the key challenges and opportunities for the children's workforce as a result of Every Child Matters (DfES, 2003) and the changing agenda for children. The moves towards interprofessional learning will be explored alongside some of the systems, processes and tools which support the integration of children's services.

Interprofessional working and information sharing: a historical policy context

The key policy drivers for recent successive changes to services for children, families and young people are set out in the introductory chapter. The move towards interprofessional working and the intention to integrate services has far-reaching intentions, demands and expectations. In order to understand why this scale of change is necessary, it may be helpful to look back at factors and events that have shaped current services.

Life for current generations of children and young people has been lived within the welfare state, which was intended to be the safety net below which no individual would be allowed to fall. Although there have been many improvements and benefits for children's and young people's lives, there have been, and still are, children who are not protected from neglect and abuse. A recurring theme from many child protection enquiries and research studies has been that agencies have not shared important information and failed to work together effectively.

Legislative changes have highlighted dilemmas about whether child welfare is a private or a public concern, and battles for power and responsibility between the state and the family have led to agencies being criticised no matter what they did.

Demographic changes have also meant significant lifestyle changes for children and families. A growing awareness of child abuse and children's rights issues alongside changes to the economy, employment patterns and family structures have also influenced changes to services.

Different understandings about children and young people, what kind of citizens we want them to be and ultimately what kind of society we want, have influenced attitudes to education, parenting and crime. Many would argue that young people's normal activity has been criminalised, which has led to the alienation of many children, young people and families. Disagreements over the 'place' of children and young people in England have been subtly fuelled by debates about rights and responsibilities and, while a children's commissioner was appointed in March 2005 to work towards the ECM outcomes, there is still a long way to go.

Every Child Matters set an agenda for change for children. The success of the ECM reform will be dependent on the degree to which organisations and individuals are enabled to work collaboratively for the benefit of children and their families. Information sharing is a crucial component of the ECM reform: it requires a collaboration for which individual professionals, systems and processes may not be fully prepared (DfES, 2006).

Since the beginning of the welfare state and despite many good intentions to work together, health, education and social care services have been segregated and fragmented, and information sharing between professionals and between agencies has been fraught with difficulties. Interprofessional working relies on effective, appropriate and confident information sharing, yet not all professionals routinely share information and it is still not uncommon for there to be duplicate referrals or for families to undergo multiple assessments.

The current policy context

Statutory guidance on the 2004 Children Act sets out clear expectations for the improvement of information sharing (DfES, 2006). Electronic tools such as the Information Sharing Index, the Common Assessment Framework and the Integrated Children's System were designed to enable authorised and trained practitioners to:

- identify and contact other practitioners delivering services to the same children;
- provide secure ways in which to share relevant information and concerns about children's welfare;
- gather information in more consistent, systematic and straightforward ways in order to assess additional needs at an early stage and help families to find responses to unmet needs;
- improve integrated working by facilitating shared understandings between practitioners, reducing the number of assessments that some children and young people may have undergone, and promoting integrated frontline services, as outlined in the 2004 Children Act.

All local authority areas are expected to implement the Common Assessment Framework (CAF) by the end of 2008. At the time of writing, an electronic CAF system is being developed with the objective of securing a nationally consistent approach. The Index and the CAF are preventive tools for children who need support over and above that provided by universal services. The Integrated Children's System is a practice tool for social care workers carrying out statutory responsibilities within a multi-agency context, based on the domains and dimensions from 'The Framework for Assessment for Children in Need and their Families' (DoH, 2000). It represents a major shift from paper to electronic recording. However, simply changing the recording systems for information will not necessarily improve the effectiveness of information sharing. Anning et al acknowledge that 'it will be a huge challenge at local and national levels to overcome the professional, ethical and technical obstacles to achieving common assessment and information sharing in multi-professional teams' (2006, p 124).

In order to understand some of the complexities of interprofessional working, integrated services and information sharing, it is worth considering first the concept of collaboration and what it might mean when applied to working together with children and their families.

The concept of collaboration

Collaboration implies 'conscious interaction between the parties to achieve a common goal' (Meads and Ashcroft, 2005, p 16). Through an interactive process of sharing expertise and knowledge an outcome can be facilitated that would not have been possible through individual working. Huxham applies the term 'collaborative advantage' (1996, p 14) to a situation in which an outcome is only achievable through collaboration and where participants, individuals or organisations also benefit in some way from the collaboration. A successful collaborative working situation would be one in which similarities between collaborators are acknowledged and differences are valued. Meads and Ashcroft (2005) suggest that there are three phases to successful collaboration, namely 'problem-setting, direction setting and implementation'. Clearly the activities associated with discussion, interaction, information sharing, assessment, agreeing priorities, action planning and working together to implement a plan, require a secure foundation of commitment to collaborate and a shared value system. Collaborative practice is characterised by action and partnership (Quinney, 2006). Across the public sector there is an impetus to refocus services around the needs of the people who use them and for professionals to collaborate with other stakeholders through the process of interprofessional working.

ECM refers specifically to the need for interprofessional and inter-agency working as follows: 'Multi-disciplinary teams of professionals and 'para professionals' should be co-located around places where children are, for example, schools, Sure Start and Children's Centres and primary healthcare centres'. This suggests that putting interprofessional teams in the same geographical location will facilitate better collaborative interprofessional working. However, simply locating people together in a workplace is not enough to establish collaborative working. Literature suggests that the opportunistic informal communication and relationship building that can be triggered by being co-located can have a positive effect on working relationships (Frost, 2005). However, if processes within an environment do not support a more formal collaborative working structure, co-location may remain a mechanism of mutual support for the staff working there, but will not necessarily improve services for children and families.

ECM also acknowledges that the reforms require supervision and continuing professional development support to be put in place to ensure 'multi-disciplinary teams are able to benefit from a wide range of professionals working together, without losing the advantages of those professionals' individual specialisms'. It is important in collaborative working that the team culture is one that facilitates shared learning and working but values the unique contributions that are made by different contributors, as this will maximise the added value of working together for continuous service improvement. As discussed in Chapter One, tools such as the CAF have been put in place to support collaborative, interprofessional working through better information sharing for the benefit of children and their families. However, it needs to be recognised that interprofessional working will not simply happen by changing systems. To make process changes effective, changes also need to be made to the prevailing culture to ensure practitioners have a positive attitude toward collaboration (Hudson, 2005). Professionals and other stakeholders need to be prepared with both the skills and attitudes to work collaboratively with one another and with children and families.

A recent study (DCSF, 2007) found that typical characteristics of effective integrated working included strong personal relationships between practitioners and the commitment of staff to working collaboratively. Factors frequently reported as helpful to integrated working included co-location and locality teams, putting the child and family at the centre of provision, preparing staff to work in new ways, providing feedback to referrers, and the adoption of the CAF and standardised referral processes. Factors most frequently reported as hindering integrated working included different ways of working, anxiety about sharing information, high staff turnover and lack of familiarity with the CAF. Given the pace and complexity of ongoing change, it is important to establish a shared understanding of the concept of interprofessional working so that all collaborators feel valued, involved and confident in their specific contribution.

Interprofessional working: defining the concept

The term 'interprofessional working' can be misleading. Taken literally it could be understood to refer only to those occupations that fall into the category of traditional 'professions', that is, those registered with a professional and regulatory body, and which have standardised minimum requirements for a qualification linked to public expectations of the role. However, national policy guidance on the integration of services uses this term more broadly (DoH, 2006), especially in relation to the education of a future workforce equipped to collaborate for improved service delivery and outcomes (DoH, 2001). ECM also uses the terms inter-agency and multi-professional. Some of the terminology used can be traced back to that used historically to describe the practice environment of different professionals.

Figure 2.1: Multi-professional working: traditional model

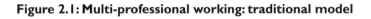

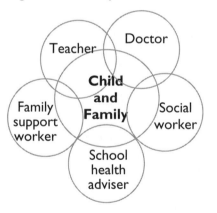

- Child and family focus of work
- Range of professionals providing separate services
- Multiple assessments/ family contacts
- Reliance on referral mechanisms between professionals
- Little or no shared working between professionals
- No formal information sharing mechanism
- Risk of duplication of work and lack of communication across agencies

Figure 2.2: Multi-professional working: integrated model

- Child and family full collaborators
- Range of professionals providing integrated services
- Reduced assessment/ family contacts
- Shared decision making mechanisms between professionals, child and family
- Role overlap between professionals acknowledged and used effectively
- Formal information sharing mechanism
- Less duplication of work
- Effective, inclusive communication with all collaborators.

Terminology aside, what is important for successful integrated working is the recognition that interprofessional working is characterised by the core social processes of interaction and collaboration. Figures 2.1 and 2.2 illustrate the transition individuals and organisations will need to undergo in order to truly work in an interprofessional way.

Figure 2.3 illustrates the shift that will need to be made in order to move towards integrated provision as described.

Figure 2.3: Towards integrated working

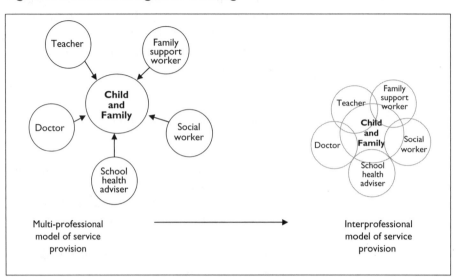

In any given service delivery setting all participants are potential collaborators, including those individuals not in traditional professional roles, such as teaching assistants or nursery support workers. Most importantly, there is a need to engage service users, in this case children, their families and guardians, as key collaborators in an interprofessional working context. Previously children and families came into contact with many professionals who rarely interacted with one another, aside from the usual referral mechanisms within organisations. Effective interprofessional working should be characterised by face-to-face interaction wherever possible, joint decision making, information sharing and shared action planning by all involved. Interprofessional working should not be inhibited in situations where face-to-face interaction is not possible. In the developing world of technology, interaction is possible by other means of communication, for example video conferencing and online discussion.

The ECM diagrammatic representation of integrated services is an all encompassing circle with several layers often described as an 'onion' (see Figure 2.4). It can be criticised for being an over simplistic portrayal of a complex practice context, for example, it does not clearly show that agencies and individuals working within children's service delivery will have a unique contribution to make. It also uses the word 'integrated' without a clear explanation and practitioners could be forgiven for being somewhat confused about where they fit in the overall picture, or even for mistakenly assuming that 'integrated' is in fact a move toward 'generic' workers for the children's workforce.

A recent research study (Machin, 2008) explored how a changing professional practice context has influenced the self perception of health visitors. Health visitors, as key health professionals working with children and families, are being urged in policy to strengthen their public health role by working more collaboratively to address the needs of communities and populations, in addition

Figure 2.4: ECM and integrated services

to their work with individual families (DoH, 2001b). There is a degree of overlap between their role and the role of others in the children's workforce, which has challenged their professional identity and called into question the unique nature of health visiting.

This concern that interprofessional working will have a negative impact on professional identity may result in a lack of willingness to engage in collaborative, interprofessional working and cause professionals to display defensive behaviour towards one another. Figure 2.5 shows a modified ECM diagram incorporating the model of interprofessional working outlined in Figure 2.5.

The key difference in this alternative diagram is that in place of 'integrated front-line delivery' is 'interprofessional front-line delivery'. The overlapping but discrete circles representing the interprofessional team illustrate that while there is role overlap and shared working, there is also something about each professional role that is unique. Acknowledging the contribution that each individual is able to make in a collaborative working situation is fundamental to them feeling that their particular role and contribution is valued.

Urie Bronfenbrenner (1979) also used a model of concentric circles to present his ecological theory of a child's development within the context of the system of

Figure 2.5: ECM and integrated services: integrated working at the core

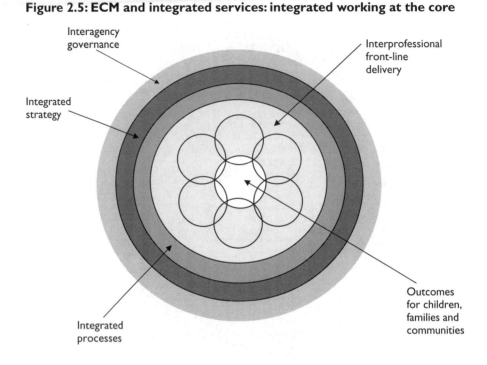

relationships that form his or her environment. He depicted how the individual at the centre is affected by the beliefs, values and customs of their parents and carers, which are, in turn, affected by the beliefs, values and customs of the wider socio-economic and cultural contexts. In examining each layer of the ECM 'onion' (Figure 2.5) and considering some of the potential influences on the success of integration at each level, the complexity of creating an integrated workforce for the benefit of children and families becomes more evident (see Table 2.1).

Clearly there is a need to prepare individuals to work together effectively in a children's workforce that is characterised by increasing complexity and change. The next section explores issues of interprofessional learning for better collaborative practice.

Learning together to work together

Where an interprofessional model of practice has not been the norm, with professionals and agencies working alongside but not necessarily with one another, there will be a need to change systems and processes and provide children's workforce development opportunities in order to empower staff to work in this way. In recognition of this, education providers are now expected to integrate opportunities for interprofessional learning in both pre- and post-qualifying programmes (QAA, 2005). Interprofessional learning as a concept mirrors interprofessional working in that it requires students to engage in interactive

Table 2.1: ECM levels of integration: influences on interprofessional working

Level		Influences
	Inter-agency governance	• shared vision for the experience of childhood in Britain • central government commitment to collaborate across departmental boundaries • shared responsibility for service improvement
	Integrated strategy	• current research • theory • policy • legislation
	Integrated processes	• organisational values • professional values • professional/service goals • professional practice principles • resources
	Interprofessional model of front line delivery	• unique charateristics of neighbourhoods and communities • personal and professional characteristics of indviduals • nature of interprofessional working relationships • location of practice
	Outcomes for children, families and communities	• individual values • family values • success of interprofessional working • engagement with child and family

learning to learn with, from and about one another for the benefit of collaborative service provision (Barr et al, 2005), again with the emphasis being on interaction and not on students simply learning the same content alongside one another.

By facilitating interprofessional learning with pre-qualifying students on different programmes of study, the development of unhelpful stereotypes of themselves and others in the workforce can be minimised (Carpenter, 1995; Freeth et al, 2005). Stereotypes, lack of understanding of other roles and different use of language across professional groups are cited as key barriers to successful collaborative working (Tunstall-Pedoe et al, 2003) and should be the focus of education programmes that aim to facilitate interprofessional learning and working. In addition to this, teaching foundational skills for collaboration such as respect for others, willingness to share, non-discriminatory and anti-oppressive practice, is essential to make the necessary cultural changes to enhance the capacity for integrated working.

A flexible workforce with transferable skills is a clear priority across health, social care and education (DoH, 2001; DfES, 2003; DfES and DoH, 2006). However, interprofessional education aims not only to help students understand what is common across professions and other roles but also affords participants an opportunity to articulate to others their unique potential contribution to the collaborative working situation; in other words, what they can offer as individuals that others involved cannot. To this end, interprofessional education is about valuing similarity and difference and about students learning to be clear about their own role in order to share that effectively with others. It does not aim to erode professional roles and identities, but to preserve them for the benefit of a balanced provision of services that maximises the use of resources by valuing general and specialist services in tandem.

ECM addresses this through the recommendation that everyone involved in providing services to children and families should undertake a Common Core curriculum to equip them with foundational skills for that work. By ensuring a parity of educational provision there is an opportunity for pre-qualifying students to understand where their roles overlap with others and where there is distinctiveness in the application of knowledge. Implementation of the Common Core curriculum also provides an opportunity for interprofessional learning to be embedded in programmes as a learning and teaching strategy. Education providers, taking best practice from successful interprofessional learning activity in other contexts; need to make the best use of this opportunity to enable students of the future children's workforce to learn together to work together. This will undoubtedly make a positive contribution towards children's workforce capacity for interprofessional working for the benefit of children and their families.

However, equipping people with the skills for interprofessional working is only one aspect of development. Organisational structures, systems and processes also need to become more integrated in order to facilitate collaborative working across the children's workforce. Putting policy into practice and collaboratively creating an infrastructure for interprofessional working is a major challenge for local organisations.

Making interprofessional working a reality

Newer initiatives such as Children's Centres will need to establish themselves in such a way that their internal processes can integrate with those of existing, mainstream services to ensure that interprofessional working for the benefit of children and their families can be achieved. One individual's reported experience of interprofessional working in one Children's Centre initiative is summarised in Table 2.2.

If they fail to establish themselves, there is a danger that Children's Centres become yet another separate organisation in an already complex health, social care and education system. Reportedly, there remains a general commitment across the local area to improving the experience of children and families through effective

Table 2.2: Collaboration and integration: a case example

Collaboration within Children's Centre	Collaboration between Children's Centre and statutory services	Implementing the CAF across organisations
• Duplication of effort between core team and three commissioned services identified as a problem • Recognised need for all involved to continue to feel valued • Recognised need for more effective use of available resource • Referral process streamlined • Collective decision making meeting established Outcome: • Better working relationships • Better use of resource • Reduced the need for multiple referral by outside agencies • Quicker response to families	• Working relationships difficult to establish • Lack of understanding of Children's Centre role and function • Information sharing particularly problematic • Duplication of effort between health visitors and Children's Centre staff in assessing, collecting and recording demographic data identified as a problem • Lack of integrated electronic recording systems • Reliance on informal information sharing which varied levels of commitment by mainstream professionals to share information • Creating a formal integrated process and system for the required level of information to be shared would take the responsibility away from individuals and provide a greater consistency and stability; however, integrated systems to support information sharing are far from a reality	• At a local level there was initial agreement that the CAF would become the priority tool for assessing children for primary and preventative support and development needs • CAF used by Children's Centre staff • In the absence of a compulsory policy directive, individuals in a range of services have reverted to using their traditional assessment documentation • Not everyone in the locality has undertaken the training to use the CAF • Some experienced professionals, have expressed a view that its reductionist format is at odds with their expert intuitive practice and that completing the CAF takes much longer than their usual mode of assessment • While CAF has been created to aid interprofessional working across agencies and sectors, its adoption as mainstream practice is problematic; the implementation of strategies and policies will not be successful unless a sharing culture is established in tandem

collaborative working. It appears that the next step is a more strategic effort across a wider population area, in order to explore more robust collaborative systems that can be replicated elsewhere. In the spirit of interprofessional working, it is crucial that representatives of the stakeholder groups involved should be included in these discussions if cross-sector systems and process are to be integrated.

Conclusion

Clearly the subject of interprofessional working is complex and there is a multiplicity of factors that will affect the success of any collaborative working venture. Table 2.3 illustrates some of the key issues.

While ECM clearly outlines the five different priority areas for meeting the needs of children and families, there is a danger that these may simply drive a new organisational structure, dissolving previous structures and ways of working and implementing new ones. For example, a safeguarding children team could be established around 'staying safe', while the 'staying healthy' team is located in the health domain. So that interprofessional working benefits the service users, children and their families, there is need for the five ECM key areas to be at the heart of everyone's practice. Taking responsibility for all areas will necessitate the involvement of other agencies and services. As professionals openly recognise the limitations of their own professional input and perspective they should seek to collaborate with others who can fill the gaps in the services that they provide to families. Information sharing is a core process in this way of working, but simply changing processes will not automatically change attitudes. Interprofessional working requires a culture of willingness to share and learn from each other. Successful interprofessional working and information sharing should therefore be driven by the needs and aspirations of children and young people as well as by the five ECM outcomes. It will rely on systems, processes and tools which value the expertise of practitioners from every professional heritage while at the same time allowing opportunities for the development of shared understandings. For the past two decades, services for children and families have been subject to unprecedented change. Maybe it is time to slow down and allow these new ways of working to embed, develop and produce the desired results of a collaborative culture which has the welfare of children at its heart.

Table 2.3: Strengths, challenges, opportunities, risks and expectations that professionals might face in working interprofessionally

Strengths	Challenges	Opportunities	Risks	Expectations
• Child and family centred practice	• Expectations of the organisation	• A chance to be involved in the 'bigger picture'	• Becoming a generic practitioner	• Improved services to children and families
• Encourages a participatory approach	• Differences in history and / or culture of the professions	• Lateral thinking	• Reduction in specialist skills and knowledge	• Reduced costs
• Encourages life-long learning	• Language and jargon	• Identify areas for your personal development	• Lack of evidence base for the collaborative	• Increased productivity
• Creates a learning culture amongst collaborators	• Unclear roles and responsibilities	• Networking	aspects of new ways of working	• Improved communication
• Respects integrity and individual contributions	• Power dynamics	• Make a contribution to evidence/ knowledge underpinning practice	• Lack of autonomy	• Seamless service provision
• Recognises similarity and role overlap while valuing differences in professional perspectives	• Communication	• Improve your service to children and families	• Power relationships	• Holistic viewpoint (whole systems approach)
• Potential increase in productivity	• Logistics / resources	• Share information effectively	• Communication	• Greater commitment
• Promotes support networks	• Finding systems that work for all		• 'Too many cooks'	• Improved job satisfaction
	• Changing well embedded working cultures		• Funding	• New systems result in new ways of working
	• Engaging individuals		• Unnecessary breach of confidentiality	

References

Anning, A., Cottrell, D., Frost, N., Green, J. and Robinson, M. (2006) *Developing multiprofessional teamwork for integrated children's services*, Buckingham: Open University Press.

Barr, H., Koppel, I., Reeves, S., Hammick, M. and Freeth, D. (2005) *Effective interprofessional education: Argument, assumption and evidence*, Oxford: Blackwell Publishing.

Bronfenbrenner, U. (1979) *The ecology of human development*, Cambridge, MA: Harvard University Press

Carpenter, J. (1995) 'Doctors and nurses: stereotypes and stereotype change in interprofessional education', *Journal of Interprofessional Care*, vol 9, pp 151-61.

DCSF (2007) *Effective integrated working: Findings of the Concept of Operations Study*, London: Stationery Office.

DfES (Department for Education and Skills) (2003) *Every Child Matters* www.everychildmatters.gov.uk

DfES (2004) *The Children Act 2004*, London: The Stationery Office.

DfES (2006) *Information sharing: Practitioners' guide*, London: The Stationery Office.

DfES and DoH (Department of Health) (2006) *Options for excellence: Building the social care workforce for the future*, London: The Stationery Office.

DoH (2000) *The Framework for Assessment for Children in Need and their Families*, London: The Stationery Office.

DoH (2000) *The NHS Plan*, London: The Stationery Office.

DoH (2001) *Learning together, working together*, London: The Stationery Office.

DoH (2001b) *Health visitor practice development resource pack*, London: The Stationery Office.

Freeth, D., Hammick, M., Reeves, S., Koppel, I. and Barr, H. (2005) *Effective interprofessional education: Development delivery and evaluation*, Oxford: Blackwell Publishing.

Frost, N. (2005) in Anning, A., Cottrell, D., Frost, N., Green, J. and Robinson, M. (eds) *Developing multiprofessional teamwork for integrated children's services*, Buckingham: Open University Press.

Hudson, B. (2005) 'Information sharing and children's services reform in England: can legislation change practice?', *Journal of Interprofessional Care*, vol 19, no 6, pp 537-637.

Huxham, C. (ed) (1996) *Creating collaborative advantage*, London: Sage Publications.

Machin, A.I. (2008) 'Role identity in a turbulent environment: the case of health visiting', PhD Thesis (unpublished).

Meads, G. and Ashcroft, J. (2005) *The case for interprofessional collaboration*, Oxford: Blackwell Publishing.

QAA (2005) Statement of Common Purpose, available at: www.qaa.ac.uk/academicinfrastructure/benchmark/health/

Quinney, A. (2006) *Collaborative social work practice*, Exeter: Learning Matters.

Tunstall-Pedoe, S., Rink, E. and Hilton, S. (2003) 'Students' attitudes to undergraduate interprofessional education', *Journal of Interprofessional Care*, vol 17, no 2, pp 161-72.

THREE

Education and Every Child Matters

Pat Broadhead and Douglas Martin

Introduction

This chapter reflects on the major role that schools and those who work within them have to play in the delivery of the ECM outcomes, in ways which are of most benefit for children. It opens by considering the climate and ethos within schools and by association, within local authorities within which ECM must now reside and grow. The once ubiquitous local education authority (LEA) has disappeared, replaced under new arrangements by one department, Children and Young People's Services within local authority directorates and federations of local services. At national level, we now have a Secretary of State for Children, Schools and Families. There is now a dual emphasis on care *and* education and Moss emphasises that 'policy is concerned with both the better protection of children and ensuring children can reach their full potential' (Moss, 2006, p 70).

In this chapter, when we refer to 'schools' we include early years services, primary and secondary schools. Our aim is to look at newly emerging roles within the wider re-modelling of the children's workforce and to consider the implications for schools and for teachers, as well as policy development. Within these contexts, we also explore the Common Assessment Framework (CAF) and the role of the lead professional (LP) in relation to schools and consider what a new teacher might expect or see as they enter this changing culture in schools and early years services.

Background: an educational heritage and new policy drivers

The educational system in England has a heritage born substantially of the 1988 Education Reform Act (ERA). A key question for ECM and education, and for this chapter, is whether and how this heritage is compatible with new policy drivers.

Since 1988, schools have been preoccupied by a standards agenda that has created competitive elements between schools linked to SAT scores, the related league tables and the naming and shaming of 'failing schools' via punitive Ofsted Inspections (Jeffery and Woods, 1996; 1998; Fitzgibbon and Stephenson-Forster, 1999; Case et al, 2000). The National Curriculum always lacked flexibility with two unsuccessful attempts by Lord Ron Dearing to slim it down. This curricular overload began to inhibit teachers from creating and sustaining a curriculum that might respond to children's own interests and agendas or that might even use children's interests and agendas as a starting point for curricular activity. Alongside this, and despite best efforts, truancy began to cause concerns in the secondary and primary sectors (Reid, 2005), although, more recently, slight improvements in attendance are emerging (DCFS, 2007a). It has also been shown that there are strong links between levels of attendance and levels of attainment (Schagen et al, 2004), which suggests that testing regimes may create disaffection for those with learning difficulties. Despite this, there is continued pressure on pupils and staff to demonstrate children's academic achievements. The early years foundation stage, to be implemented from September 2008, identifies targets to be achieved by children by the end of their foundation stage, aged 5 years. In primary schools, sport and physical education – a key form of self-expression for many children – were almost entirely removed from the curriculum to make way for the daily and extended diet of literacy and numeracy. Ironic now that our concerns are national levels of obesity (Hawkins et al, 2007). Drama and music similarly became marginalised. It is hard to believe now that in the early days of assessment policy development it was proposed that all areas of the National Curriculum would be subject to Standard Assessment Tasks (as they were first named) to bring parity across subjects but was, as we know, reduced to maths and English, with science being included and excluded at various times. A curricular hierarchy and emphasis emerged in our schools and this has subsequently threatened other subjects, especially in our primary schools.

In this climate of striving for measurable and comparative academic excellence and regular inspections, schools (generally but not of course exclusively) gradually distanced themselves from the affective, to focus on the cognitive. With an emphasis on subject knowledge acquisition, especially in relation to testing and with particular subjects having primacy and dominance, a pedagogy of child/student-direction, based on personal interests and agendas gradually disappeared; there was no time for it. The curriculum became substantially teacher-determined. Alongside this, the playful learning agenda disappeared from debate and from many Year 1 and reception classrooms (Wood and Attfield, 1996; Anning, 1997; Broadhead, 2004). With its disappearance went yet another opportunity for pupils to believe that their interests and agendas had a welcome place within their school setting.

In recognition of this unrelenting stream of policy imperatives being imposed on schools, in June 2007, the Cabinet Office launched a better regulation strategy for the public sector, under the heading of the New Relationship with Schools (NRwS), aimed at reducing unnecessary bureaucracy in schools. This was is in direct response to the recognition of the difficulties facing schools in implementing the ECM agenda with their present educational heritage. But will this be sufficient in re-introducing a child/student initiated pedagogy to sit alongside a teacher-determined pedagogy? This chapter argues that this is a key part of having the chance to 'reach one's full potential' in an educational setting.

The five outcomes of ECM represent a return to a holistic perspective on children and young people and to an emphasis on well-being as a right. Section 10 of the 2004 Children Act, gave a duty to local authorities to promote inter-agency co-operation to improve children's well-being as part of the five outcomes of ECM. Given the prevailing educational climate and its tight grip on school ethos, it was unsurprising that, in the first instance, many schools thought that ECM was someone else's agenda. A poll of 805 head teachers in 2005 found that 37% of heads were opposed to the policy and only 11% were fully in favour, suggesting that, even if this is changing, large-scale change may take time (Lewis, 2006).

Well-being as a right is also emphasised by the UN Convention on the Rights of the Child:

- Article 12 identifies the child's right to express views;
- Article 29 endorses holistic approaches to education being about the child's right to develop fully;
- Article 31 identifies the child's right to rest, play and do things they enjoy wherever they are.

In educational terms we might argue that substantial change is needed in many of our schools to bring these rights to full expression in educational settings.

These debates about learning and enjoyment are not new in education but never before has the wider agenda of the five outcomes prevailed. Schools may say they have always emphasised these aspects, but the standards agenda has, to various extents, driven them away from the implied inter-connection between 'enjoying and achieving' creating an emphasis on 'transmissive teaching' rather than 'transformative learning' (O'Sullivan, 1999). Children and young people need to feel valued, recognised and included, and schools now have a responsibility to ensure all children experience learning in these ways (Cassen and Kingdom, 2007).

The current position

The growth of extended services around schools and Children's Centres

An announcement by the Secretary of State for Children, Schools and Families in July 2007 stated that, with an injection of £1.3 billion into the Extended Schools' expansion the intention was to move towards every school offering access to extended services by 2010. The Secretary of State announced:

> As the best schools demonstrate, you cannot raise standards and close achievement gaps without focussing on all the needs of every single child and tackling every obstacle to their learning. Extended schools do just that – improve children's lives, boosting their attainment and placing schools at the heart of communities. (DCSF, 2007b)

The core offer that all primary and secondary schools will be required to make by 2010 includes:

- a varied menu of study support activities such as homework, sports and music clubs;
- high-quality childcare provided on primary school sites or through local providers, with supervised transfer arrangements where appropriate, available 8am-6pm all year round;
- parenting support, including information sessions for parents at key transition points, parenting programmes run with the support of other children's services, and family learning sessions to allow children to learn with their parents;
- identifying children with particular needs to ensure swift and easy referral to a wide range of specialist support services such as speech therapy, child and adolescent mental health services, family support services, intensive behaviour support and sexual health services;
- ICT, sports and arts facilities, and adult learning for the wider community.

Not every school will provide all of these. The models emerging are ones of partnership in which clusters of schools are working together in local communities. Where they are well-developed, these partnerships include not only primary and secondary schools but also youth services or voluntary groups providing after-school and holiday clubs, school attendance officers, social services, educational psychology services and the school nurse, amongst others. One head teacher we spoke to talked of key personnel (such as social workers) now progressing with children through their primary and secondary schooling bringing continuity for everyone. In many cases, these local partnerships also include a Children's Centre and, in providing childcare, can include private and voluntary sector providers within the local community. Much of this has grown out of earlier initiatives such as Early Years Development and Childcare Partnerships (EYDCPs) and their related work and the Early Excellence Centres and local Sure Start programmes. It became apparent that there were substantial costs associated with providing and maintaining a Children's Centre in every community. Although new buildings emerged across the country, the broader spectrum of activity is now through partnership developments relating to school-based, extended services.

Full service schools and community schools, as they were previously known, have been established for some time (Ball, 1998; Cummings et al, 2004); these have formed the blue-print for the national roll-out. Early work was focused on areas of economic disadvantage because it was recognised that pupil disaffection was higher in these areas and that the associated challenges for schools were greater. But is ECM enough? As MacBeath et al state:

> There are systemic reasons why some schools are on the edge. These are not easily addressed by purely educational interventions. They require more joined up social and economic policy. Every Child Matters

goes some way to recognising the need for more coherent delivery of services but is obliged to work within local infrastructures which do not address wider systemic issues. (MacBeath et al, 2007, p 137)

A school's core business is education – teaching and learning; in order to holistically address their students' lives within the wider community and the impact of this on teaching and learning, schools are being required to change. What MacBeath et al ask is whether the wider social context is changing sufficiently to support schools. We have already considered the impact of the testing regime on the ethos of the school and the tensions for pupils who find it hard to learn. Dyson also notes differences in the way schools operate:

> Some community-orientated schools focus very much on what people lack or cannot do – their low aspirations, their disengagement from learning, their poor parenting skills and so on – and try to find ways of changing these negative or dysfunctional aspects of individuals and families. Others focus on the disadvantaged conditions and limited opportunities that people experience and set about changing these external circumstances rather than the people themselves. (Dyson, 2006, p 99)

All schools have a prevailing ethos that drives their attitudes towards and their relationships with the local community. This ethos is driven mainly by those in management and leadership roles. One way in which new teachers may experience this ethos is in how their colleagues talk about students and their families in both informal and formal contexts. In the examples described by Dyson above, conversations in the former type of school are more likely to be disrespectful and disregarding than in the latter schools he describes. With greater numbers of professionals in and around schools who better understand the challenging nature of some children's and young people's lives outside school, the more likely it would seem, that schools will move towards the latter, more understanding ethos; only time will tell.

The curriculum and personalisation

Personalisation of learning has been placed at the centre of innovation and reform in education and is a key part of the ECM agenda in schools. Personalisation is depicted as a way in which a young person's learning experience becomes better matched to their needs, aspirations, interests and knowledge. It is about the learner's active engagement in their own learning process. Many schools are using individual learning plans (ILPs) to achieve this. There is no one model in use and schools and colleges are developing their own models and processes based on local authority guidelines. With the support of their teachers or from learning mentors, pupils record their successes, assess their progress and think through their needs, goals and aspirations. Some schools are assigning learning mentors to individual pupils or pupils are being located in small coaching groups, having ongoing links with key individuals, usually also learning mentors, to bring stability to their learning experiences and forward planning.

We argue that personalised learning is about much more than ILPs, important as they are. It should encompass what happens in classrooms within teaching–learning contexts. It is also, as Kirk and Broadhead note:

> an invitation to assume ownership of the teaching and learning process, to be suspicious of one-size-fits-all prescriptions and to reject a model of the learning process in which a uniform curricular diet is rigidly dispensed to all. It challenges teachers' pedagogical resourcefulness, demanding of them a capacity to draw on an extensive repertoire of strategies to promote learning. (Kirk and Broadhead, 2007, p 12)

The building of 'an extensive repertoire of strategies to promote learning' is a clear indication of the need for continuing professional development (CPD) for teachers in relation to these aspects of ECM. Schagen et al's (2004) work on truancy also indicated links for primary and secondary schools between the attitudes of pupils to the school and the relationships between schools and parents. Extended services around schools and Children's Centres are expected to support parental and family learning; many schools now have staff responsible for family support links, often not trained teachers, and these roles will grow in the future, hopefully making school a more meaningful experience for the once disaffected pupils. With the re-focusing on personalised learning and an extending pedagogical repertoire, hopefully the child and their learning, rather than their capacities in relation to 'boxes being ticked' will be to the fore.

We also make a plea here, albeit brief, for playful learning to be valued as personalised learning, especially for young learners. This chapter does not allow the space for extended argument of this position, but we offer the following quote to highlight the integral links between play and personalised learning:

> Play offers opportunities for emotional exploration and expression, opportunities to make and strengthen friendships, opportunities for deepening language skills and, perhaps most of all, the chance to take ownership of learning, to construct understandings and in facilitative environments, the chance for adults and children to co-construct the curriculum. While play belongs to children, its facilitation offers a bridge for adults into the child's thinking and understanding. (Broadhead, 2004, p 130)

Understanding what this means in practice has implication for teachers' CPD needs. Personalised learning is not a simple issue and not just a matter of ILPs if significant changes are to be made to the learning experience for all pupils in schools. Despite the growing range of professionals in schools, and their contributory roles, there are clear implications for how the curriculum is delivered in classrooms, by teachers, and, as we have indicated above, there are clear implications for policy in relation to our present educational heritage.

The changing face of the local authority

From the 1988 Education Act onwards, through various further Education Acts, LEAs have had their powers to call schools to account eroded. There had been a strong push during the extended period of Conservative government to undermine and, many believed, to eradicate LEAs, especially when, under the 1988 Education Act, schools were given the power to opt out of their LEA and become grant-maintained – an option that predominantly secondary schools took up. In opting out, they gained substantial control of huge budgets and as local authorities lost this income, staffing was also affected. Schools were no longer required to buy into local authorities support services and many became isolated from networks of schools; a situation exacerbated by the competitiveness of local league tables.

A key part of ECM has been the move towards multi-agency working and multi-professional practice (Anning et al, 2006). In many ways, changes in early years services have led the way in this. The Childcare Bill 2005 aimed to remove the distinction between care and education by creating the early years foundation stage from birth to the start of key stage 1 (during Year 1 in school); to be implemented by all registered early years settings and services. The Bill also placed a duty on local authorities to secure sufficient childcare for working parents. Moss (2006) identified this requirement as a potentially detrimental shift away from 'education' to 'childcare' to meet the needs of the economy rather than to address the rights of the child. The Bill also expanded the requirement in the 1989 Children Act to provide for 'children in need'. This had led to the growth of before- and after-school clubs, some on school premises, but usually led by volunteers or private providers and seldom seen as integral to the business of the school. These clubs were to be a small part of much bigger organisational shifts for schools as extended services began to emerge.

The roles and responsibilities of local authorities have recently begun to expand in relation to government policy. The 2006 Childcare Act gave new duties to work with NHS and Jobcentre Plus partners, to apply and improve on the five ECM outcomes in their areas and thereby to reduce inequality. These duties commenced on 1 April 2008. We can see that within 20 years there have been huge changes for local authority structures and duties, as well as huge shifts in the autonomy of schools within a rapidly expanding climate of service provision for children and families. It is onto this shifting ground of duty and autonomy that ECM is now located.

The education workforce

Entry into teaching

Teaching has been a graduate profession since the early 1970s; prior to that a teacher would qualify with a Certificate in Education. Now graduation is accompanied by qualified teacher status (QTS), which is awarded by the General Teaching Council. The traditional and most well-established route is through a three-year (or in a small number of cases four-year) undergraduate course with QTS. Another well-established option is for graduates to follow an intensive and highly demanding one-year route into teaching – the Postgraduate Certificate in Education (PGCE); an increasing number of these are now being offered at masters level, indeed, the government has signalled its intent to make teaching a 'Masters level profession' (DCSF, 2007c).

QTS routes are offered for early years (children aged 3-7), at primary (children aged 5-11) and with a subject specialism at secondary level. Early years and primary routes are generalist courses with the teacher expected to offer all subjects of the national curriculum plus others such as Citizenship or perhaps a foreign language. There have been opportunities in the past to develop specialist courses within early years and primary routes but are no requirements to do so at the moment. There are professional standards for assessing student progress and structuring courses and all courses are inspected by Ofsted.

All courses require A-levels, although higher education institutions set their own entry requirements, so the level of achievement demanded may vary. There are minimum standards relating to QTS. All candidates must have GCSE in English and maths at grade C or above and those on early years and primary courses require GCSE science at grade C.

There other entry options into teaching. A graduate can participate in a school-centred initial teacher training (SCITT), where local authorities and schools are closely involved in course delivery and assessment. Teach First is designed to allow top graduates to spend two years working in challenging secondary schools in London, Manchester and the Midlands, qualifying as a teacher while completing leadership training and work experience with selected employers. This is a two-year course. There are other employment-based options such as the Graduate Teacher Programme and the Registered Teacher Programme; there are also specific opportunities to receive QTS for those trained to teach overseas. PGCE and SCITT students currently receive a tax-free bursary but there will be reductions in these from August 2008.

A newly qualified teacher (NQT) is entitled to be given time to build their identity, confidence and expertise as a classroom practitioner and to develop subject knowledge and pedagogical expertise without having to take on wider responsibilities. However, they do need to know how schools are changing and to know about the potentially wide range of other professionals with whom they may work, even if they are not yet in a lead role. This has implications for initial teacher training.

New professional roles in schools

Teaching assistants are now widespread and other roles, for example learning mentors, are becoming common, perhaps more so in secondary than in primary schools. Learning mentors in secondary schools often have backgrounds in youth work, while in primary schools, they often come through volunteering roles, going on to receive training as learning mentors. Very often people in these roles have a greater understanding of children's lives outside school and the impact this can have on their learning, because teachers have a greater preoccupation with knowledge acquisition and learning processes in the classroom. Together, they can see and reflect on the holistic needs of the child.

Interprofessional working and the CAF

Some schools are better than others at creating opportunities for professional interaction to facilitate this, but all schools will need to think about this under the new agenda. New types of partnerships are forming with the pupil at their centre and there are particular links with personalised learning here, especially for those children whose life experiences create learning difficulties.

While senior staff members in school might have overall responsibility for the development of the extended services around schools and Children's Centres and for the multi-professional dimensions of this work, there is no doubt that new teachers will need to engage with family link workers, social workers, health visitors, speech therapists and others, to a far greater extent than has been the case in the past.

> They must therefore understand the importance of professional dialogues and interaction and learn respect for the contributions made by other professional agencies in supporting children and families, key features within workforce re-modelling and a core feature of professionalism. (Kirk and Broadhead, 2007, p 20)

Once again, there are implications here for both initial training and for CPD.

One new role that should be manifest within schools at some point is that of the lead professional (LP). This may be a teacher, it may be a learning mentor; it will need to be a person who has been trained for the role and who has the time to fulfil the requirements in support of a child for whom a common assessment (CA) has been undertaken and who is recognised as having needs to be met in order to make the most of their educational experiences. The CA should be undertaken with the family, who are helped to identify their strengths and needs. The Common Assessment Framework used for this (see Chapter Two) is designed to be an early identification and intervention tool. Once a CA has been undertaken, a multi-agency team, which may include a class teacher, convenes around the child. Flexible schools will provide cover for multi-agency team meetings so that class teachers can attend. Not all multi-agency teams will meet on school sites, but some will.

It is not likely that a class teacher would have the time to be an LP in a multi-agency team, but a senior teacher may do so and may see it as a welcome professional development opportunity. At the time of writing several local authorities are trialling budget-holding LPs who have quicker access to financial solutions for children and young people in need, and the intention is to mainstream this role of budget-holding LPs from 2008.

Case example: Lead professional

While a class teacher is unlikely to be an LP, teachers or learning mentors may be well placed to recognise a child in difficulty for which a CA may be helpful. One example given to us was of a secondary pupil who never completed her homework and was always tired. It was discovered that she was sleeping three-in-a-bed and her youngest sibling was wetting the bed; the elder child was taking responsibility for changing sheets. A team was gathered to assess the student's needs and what support was available. An LP was identified and they were able to draw down funds to buy an extra bed and bedding for the family. The practical solution immediately improved the quality of her daily life and her capacity to re-engage with the curriculum and learning and to complete her homework.

The contribution of education to ECM

The five outcomes of ECM aim to release the learning potential of all children and young people, to help them get more out of learning and have more influence on their own futures. Schools have a substantial part to play in this and we have summarised below, under each of the five outcomes, the potential contribution of services, schools, teachers and other school-based professionals to ECM.

Being healthy

To contribute here, schools need time to bring back sport, physical education and dance: subjects marginalised for many years as some schools sold off their playing fields and as primary schools succumbed to the demands of the high status subjects dominated by SAT scores. An initiative that may contribute here is the new secondary curriculum emerging from the Qualifications and Curriculum Authority (QCA) which aims to reinstate some of these 'lost subjects' in order to bring a more balanced curriculum back into secondary schools. We would argue for the same consideration in primary schools.

Staying safe

Teachers have a clear role to play within multi-professional teams that gather around a child or young person after a CA has been undertaken. Early years and primary teachers, learning mentors and teachers with pastoral roles in secondary schools can be trusted confidantes if they have time to build good relationships and if they have access to the appropriate training to build these skills.

Enjoy and achieve

We have argued above for the need to acknowledge how the policy climate since 1988 has emphasised 'achieve' above 'enjoy'. The new secondary curriculum is addressing this aspect by placing less emphasis on subject knowledge and more on subject integration and learning process; it will need time to have an impact. The workforce is also being re-modelled; fewer teachers are being trained and a greater number of other school-based professionals are emerging. Schools are operating in new and different ways. The establishment of extended services around schools means that there will be a greater number of professionals available to hear the child's voice and to recognise the influence of barriers to learning within the child or young person's life. This will lead to new career opportunities for teachers as well as, hopefully, more meaningful learning experiences for pupils.

What we still do not have are deeply embedded, well articulated and commonly understood principles of pedagogical practice, applicable across all age ranges. Without these, new curriculum initiatives continue to run the risk of being 'reactive or opportunistic appropriation' (Alexander, 2004, p 29) as the curriculum re-modelling continues to swing pendulum-like from knowledge to process and back again without any clear connections being made in terms of what happens during the teaching and learning.

Make a positive contribution

We have argued that personalised learning must find voice in all classrooms and not only through ILPs. CPD should help teachers to develop their pedagogical repertoires to take account of children's and young people's interests within the curriculum as planned and delivered, within early years and in primary and secondary schools. There are still questions about whether schools can truly address an entitlement agenda if they do not address the ways in which they may be perpetuating disadvantage and discrimination through the curriculum and through testing. The children and families most at risk remain at risk of being disenfranchised from educational services and from learning opportunities; those risks are not yet past.

Achieve economic well-being

Schools play a disproportionately significant role in academic success, but they are only one of many variables required for educational success and the associated factor of quality of life through economic viability (West-Burnham, 2006). Changes happening in schools now will, we believe, only make a real difference in beginning to combat poverty if schools can shake off the legacy of the ERA and, on behalf of their pupils, begin to reap the benefits of these significant new reforms.

Summary

In the early part of this chapter statistics noted that, in 2005, only 11% of heads were fully in favour of applying ECM in schools. A key barrier might have been their preoccupation with the standards agenda and testing, an ethos that has now prevailed for almost 20 years. With the global pressures for economic viability and the inherent links with the perceived need for an increasingly skilled workforce, schools remain in an especially challenging position in relation to implementing ECM. In a recent survey, schools identified other barriers to implementation, including, for example, their reluctance to charge for services because they might exclude some parents and children from services. A challenge was also recognised in relation to taking time to develop interconnections with cluster partners (DCSF 2008). Of all professionals, teachers have the most frequent and regular contact with children and young people, and yet may still see themselves substantially constrained by the pressures relating to the standards agenda to focus on knowledge transmission rather than relationship building. The increasing numbers of other adults working in schools may go some way towards ameliorating this, but teacher–pupil relationship building centred on inclusive pedagogies is one way forward and might most substantially capture the spirit of ECM in practice in schools. A consultation process, ongoing as we conclude this chapter, is looking at the role of schools in promoting pupil well-being. 'Unlocking potential' is seen as the core business of schools and as being closely associated with achievement, but there may be some way to go to shift the ethos. Schools are changing; their managerial and staffing structures are changing and, in some cases, their commitment to closer community links is also influencing the way they are developing. It will be a loss for all schools if ECM is seen as only being for the economically disadvantaged or at risk communities. It is, after all, an entitlement for every child and young person and given the amount of time they spend in school, surely that entitlement should be reflected in their day-to-day experiences.

Acknowledgements
Thanks to those who gave their time to be interviewed in support of the development of this chapter: your input was immensely helpful.

References

Alexander, A. (2004) 'Still no pedagogy? Principle, pragmatism and compliance in primary education', *Cambridge Journal of Education*, vol 34, no 1, pp 7-33.

Anning, A. (1997) *The First Years at School*, Buckingham: Open University Press.

Anning, A., Cottrell, D.M., Frost, N. and Green, J. (2006) *Developing multi-professional teamwork for integrated Children's Services*, Maidenhead: Open University Press.

Ball, M. (1998) *School inclusion: The school, the family and the community*, York: Joseph Rowntree Foundation

Broadhead, P. (2004) *Early years play and learning: Developing social skills and cooperation*, London: Routledge.

Case, P., Case, S. and Catling, S. (2000) 'Please show you're working: a critical assessment of the impact of Ofsted inspection on primary teachers', *British Journal of Sociology of Education,* vol 21, no 2, pp 605-21.

Cassen, C. and Kingdom, G. (2007) *Tackling low educational achievement*, York: Joseph Rowntree Foundation.

Cummings, C., Dyson, A. and Todd, L. (2004) *Evaluation of the Extended Schools Pathfinder Project*, RR530, London: DfES.

DCFS (Department for Children, Schools and Families) (2007a) *Contribution of schools to Every Child Matters outcomes: Evidence to support education productivity measures*, London: DCSF.

DCSF (2007b) '£1bn boost for extended schools', London: DCSF, available at www.everychildmatters.gov.uk/news/.

DCSF (2008) *Extended schools testing the delivery of the care offer in and around extended schools*, Final report No DCSF-RW037, London: DCSF.

Dyson, A. (2006) 'What are we learning from research?', in J. Piper (ed) *Schools Plus to Extended Schools: Lessons from the last five years*, Coventry: ContinYou.

Fitzgibbon, C.T. and Stephenson-Forster, N.J. (1999) 'Is Ofsted helpful?', in C. Cullingford, (ed) *An inspector calls: Ofsted and its effects on school standards*, London: Kogan Page.

Hawkins, S.S., Cole, T. and Dezateux, C. (2007) *Millennium Cohort Study: Childhood obesity*, Briefing 12, London: Institute of Education.

Jeffery, B. and Woods, P. (1996) 'Feeling de-professionalised: the social construction of emotions during an Ofsted inspection', *Cambridge Journal of Education*, vol 26, no 3, pp 375-91.

Jeffery, B. and Woods, P. (1998) *Testing teachers*, London: Falmer Press.

Kirk, G. and Broadhead, P. (2007) *Every Child Matters and teacher education: A UCET position paper*, Occasional Paper 17, London: University Council for the Education of Teachers.

Lewis, J. (2006) 'The school's role in encouraging behaviour for learning outside the classroom that supports learning within: a response to the 'Every Child Matters' and Extended Schools initiatives', *Support for Learning*, vol 21, no 4, pp 175-81.

MacBeath, J., Gray, J., Cullen, J., Frost, D., Steward, S. and Swaffield, S. (2007) *Schools on the edge: Responding to challenging circumstances*, London: Paul Chapman Publishing.

Moss, P. (2006) 'Farewell to childcare?', *National Institute Economic Review*, no 195, pp 70-83.

O'Sullivan, E. (1999) *Transformative learning: Educational vision for the 21st century*, London: Zed Books.

Reid, K. (2005) 'The causes, views and traits of school absenteeism and truancy: an analytical review', *Research in Education*, vol 74, November, pp 59-82.

Schagen, I., Benton, T. and Rutt, S. (2004) *Study of attendance in England: Report for the National Audit Office*, December, London: National Foundation for Educational Research.

West-Burnham, J. (2006) 'Extended Schools 2020: prospects and possibilities', in J. Piper (ed) *Schools Plus to Extended Schools: Lessons from the last five years*, Coventry: ContinYou.

Wood, E. and Attfield, J. (1996) *Play, learning and the early childhood curriculum*, London: Paul Chapman Publishing.

FOUR

Early years, childcare and Every Child Matters

Joan Santer and Lindey Cookson

Does *every* child *really* matter in the early years? Early years ideology focuses strongly on the holistic needs of the individual child, although the extent to which this rhetoric has been realised in practice can be questioned, due to the chequered history of provision, and generally low status of the workforce. This chapter will look at some of the key developments in provision and practice by providing a brief history of early years and childcare, considering the current position in relation to the ECM agenda, exploring key challenges for the workforce, providing illustrations from practice, and concluding with a discussion of issues and dilemmas.

The historical context

Early years education and childcare provision has only recently become the focus of government policy and has been vulnerable due to its non–statutory status and subsequent lack of funding, particularly in the private, voluntary and independent (PVI) sectors. Provision has had a turbulent and complex history, reflecting changing government priorities, which, in recent years, have evolved from a desire to enhance economic prosperity to prioritising the needs of children.

The role of women in society changed dramatically during the 20th century, with women entering education, training and employment in even larger numbers. There have also been significant changes to family structures, such as rises in divorce rates and increasing numbers of lone parent families (Yeo and Lovell, 2002), as well as more people moving away from wider family support networks. These social changes have led to increases in demand for childcare.

At certain points, such as during the Second World War and during the welfare state expansion of the 1960s, women were actively encouraged to enter the workplace and there was an accompanying increase in state provision of childcare. This was equally rapidly run down when women's contribution to the labour market was perceived as less important.

With the exception of the influence of Bowlby's work (1951), which suggested that crèches had serious and permanent effects on children, early provision for young children appears to have been created and withdrawn more for pragmatic reasons than because of a genuine concern about the potential adverse effects of childcare outside the home.

'Casual' childminding grew from 1946 and in the 1960s the Pre-school Playgroups Association (now the Pre-School Learning Alliance) was established to ensure that pre-school provision would meet children's social and educational needs. State funded nursery education and childcare was provided according to the priorities of the local authority, so PVI provision developed alongside local authority maintained provision. These different services tended to serve different groups, with social services day nurseries more likely to serve disadvantaged communities, while middle class families predominantly used playgroups.

This historic diversity of provision led to the fragmentation of services and the separation of 'care' and 'education'. Provision in nursery schools and nursery and reception classes has traditionally been associated with the 'education' of the child, with 'care' a strong feature of day care. Today children from birth-5 years can still be found in various different types of provision, including local authority maintained, non-maintained and private. Nursery schools and reception classes are maintained forms of provision usually housed within schools. Other types of provision supplied by the PVI sector such as playgroups, daycare, crèches and childminders can be found in many different locations. Settings vary to cater for different age groups, they are open for different hours over the day, week and year, some are free while others charge, curriculum experiences differ, and staff have different levels of training and qualifications.

More recently, research findings highlighted the importance of providing for the educational needs of young children, and the integral role that parents play in this process. This led to the development of family centres and integrated centres in which a number of services endeavoured to work on behalf of both children and families. These were the forerunners of the recent Sure Start initiative.

The current position

It is now generally accepted that pre-school provision brings social and cognitive benefits to children, particularly those in areas of disadvantage (Lazar and Darlington, 1987; Osborn and Milbank, 1987; Schweinhart and Weikart, 1993; Hohmann and Weikart, 1995; Sylva et al, 2004). These benefits can have long lasting effects on both later academic achievement and social responsibility (Athey, 1990; Schweinhart and Weikart, 1993; Sylva et al, 2004; Mathers et al, 2007). A number of research projects have sought to look more closely at the relationship between type of setting and quality of provision, but findings have been confusing and, at times, conflicting. Jowett and Sylva (1982) comparing playgroups with local authority pre-school provision, found that the latter provided more cognitive challenge and creativity for children than the former. In contrast, Osborn and Milbank (1987) suggested that home-based playgroups did particularly well. Ofsted (2001) and the Effective Provision of Preschool Education (EPPE) project noted that playgroups performed slightly less effectively than other providers (Sylva et al, 2004).

The EPPE project (Sylva et al, 2004) found that good-quality provision occurs across all types of settings, but integrated centres combining education and care, and nursery schools that also have a high proportion of trained teachers tend to promote better intellectual outcomes for children. This was supported by Sammons et al (2004) who reported that traditional nursery schools and integrated centres had highest scores, followed by nursery classes.

The National Childcare Strategy (DfEE, 1998) brought about a key change in social policy which aimed to ensure that quality, affordable, accessible childcare was available in every community for 0- to 14-year-olds. The ECM agenda (DfES, 2004a), and subsequent proposals for early years and childcare in the Ten Year Strategy for Childcare (DfES, 2004b) have built on this by addressing some of the ongoing difficulties for those working with young children. This has heralded significant changes in provision for young children and their families. Table 4.1 provides details of some of the developments in policy and practice in early years and childcare.

The 2004 Children Act provides 'the legislative framework to build services around the needs of children and young people', while the 2006 Childcare Act states as follows.

All providers must comply with the Childcare Act 2006 which charges local authorities to improve the well being of, and reduce inequalities between, young children in their area. They are responsible for the education, care and health of young children specifically:

- physical and mental health and emotional well-being
- protection from harm and neglect
- education training and recreation
- contribution made by children to society
- social and economic well-being (DfES 2006, s 40)

How this is to be achieved will be discussed under the themes of the Ten Year Childcare Strategy.

Choice and flexibility

Hudson et al (2004) found that some mothers who returned to work early only did so for financial reasons, and that fathers increasingly wanted to play a greater role in their child's first year of life. Taking cognisance of this and recognising the influential role that parents play, the government has sought to develop a package of 'family friendly' benefits, giving more choice, with flexible and increased maternity and paternity leave for the child's first year, followed by entitlement to flexible working hours as well as a phased return to work. This initiative aims to improve retention rates in employment and bring an increase in the skilled workforce. To support parents in balancing their work with their family life, free early education provision, with flexible availability, has been increased from 12.5 to 15 hours per week (DfES, 2004b).

Table 4.1: Recent developments in early years and childcare policy and legislation

1989	The Children Act emphasised the welfare of the child, parental responsibilities, co-operation between agencies.
1989	UN Convention on the Rights of the Child
1994	The Early Years Task Force provided the foundation on which later early years policy was built
1996	Voucher scheme for nursery education: the first state funding for a universal early years service
1996	Desirable Outcomes for Children's Learning on Entering Compulsory Education introduced six outcomes for children's learning
1998	The National Childcare Strategy was launched as part of government's anti-poverty strategy to expand good-quality childcare to enable parents to return to work
1998	Early Years Development and Childcare Partnerships (EYDCPs) drew together representatives from different early years and childcare sectors, to realise the aims of the National Childcare Strategy
2000	Foundation Stage (for children 3-5 years): curriculum guidance for the Foundation Stage was published
1997-2006	Early Excellence Centres established to foster the integration of care and education of young children
1999-2006	Sure Start Programmes emphasised family support and integrated services to tackle child poverty and social inequalities
2000-2006	Neighbourhood Nursery Initiative provided new provision in disadvantaged areas
2001	National Standards for Daycare and Childminding
2002	Sure Start Unit established
2003-present day	Children's Centres: the Labour government committed itself to providing 2,500 Children's Centres by 2008 and 3,100 by 2010.
2003	Birth to Three Matters Framework: now subsumed in the Early Years Foundation Stage 2008
2003	Every Child Matters
2004	The Children Act
2004	Choice for parents, the best start for children: A ten-year strategy for childcare
2005	Ofsted inspections began to focus on the ECM outcomes
2006	The Childcare Act speaks of high-quality childcare for under-fives and their families
2006	Transformation Fund: the government committed £250 million over two years to support the growth of EYPs particularly in PVI settings
2006	The first early years professional training: around 400 candidates achieving Early Years status by March 2007
2006	Consultation on early years foundation stage (birth-5 years), implemented in September 2008
2007	*The Children's Plan: Building brighter futures.* Detailing the government's commitment to provide more support for parents and families, safe play places for children and further develop the early years workforce)

Availability and affordability

There are duties placed on local authorities not only to promote social mobility and reduce inequalities, but to deliver integrated services ensuring a seamless experience for parents and children. The government aims to have 3,500 Children's Centres by 2010 offering easy access to integrated services in each local community.

Section 6 of the 2006 Childcare Act states that parents must have sufficient provision to enable them to work or retrain. Local authorities have a duty to undertake a comprehensive and robust Childcare Sufficiency Assessment (DfES, 2007b) to identify gaps in provision by proactively consulting with parents, communities and employers. This is to be published widely, regularly reviewed and updated. In this way services will be reshaped and duplication of provision minimised. Systems of data collection will pay special attention to demographics, the needs of disabled children, ethnic minorities, looked after and foster children, and children from socially excluded groups. The patterns of training and adult learning, working patterns (shifts outside 8am-6pm), property development, population composition and density will all be key factors in informing provision. Providers are to work together to this end and systems are to be created which will alert where families' needs are not met. One measure of success will be the ease with which families can access provision.

The Children's Information Service is the starting point for gathering information. It will act as a brokerage agent within each local authority to assist parents in accessing suitable childcare by providing advice, information and guidance on holiday schemes, childcare costs, tax credits and parental employment laws. Sure Start Children's Centres and Extended Schools will be key information points acting as gateways to other services. Job Centre Plus is to improve the information available so that parents become 'informed consumers'. There will also be a strong commitment to consulting with employers, parents, and other key stakeholders on the details of the proposed measures as well as listening to the voices of children.

Quality

The government's expressed aim is that childcare provision in this country should be amongst the best in the world, based on the understanding that when children experience good-quality childcare there are improved outcomes (Athey, 1990; Hohmann and Weikart, 1995). *Desirable outcomes for children's learning at age 5* (SCAA, 1996) was the first move towards developing a consistent learning experience for children across all types of settings, followed in 2000 by the introduction of the foundation stage for children aged 3-5 years. Subsequently, the Birth to Three Matters Framework (DfES, 2004) focused on good practice for babies and toddlers, and the National Standards for Under 8's Daycare and Childminding (DfES, 2003) gave guidance on standards required for registration. These documents were drawn together to become the EYFS for children aged 0–5 years (DfES 2007a). Quality services are to be achieved primarily through the early years foundation stage (0–5 years), which outlines the introduction of a new professional role, the development of a career structure for those who work with young children, an integrated inspection service and closer partnership with parents. The EYFS aims to provide a consistent approach to care, learning and development across all settings and is the key means of meeting the ECM outcomes in the early years.

The Rumbold Report (DES, 1990) identified concerns regarding the educational experiences of 3- to 4-year-olds, specifically that a high proportion of practitioners were either unqualified or had low levels of qualifications. Since 1998 attempts have been made to raise the qualifications of the workforce. Today, maintained settings are typically led by graduates with qualified teacher status (QTS) and supported by staff with level 3 childcare qualifications. The current requirement for other registered early years and childcare providers is that leaders and supervisors be qualified to level 3, with 50% of the remaining staff having a level 2 qualification. While many childminders are working towards a level 3 qualification, this is not at present a requirement for registration. They are, however, expected to complete an introductory childminding course as well as a first aid course in order to register. This is moving in the right direction but still leaves many practitioners unqualified (Baldock et al, 2005).

Recent debate has also focused on the disparity in employment conditions and pay between early years and childcare workers in PVI settings and teachers in maintained provision (Osgood, 2004). The distinction between the 'care' and 'education' of young children in the UK and the perceived lower status of 'care' have been two drivers for reform of this area. The present discourse is not solely about accessing qualifications, but ensuring that qualifications are appropriate for the present models of early education and childcare. Moss suggested that a new type of worker is needed: 'a worker on a par with school teachers in terms of training and employment conditions' (2003, p 5). A new role of 'early years professional' (EYP) has been introduced to provide leadership in the implementation of the EYFS. This marks a commitment to introducing progression routes both in terms of qualifications and career paths. EYPs are recruited from a variety of backgrounds but must be graduates who can demonstrate competency against 39 standards that are closely related to work in early education and care (CWDC, 2007a). Furthermore, the government committed a £250 million 'Transformation Fund', which has been superceded by the Graduate Leader Fund of £305 million, to drive forward the development of EYPs, and ensure that one is employed in each Children's Centre by 2010 and all full day care settings by 2015. PVI settings will be eligible to receive various streams of funding to assist them in the recruitment and retention of staff. Childminder quality will be developed through training opportunities leading to level 3 qualifications, dissemination of good practice, childminders' networks and more integrated working with local provision.

From September 2008 Ofsted inspects against the EYFS statutory guidance using a more robust process aimed at enforcing standards and providing information to inform parents' choices. Settings and Sure Start Children's Centres must work in partnership with parents. They are to hear parents' voices, provide information to aid decision making, provide opportunities for observation of practice and enable them to participate in decision making. It is also important that they work together on the early identification of children with special educational needs.

The four key challenges for the workforce

The 2005 government vision for the children's workforce was built around meeting the needs of and improving outcomes for children. The four main areas identified as strategic challenges to children's services are recruitment, retention of staff; strengthening multi-disciplinary working and promoting stronger leadership and management.

Recruitment and retention

Recruitment and retention, which have always been problematic, have remained so due largely to poor employment conditions, confusion around qualifications and employment roles within the sector, and lack of clear progression routes and promotion opportunities. Early years workers are paid far less on average than other similarly qualified occupations, and are currently the lowest paid within the children's workforce (DfES, 2005a). Settings report high levels of staff turnover.

Childcare has traditionally been viewed as a natural extension of women's caring role and, despite a national recruitment drive to create a more diverse workforce, it remains a predominantly female domain (98%). This stereotypical perception often operates against men who may be viewed with suspicion for seeking work with young children. Lack of career structure and status has also been reported as deterring men from working with children. Minority ethnic groups, disabled people and older people are also under represented. Many local authorities have been proactive in their recruitment campaigns to target males. The following case study describes two such initiatives.

Case study: Local authority recruitment campaign

One local authority decided to begin recruitment activity early and in partnership with other agencies, and developed a package of 'Working with Children' workshops to be delivered to Year 9 students who were approaching their GCSE options. This introduced the concept of 'working with children' to both boys and girls.

This activity also led to the development and delivery of 'babysitting' courses which proved to be popular with boys as well as girls.

The local authority also commissioned a local theatre company to write a performance about working with children, which featured a male as one of the main characters and raised many of the issues facing men as a minority in the childcare workforce. The performance was delivered at recruitment events across the authority.

The introduction of the Common Core of Skills and Knowledge (DfES, 2005b), the Integrated Qualifications Framework (CWDC, 2007b) and the government's national recruitment campaign may assist employers in recruiting more diverse employees.

Attempts have been made to introduce new qualifications and job roles in the sector, but without long-term state funding it has proven difficult to improve career progression pathways. The recent development of Early Childhood Studies degrees and foundation degrees in Early Years have given practitioners access to further qualifications, but genuine promotion opportunities have remained limited. The newly introduced EYP role marks a commitment to introducing clear progression routes and aims to address many of the recruitment and retention issues facing this sector.

Debbie's case study is typical of the way in which many early years and childcare practitioners enter the workforce.

Case study: Flexible career paths

"I was a school governor at my children's school and we became increasingly concerned that our school had a falling school roll, largely because we did not have any pre-school provision. I approached the Head about setting up a play group but realised I was not qualified and it would take some time. There began a long journey that I would never have dreamt of! In 1994 I studied for a Diploma in Pre-School Practice (level 3) which meant I could be the leader. I set up the playgroup with myself and two other staff: both had their NNEB qualification. We started off with 12 children in a mobile attached to the school and operated for three mornings each week.

"Thirteen years on and I have seen huge changes in both provision, and in my own knowledge and experience. In terms of the provision, we now operate for ten sessions each week, delivering the foundation stage curriculum to three-fives, and our most recent Ofsted inspection gave us 'outstanding' in all areas.

"I have completed a foundation degree in Early Years and I am currently in my final year of a BA (Hons) in Learning in Families and Beyond. I am hoping to achieve EYP status in the near future. At the moment I am working with our local authority foundation stage consultant to identify the best way to train my staff team on the EYFS, ready for its introduction next year. It has been a long and exciting professional journey."

Multi-disciplinary working

A multi-disciplinary approach is another means by which better outcomes for children are to be achieved. The mandate to work more closely with other agencies is not new (DES, 1990). The 1989 Children Act enshrined in legislation the principles of collaboration and co-ordination in children's services. In practice, this has been difficult to achieve, as agencies bring different professional cultures and knowledge that influence them in formulating their ethos, aims, priorities, timescales and ways of working (Easen et al, 2000). Practitioners can see multi-disciplinary work as threatening their professional status, creating extra demands on already limited time and resources, and potentially bringing change to their conditions of service (Anning, 2001). Some agencies consider that the highly confidential nature of information they possess makes it ethically difficult for this to be shared; others that different agencies are encroaching on their professional territory and in response create boundaries. Critical issues for multi-agency work have been identified as communication and trust between groups, the breaking down of professional boundaries and a willingness to explore new ways of working. Abbott and Hevey believe that working together needs more than 'benign co-operation' (2001, p 180). They highlight the need for flexibility in approach and sharing of values and attitudes. Anning et al (2006) identify four levels of partnership in which partners move from:

1. **Co-operation**: working together to consistent goals but maintaining independence.
   to
2. **Collaboration**: planning together and identifying and addressing where their work overlaps and working towards common outcomes.
   to
3. **Co-ordination**: working and planning together in a systematic way with shared and agreed goals.
   finally to
4. **Integration**: merger; becoming one in order to enhance services.

This final level does not signify the creation of a homogenous professional group but reflects a commitment to sharing unique skills, expertise and knowledge for the benefit of children and families.

Early Years Development and Childcare Partnerships (EYDCP) were early models of working that pulled together representatives from different providers to develop and expand provision and support the growth of the workforce. A key duty in the new legislation is that local authorities via the Director of Children's Services and Lead Members for Children's Services are to lead on drawing together multi-agency services in strong and co-operative partnerships. Core services to be included for early childhood services are the agencies that have direct responsibility for children:

- early years provision;
- social services (parenting classes and family support);
- health services (midwifery, health visitors and speech and language therapists);
- Jobcentre Plus.

Through joint working to inform the Common Assessment Framework (CAF), children are to receive earlier and speedier assessment, improved quality of referrals and easy access to effective and specialised services.

The ECM agenda recognises that the delivery of more integrated services is a significant challenge that will require 'new ways of working and significant culture change for staff used to working within narrower professional and service-based boundaries' (DfES, 2004a, p 17). Anning et al (2006) assert that when individuals are confident in their professional identity then they will be able to transform it.

Case example: Successful joint working

Northumberland has introduced a Foundation Stage Liaison Programme which brings PVI settings and schools together. In some cases this has been so successful that the two providers are combining to provide Foundation Stage Unit provision where it is impossible to see where one form of provision ends and the other begins. Sunderland, a neighbouring authority, piloted the extended offer of early education to parents, which increased the hours of provision from 12.5 to 15 per week. An evaluation of this initiative revealed that many of the most successful strategies had involved close working between PVI and school settings.

Leadership and management

Research highlights the link between highly qualified managers and quality of provision (Sylva et al, 2004) and this has informed the agenda for the development of national and local initiatives to promote more effective leadership and management skills in early years and childcare settings.

There has been a growth in leaders and managers holding qualifications at level 4 and above, yet there remains a large number with no training beyond level 3. Rodd (1997) found that when training courses were offered to staff, they tended to be 'in-house', short courses offering little or no accreditation or qualification. Thus, many leaders are left to draw on knowledge gained from their level 3 training, which does not fully prepare them for a range of 'real life' management issues. Rodd's research identified a lack of confidence among managers and a reluctance to label themselves as 'leaders', which formed barriers to their development of management and leadership skills. Siraj-Blatchford and Manni (2006) reiterate these concerns and suggest that the core challenge is to make a transition from managing children to managing adults.

These issues need to be considered in the development of appropriate leadership and management training in this area. The National Professional Qualification in Integrated Centre Leadership (NPQICL) is now in place to support leaders of integrated centres, but this is a level 7 qualification and was not designed as an appropriate progression route for a manager of an early years setting who may currently hold a level 3 qualification. The role of the EYP does address leadership of the EYFS, but it is not intended that the EYP will be the person with management responsibility for the whole setting. Therefore, neither the NPQICL nor the EYP role directly fulfils the specific need to develop more highly qualified managers in early years and childcare settings. While there are some examples of local authorities working in partnership with training institutions to provide sector-specific leadership and management opportunities beyond level 3, there is currently no national strategy to meet this need.

A further difficulty in developing leadership and management training for the sector is that many established models of leadership theory have been developed in the male-dominated world of industry and business and therefore do not capture the distinct nature of leading an early years and childcare setting (Savage and Leeson, 2006; Siraj-Blatchford and Manni, 2006). A more progressive approach is one that favours 'authentic' leadership (Turner and Mavin, 2007) and adopts a self-evaluative and reflective approach such as that promoted in NPQICL.

Case example: Training and development

Durham local authority established training and development plans to develop a local supply of EYPs. However, concern over a lack of progression paths for the managers who then appeared to be left behind, led them to develop their own package of training specifically focused on managing an early years setting. The qualification – Effective Leadership and Management in Childcare – covers all aspects of leading and managing a childcare setting and has reflective practice as a central theme. It has been accredited with 40 credits at level 5 from Northumbria University. The course is paid for by Durham local authority, delivered at flexible times and supply cover is allocated to settings.

The contribution of the early years workforce to ECM

A key contribution of the early years and childcare workforce to the ECM agenda is through the delivery of the EYFS. Materials to support settings in the implementation of EYFS emphasise that it builds on the good practice already developed within the Birth to Three Matters Framework and the Foundation Stage (3-5 years). Therefore, for many practitioners, the skills, knowledge and competencies they have developed will continue to be utilised when working with children and parents within the four EYFS themes integral to effective practice.

The four EYFS themes

- **A unique child:** every child is a competent learner from birth who can be resilient, capable, confident and self assured.
- **Positive relationships:** children learn to be strong and independent from a base of loving and secure relationships with parents and/or a key person.
- **Enabling environments:** the environment plays a key role in supporting and extending children's development and learning.
- **Learning and development:** children develop and learn in different ways and at different rates, and all areas of learning and development are equally important and interconnected.

The government has provided detailed practice guidance (DfES, 2007e) which describes the elements of a 'principled approach' based on five statements.

1. Setting the standards

Practitioners are to be aware of the experiences that children share with their parents at home and build on these, so that the experiences children have in the setting will be both consistent and meaningful. Practitioners should offer children learning experiences that are individual to them, ensure that they progress at an appropriate pace, and have access to extra support if this is necessary.

2. Providing for equality of opportunity

Practitioners are to ensure that positive attitudes to diversity and difference are adopted so that from their early years children value diversity in others and by doing so make a positive contribution to society. This can be done in several ways by the appointment of staff both male and female, and individuals from different cultures. Environmental provision and resources such as play materials and utensils, wall displays and books should reflect diversity. Practitioners are to adopt individualised learning strategies, set appropriate challenges, and ensure that practice is anti-discriminatory. They are to recognise and respond appropriately to signs of early difficulties and alert other agencies as appropriate.

3. Creating the framework for partnership working

Practitioners are to ensure smooth transitions between settings by sharing information with parents, and other providers. Parents are to be supported in their relationship with their children by information sharing and provision of support in the home if this is necessary. Practitioners are also to work with professionals from other agencies to provide the best social care, learning opportunities and environments for *all* children. These include the emotional, as well as outdoor and indoor environments.

4. Improving quality and consistency

Practitioners are to meet the learning and development, and welfare requirements for the EYFS. The former includes the three elements of the early learning goals, the educational programme of experiences, skills and the process of teaching young children, and assessment arrangements. The latter includes safeguarding and promoting the welfare of children, promotion of good health and effective behaviour management, ensuring a safe physical environment, and providing a healthy and balanced diet. In this way the problematic distinctions between care and learning, and between birth-3 years and 3-5 years are being addressed.

5. Laying a secure foundation for future learning

Practitioners are to ensure that they lay secure foundations for learning by making it relevant, appropriate to the child's individual development, incorporating elements of challenge and ensuring that it is enjoyable. This will be achieved by carrying out ongoing observational assessment, and systematic recording and analysis of data based on a sound knowledge of children's development and learning. Observations will be matched to the early learning goals and used to plan children's subsequent play experiences. The EYFS is underpinned by a play-based approach; therefore practitioners are to have a sound knowledge of play and its contribution to children's development and learning.

It is important to note that in settings there will be a key person identified for each child; a co-ordinator responsible for children with special educational needs; and someone with lead responsibility for safeguarding children. Practitioners will contribute to the early years foundation profile and participate in moderation procedures. They will also work alongside other professionals in contributing to the CAF, interpreting data and measuring outcomes against action plans.

Settings are inspected against four of the five ECM outcomes: making a positive contribution; staying safe; being healthy; and enjoying and achieving. However, it is acknowledged that the provision of good-quality childcare makes an important contribution to the economic well-being of children, as it supports parents in their return to work (Ofsted, 2005).

The following case studies illustrate how the ECM outcomes are met in everyday activities.

Outcome: Making a positive contribution

Children are provided with experiences which will encourage a positive sense of self and independence, help them to develop positive relationships and to see themselves as part of a wider community. Children's voices are heard and valued, and young children are encouraged to value and respect each other.

Example: Children were involved in a range of activities which explored the environment and recycling. During circle time the children were given the challenge of trying to bring a heavy bag of recyclable items into the ring. This was too much for one child and gradually, one by one, the rest of the group got up to help. The children realised the benefits of working as a team rather than trying to do things for themselves. One child said: "Everyone had a go".

Outcome: Staying safe

Practitioners understand how to provide a calm, stable, child-friendly environment, which keeps children safe from harm. Young children are encouraged to develop their awareness of keeping safe, while also being encouraged to develop their own boundaries and to manage risk.

Example: The story of *The Gruffalo* was used to encourage children to think about feeling safe and to identify times when they felt frightened. Children took part in conversations about getting lost and one child shared his experience: "Two gentlemens helped me … workers … my name was on the microphone".

Others were able to describe what to do if lost:
"Tell the person in the shop."
"Cry."
"Go to the police."
"Ask someone on the till."
"Wait for someone to come."
The story was also linked to a trip to the park during which children were encouraged to identify potential risks. Children's ideas included:
"I think they need a gate so children don't run off."
"You might get cut on broken glass."
"You need your shoes on to stay safe."

Outcome: Being healthy

Practitioners understand the links between emotional and physical well-being of the young child, and value the importance of encouraging both. Children are offered a range of indoor and outdoor activities which stimulate healthy development and help children to make healthy choices. Babies and young children are offered healthy foods and drinks, and feeding and sleeping routines are flexible to take into account individual needs.

Example: Settings in Northumberland took part in a 'Healthy Pathways Award' pilot scheme, which was based on aspects of the National Healthy Schools Programme. Focusing on children's personal, social and emotional development, practitioners involved children and their parents in a range of activities to encourage healthy lifestyle choices. Positive changes were made to many aspects of provision and practice. In response to the introduction of fruit at snack time, one child said: "I didn't like fruit and wanted biscuits, but there aren't any at nursery, so I have fruit now, and it's quite nice".

The involvement of parents as partners was identified as key to the success of the project and parents were also invited to make healthy choices. One parent commented:"because he came home and told us how bad it was, and how bad it was for everybody else, me and my partner have given up smoking".

Outcome: Enjoying and achieving

Practitioners understand how children learn and develop and are able to engage children in challenging play based activities which promote all aspects of their development; intellectual, social, emotional and physical. Children's natural curiosity is encouraged, supported by adults who are interested in what they do and say. Practitioners are skilled observers of children who plan appropriate activities based on the child's interests and individual needs.

Example: Children were already familiar with 'Dansi', a puppet used during circle time to promote social and emotional development. They decided that Dansi needed a home and, supported by the practitioner, they worked together to design and create one. The final result was Dansi's cave, which, one year later, still took pride of place in the setting. The project lasted for months as children decided that Dansi needed further additions to his lifestyle. They gave him a 'water park' to play in and at Christmas made Dansi a tree and some presents. Throughout the project all children were encouraged to take part and they all showed a great sense of pride in their achievements.

Issues and dilemmas

The ambitious current programme of reform has produced some tensions and dilemmas to be faced. Most significantly, concerns have been expressed regarding the continuing outcomes focus of the EYFS, and the broadening of these to encompass our youngest children from birth to three. An outcomes-led curriculum may result in inappropriate experiences for children if practitioners are not fully aware of, and sensitive to, their developmental and individual learning needs. Developmental grids such as those presented in the practice guidance (DfES, 2007a) may be understood to suggest fixed norms, which lead to target setting for babies and young children. Close monitoring and evaluation of this new initiative is necessary to ensure that training of practitioners is of a high standard and that practice is guided by a sound knowledge of children's development and learning, rather than targets.

The impact of EYP status on provision is as yet uncertain. A new professional identity is being created which as yet lacks clarity in relation to other roles within the early years and childcare workforce, particularly QTS. The recent proposal in the Children's Plan (DCSF, 2007) to make teaching a masters profession introduces an additional tension. In addition, there may be reluctance by some settings and practitioners to embrace the leadership of the EYP. This and multi-agency work are major challenges for the early years and childcare workforce, requiring a substantial revising of priorities and an investment of time if the sector is to overcome historical tensions that impede the action of safeguarding children and development of seamless high-quality provision.

Positive relationships and trust between settings are crucial in achieving the ECM outcomes. In the past providers have been in competition for funding to ensure their sustainability, which has led to lack of trust and poor transition arrangements between settings. Many authorities recognise some of these systemic tensions and are addressing them proactively.

The ECM agenda draws together key recommendations of respected research, and evidence-based reports within a legal framework. Some believe that this is a radical reform (Roche and Tucker, 2007), others that it contains nothing new, and yet others that it is the latest political 'bandwagon'. What is undeniable is that it is an ambitious undertaking that has placed an unprecedented focus on children and families, and on the early childhood workforce. While parenting and childcare are still legally the responsibility of the family, recent legislation within the ECM agenda has placed greater responsibility on local authorities for meeting the needs of young children and their families. Long-term success, however, depends on this ideology being adopted across political boundaries as well as becoming embedded within society. The Labour government has been criticised for creating a nanny state, one that removes responsibility from families; a form of social control. If every child really does matter then who is responsible for our children? In the ECM agenda responsibility has become more of a shared endeavour than has previously been the case. The key challenge in our opinion is to keep children at the centre.

Summary

This chapter has shown how the ECM agenda has in many ways drawn together and given political force to elements of early years and childcare already established in high-quality provision. It has created a consistent approach for children from birth to five, and placed equal emphasis on care and education, while at the same time promoting diversity of provision and choice for parents. There has been financial investment to support and improve the qualifications and training of those working in the sector, thus raising their status. The chapter also outlines the major challenges that are still to be faced.

References

Abbott, L. and Hevey, D. (2001) 'Training to work in the early years: developing the climbing frame' in G. Pugh (ed) *Contemporary issues in the early years, working collaboratively for children*, London: Paul Chapman, pp 179-93.

Anning, A. (2001) 'Knowing who I am and what I know: developing versions of professional knowledge in integrated service settings', Paper presented at the British Educational Research Annual Conference, University of Leeds, 13-17 September.

Anning, A., Cottrell, D., Frost, N., Green, J. and Robinson, M. (2006) *Developing multiprofessional teamwork for integrated children's services*, Buckingham: Open University Press.

Athey, C. (1990) *Extending thought in young children: A parent–teacher partnership*, London: Paul Chapman.

Baldock, P., Fitzgerald, D. and Kay, J. (2005) *Understanding early years policy*, London: Paul Chapman.

Bowlby, J. (1951) *Maternal care and mental health*, Geneva: World Health Organisation.

CWDC (Children's Workforce Development Council) (2007a) Prospectus: Early Years Professional Status, Leeds: CWDC.

CWDC (2007b) *Integrated Qualifications Newsletter*, 5th edition, Leeds: CWDC.

DES (1990) *Starting with quality: Report of the Committee into the Quality of Education offered to 3-4 and 4-year olds*, London: HMSO.

DfEE (Department for Education and Employment) (1998) *Meeting the childcare challenge*, London: HMSO.

DfES (Department for Education and Skills (2002) *Birth to three matters: A framework to support children in their earliest years*, London: DfES Publications

DfEES (2003) *National Standards for Under Eights Day Care and Childminding*, London: DfES Publications.

DfES (2004a) *Every Child Matters: Change for children*. London: DfES Publications.

DfES (2004b) *Choice for parents, the best start for children: A ten year strategy for childcare*, London: DfES publications.

DfES (2005a) *Children's Workforce Strategy: A strategy to build a world-class workforce for children and young people*, London: DfES Publications.

DfES (2005b) *Common Core of Skills and Knowledge for the Children's Workforce*, London: DfES Publications.

DfES (2006) *Childcare Act 2006*, London: The Stationery Office.

DfES (2007a) *Statutory Framework for the early years foundation stage: Setting the standards for learning, development and care for children from birth to five*, London: DfES Publications.

DfES (2007b) *Child Sufficiency Assessments: Guidance for local authorities: Every Child Matters: Change for children*, London: DfES Publications.

DfES (2007c) *Transformation Fund Guidance* (updated), available at www.everychildmatters.gov.uk/resources-and-practice/IG00056/

DfES (2007d) *Primary National Strategy, developing quality through leadership: Action research in private, voluntary and independent sector early years settings*, London: DfES Publications.

DfES (2007e) *Practice Guidance for the early years foundation stage: Setting the standards for learning, development and care for children from birth to five*, London: DfES Publications.

Easen, P. Dyson, A. and Atkins, M. (2000) 'Interprofessional collaboration and conceptualisation of practice', *Children and Society*, vol 14, no 5, pp 355-67.

HM Treasury, DfES, DWP and DTI (2004) *Choice for parents, the best start for children: A strategy for childcare*, London: The Stationery Office.

Hohmann, M. and Weikart, D.P. (1995) *Educating young children*, London: High/Scope Educational Research Foundation.

Hudson, M., Lissenburgh, S. and Sahin-Dikmen, M. (2004) *Maternity and Paternity rights in Britain 2002: Survey of parents*, London: The Stationery Office.

Jowett S. and Sylva, K. (1982) 'Does kind of pre-school Matter?', *Educational Research*, vol 28, no 1, pp 21-3.

Lazer, I. and Darlington, R. (1987) *Lasting effects of early education*, Oxford: Blackwell Publishing.

Mathers, S., Sylva, K. and Joshi, H. (2007) *Quality of childcare settings in the Millenium Cohort Study*, Sure Start Research Report, SSU/2007/FR/025, London: HMSO.

Moss, P. (2003) *Beyond caring: The case for reforming the childcare and early years workforce*, London: Daycare Trust.

Ofsted (2001) *Nursery education: Quality of provision for 3 and 4 year olds 2000-2001*, London: Ofsted.

Ofsted (2005) *Every Child Matters: Framework for the inspection of children's services*, London: Ofsted.

Osborn, A.F. and Milbank, J.E. (1987) *The effects of early education*, Oxford: Clarendon Press.

Osgood, J. (2004) 'Time to get down to business? The response of early years practitioners to entrepreneurial approaches to professionalism', *Journal of Early Childhood Research*, vol 2, no 1, pp 5-24.

Roche, J. and Tucker, S.A. (2007) 'Every Child Matters: "tinkering" or "reforming"?: an analysis of the Children Act (2004) from an educational perspective', *Education 3-13*, vol 35, no 3, pp 213-23.

Rodd, J. (1997) *Leadership in early childhood*, London: Paul Chapman Publishing.

Sammons, P., Elliot, K., Sylva, K., Melhuish, E., Siraj-Batchford, I. and Taggart, B. (2004) 'The impact of pre-school on young children's cognitive attainments at entry to reception', *British Educational Research Journal*, vol 30, no 5, pp 691-712.

Savage, J. and Leeson, C. (2004) 'Leadership in early childhood settings', in J. Willan, R. Parker-Rees and J. Savage (eds) (2004) *Early childhood studies*, Exeter: Learning Matters, pp 119-31.

SCAA (School Curriculum and Assessment Authority (1986) *Nursery education, desirable outcomes for children's learning*, London: DfEE.

Schweinhart, L.J. and Weikart, D.P. (1993) *Significant benefits: The High/Scope Perry Pre-School Study through age 27*, Ypsilanti, MI: High/Scope Press.

Siraj-Blatchford, I. and Manni, L. (2006) 'Effective Leadership in the Early Years Sector (ELEYS) Study', London: Institute of Education, University of London.

Sylva, K., Sammons, P., Melhuish, E., Siraj-Blatchford, I. and Taggart, B. (2004) *The Effective Provision of Pre-School Education (EPPE) Project: Final report*, London: DfES Publications.

Turner, J. and Mavin, S. (2007) 'Exploring individual leadership journeys through authentic leadership theory', Paper presented at the 8th International Conference on HRD Research and Practice across Europe, Oxford Brookes University, June 2007.

Yeo, A. and Lovell, T. (2002) *Sociology and social policy for the early years*, 2nd edn, London: Hodder & Stoughton.

FIVE

Sure Start Children's Centres and Every Child Matters

Sue Barker

Sure Start Children's Centres occupy a pivotal role in the development and delivery of the services required in response to the ECM agenda (DfES, 2004). They are essential to the integration of holistic service delivery for parents and young children and it is vital that they occupy a clearly understood position within the tiers of preventative, targeted and specialist children's services.

Recent history

The broader history and development of Children's Centres can be viewed from a number of perspectives because, although Sure Start Children's Centres are being developed as a result of the current government agenda they are building on, changing and developing existing facilities and services. In this chapter, the author is writing from a background in social care, including management of nurseries, childminding and family centres, involvement in the development of Early Excellence and Early Years Development and Childcare Partnerships (EYDCP) and in the development of Sure Start Children's Centres.

Family centres within social care have, since the 1970s, offered similar services to those being developed in a more co-ordinated, consistent and defined way in Sure Start Children's Centres, although family centres often had more emphasis on social care and less on education and interprofessional working (Holman, 1987). The term 'family centre' covers a range of different models. Tunstill et al suggest that 'The insight provided into the work of family centres is fundamental to the current aspirations of government for children's services, including children's trusts, children's centres and extended schools', and that their information 'provides an opportunity for policy makers, in the process of developing children's centres and extended schools, to draw on the long-standing expertise, skills and experience of their local family centres' (Tunstill et al, 2007, p 9).

Nurseries and childminders have also offered services to children and parents for many years – often focused on the needs of working parents or on preparing children for school, and sometimes sponsored childminders provided a social care function. Early Excellence Centres have also developed multi-disciplinary, child-focused services since the late 1990s (Bertram et al, 2001).

The first Sure Start Local Programmes (SSLP) were set up in 1999 with a remit to bring together childcare, health and family support for children from birth to four years living in disadvantaged areas (Glass, 1999). This was an area-based initiative focusing on the most disadvantaged wards within the most disadvantaged local authority areas. There were 524 original programmes with multi-agency stakeholder advisory boards steering the development of services according to government guidelines, with the aim of improving the health and well-being of families and children so that young children living in disadvantaged areas would be better able to achieve when they started school. The leadership and development of the Sure Start Programme varied between local authorities, some being led by health, some by education and some by social services. The intention was that over a period of some 7-10 years Children's Centres would become the vehicle for delivery of mainstream services for young children and their families, with new ways of working having been developed and improved outcomes having been demonstrated.

However, the National Evaluation of Sure Start (NESS) has had very mixed findings from their studies. They found that:

> There is substantial evidence that Sure Start Local Programmes have empowered individual parents, so that they feel less isolated, more valued (especially as mothers) and more confident in their parenting activities. As a result, individual parents report feeling a closer bond with their children, whom they say are happier, easier to relate to, mixing better and better prepared for learning. (Williams and Churchill, 2006, p 1)

While in another NESS study, they found that 'few programmes were delivering evidence-based parenting support, but some were doing this well'. In relation to home visiting programmes they found that 'some addressed common behaviour problems, but few were providing the intensive evidence-based home visiting programmes that have been shown to improve parenting. Additional training is needed to prepare staff to provide such support' (Barlow et al, 2007, p 1).

The development of Sure Start Children's Centres is intended to build on previous work in all sectors working with young children and their parents to provide an integrated, holistic service that meets locally identified need. Learning the lessons from the past will need to be carefully and skilfully integrated into the education and training of staff working in the new Sure Start Children's Centres. The information and expertise within family centres, SSLPs, nurseries and childminders can provide local authorities with resources to enable learning from one another if well-informed and evidence-based.

The current position

The Sure Start, Extended Schools and Childcare group within the Department for Children, Schools and Families (DCSF) is responsible for delivering Sure Start Children's Centres. In the autumn of 2006 it commissioned an organisation called Together for Children (TfC) (see www.togetherforchildren.co.uk) to assist by providing support for and challenge to local authorities in the development of their Children's Centre programmes.

Sure Start Children's Centres are being developed incrementally towards the provision of a universal service through 3,500 Children's Centres by 2010. At mid-2008 there are in the region of 3,000 designated Children's Centres nationally. A total of 2,500 Children's Centres were designated for the end of Phase 2 by March 2008, with a further 1,000 to be designated by 2010 as part of Phase 3.

- In Phase 1 local authorities were given a target number of children to reach with services through Sure Start Children's Centres and a target number of new childcare places to create within the areas of greatest need.
- In Phase 2 local authorities were given a target number of children to reach through a target number of new Sure Start Children's Centres in areas of disadvantage and in other areas. The concept of a mixed economy of childcare provision has been developed in Phase 2 with many Children's Centres having service level agreements or affiliation schemes with private providers of childcare rather than creating new places. In response to the duty in the 2006 Childcare Act, local authorities have been carrying out their sufficiency assessments, which are important in informing local authority strategic planning for sustainable childcare.
- In Phase 3 local authorities have been given indicative targets of new Sure Start Children's Centres to develop in 2008-2010, the majority of these being in less disadvantaged areas and therefore requiring less intensive levels of support. The levels of service will be expected to vary according to the levels of local deprivation; however, all Centres must deliver the minimum service described below, with rural areas having greater flexibility in how services are delivered.

What do Sure Start Children's Centres provide?

To be officially designated, a Sure Start Children's Centre has to provide a basic level of service. A designated Children's Centre in an area of high disadvantage provides a minimum of Ofsted registered integrated early learning and childcare for 0-5 year olds for 10hours each day, 5 days per week, 48 weeks per year and have agreed links with JobCentre Plus. The Centre has to have a Centre manager and a 0.5 qualified teacher and there must be a service plan in place that outlines services currently provided, future arrangements for health and outreach services, plans to develop a childminding network and any other services the Centre intends to provide.

In a less disadvantaged area a designated Children's Centre provides a minimum of drop-in activity sessions and links with JobCentre Plus and its hours of opening are to suit local need. The Centre has to have a Centre manager and there must be a service or business plan in place that outlines the services currently being offered and future delivery arrangements for health, outreach services, childminding support and other services the Centre intends to provide as part of it's 'full core offer'.

A centre is recognised as a Sure Start Children's Centre when it has been officially designated however this is the basis from which it must develop the 'full core offer' described below.

The full core offer stage is the operational (3rd) stage of the 4 stage process and once having all staffing, services, accommodation, managing and monitoring arrangements fully in place each Sure Start Children's Centre will be in a position to identify plans for improvement.

Children's Centres are intended to provide universal services for families and young children within a community. The services provided should reflect local need and, according to the government practice guidance (DfES, 2006b), must include a minimum of information about childcare and early years provision, information and support regarding wider services, information and advice for parents, support to childminders, drop-in sessions for parents and children, and links to Jobcentre Plus and health services.

In the planning and performance management guidance (DfES, 2006c) the description of this minimum expectation is expanded to include:

- offer of appropriate support and outreach services to parents/carers and children who have been identified as in need of them;
- information and advice to fathers, mothers and carers on a range of subjects including local childcare, looking after babies and young children and local early years provision and education services for three- and four-year-olds;
- support to childminders through a co-ordinated network and also to other childminders in the area by providing training, loan of toys and equipment, and drop-in sessions;
- drop-in sessions and other activities for children, parents and carers at the centre, including parent groups, play groups and adult education;
- links to Jobcentre Plus services, to support and encourage parents to take up employment and help to combat poverty appropriate to local circumstances and the identified needs of the community;
- access to community health services, including local midwives and health visitors who provide visits to families with newborn babies with information about services and support; access to the Child Health Promotion Programme, information and guidance on breastfeeding, nutrition, hygiene and safety; antenatal advice should also be available together with support to all pregnant women and their families in the area;
- health promotion, such as encouragement to parents who smoke to attend smoking cessation clinics, encouragement for children to take up opportunities for physical activity from an early age;

- an opportunity for identification of children with special needs and disabilities, and multi-agency plans to address their needs; identification of particularly disadvantaged families so that the centre can offer appropriate support.

The development of Children's Centres in the most disadvantaged areas has been more strictly prescribed, and according to central government guidance (DfES, 2006c) must offer the following.

Early years provision: Early years provision should include integrated early learning and childcare for 0- to 5-year-olds, suitable for working mothers, fathers and carers, for a minimum of 48 weeks per year, five days per week and for ten hours each day. Childcare places should be open for all – not just for families living in the area – with admission and fee policies set locally and priority given to disadvantaged families. There is to be support for childminders, including a network, provision of inclusive services and support for families of children with special needs and disabilities (including early identification) and links to local schools, including to extended services and Healthy Schools.

Outreach: This includes visits to all families in the catchment area within two months of a new birth, either through the Child Health Promotion Programme or other agreed arrangements. There should be activities to raise community awareness, a co-ordinated programme of home visits, a system for referring families to other services or signposting, a system for monitoring service usage and a keyworker system where possible.

Family support: This should include information about family support services and activities for families and children in the area, support and advice on parenting, access to targeted or specialist services for families who need them, activities to help parents and carers understand child development, and strategies or activities to increase the involvement of fathers.

Child and family health services: Child and family health services should include antenatal advice and support, access to the Child Health Promotion Programme, advice on breastfeeding, hygiene, nutrition and safety, promoting well-being, including positive mental health and identifying and providing support for families where there is maternal depression, specialist support such as speech and language therapy, healthy lifestyle support and smoking cessation advice and support.

Parental involvement: There should be systems for user feedback and consultation, as well as information sharing and continuous arrangements for parents and carers to have a say in the provision of services, for example through a parent's forum.

Links to training and employment: Sure Start Children's Centres must link with Jobcentre Plus and encourage and support parents who want to train or work. They may also offer help with gaining access to training, with work advice and information, and may provide other services with additional funding from a variety of sources. These can include links with education institutions and local training providers, training in basic skills and English as an additional language, or other topics identified as needed to assist parents to take up employment.

Other additional services: Benefits advice, relationship support, Contact Centres and toy libraries can be available or signposted, as can childcare and other extended services for older siblings. Other initiatives such as Bookstart (www.bookstart.co.uk), I CAN (www.ican.org.uk), or Early Support may be located in Children's Centres or signposted.

What do Sure Start Children's Centres look like?

A variety of different building models are emerging and, within these models, services are being developed, not only according to whether the Children's Centre is in a disadvantaged or less disadvantaged area, but also to meet locally determined need. This is providing a complex picture of Children's Centre service provision and delivery.

Single site, single building: Many Phase 1 Children's Centres are single buildings specifically designed for the services being delivered through a Children's Centre offering a full range of services. Others were previously Sure Start Local programmes or Early Excellence Centres. Often purpose built or having had a high-quality refurbishment, these centres usually include early years provision and a childminding network, drop-in facilities for children and families, and services for parents with a 0.5 qualified teacher providing support as part of the Children's Centre. These Centres will be providing, or working towards the provision of, the 'full core offer' of services described in more detail later in this chapter. The Centre will be working with at least one local school with a newly developing or well-established relationship and will be moving towards a relationship with all schools serving the population of children served by the Children's Centre. This type of Children's Centre is often in an area where there are other initiatives and has relationships with those initiatives providing services related to the aims of the Children's Centre. The involvement of health, social care and Jobcentre Plus in these Centres is usually well established. The manager of the Centre will be supported by an advisory board (DfES, 2007) with representation from all stakeholders particularly including parent representation.

Single site, multi building: This model is more likely to be used for a Phase 2 Children's Centre and comprises two or three buildings adjacent to one another or located nearby (the distance between these buildings of up to 0.5

miles being described as 'pram-pushing' distance). This model is likely to have emerged from existing services or settings with additional new buildings or refurbishments planned in response to the Sure Start Children's Centre programme of development. It often includes a primary or first school, family centre or private/voluntary daycare setting and may have additional venues in the local community where Children's Centre services are provided on a sessional basis. There is usually a Centre manager or leader with overall responsibility for service co-ordination and reporting, although there can be quite complex arrangements for line management and resource allocation, with linked sites having a head teacher or operational manager responsible for service delivery on the site.

Cluster/locality management: Some Children's Centres are arranged in 'clusters' within localities. These include both single and multi-building sites and often have a management line through a Children's Centres manager or co-ordinator. As Children and Young People's Services within local authorities become more decentralised and locality-focused, along with the range of council services, this model is increasing. Clusters of Children's Centres are likely to be supported by one or more Children's Centre Local Advisory Board.

Rural Children's Centres: In the multi-building model a Children's Centre with more than one building or site is meant to include up to three buildings within pram-pushing (0.5 mile) distance of one another, to enable parents to easily use the various services being delivered. This arrangement is proving to be a challenge in many areas, especially in rural communities. With very low numbers of children in most rural areas, it is not possible to develop a Children's Centre for a community of around 800 children, delivering services from buildings within pram-pushing distance. Although Phase 3 guidance has amended the number of children to be reached by a centre to between 600 and 1,200 children this is still not usually feasible for rural areas.

The range of rural models is therefore the most complex to describe due to the variation of need and the choice of and distance between buildings or delivery points. They are likely to include drop-in services for children and families, childminding networks, links with schools, information about services for children and families, and links with Jobcentre Plus, together with plans for developing outreach services and services integrated with health, social care and with PVI childcare providers where this is appropriate. There are similarities between rural models and the multi-building model, but rural services cover greater distances, and are likely to use innovative approaches to service provision and a range of service delivery points, which may include mobile facilities.

Local authority management

The development of Children's Centres is managed and directed through the local authority. The task is a challenging and complex one encompassing planning and project management, management of capital and revenue budgeting and the process of developing new buildings, planning restructuring or refurbishment in addition to setting up new services, integrating existing services, winning the hearts and minds of stakeholders and scoping the needs and expectations of the community.

Local authorities have a variety of management structures to meet these challenges partly depending on the size of the local authority and complexity of the Sure Start Children's Centre programme and partly depending on the management and service structures in the local authority. The local authority management structure has been further complicated by the many changes in local authority children's services structures to meet the needs of the ECM agenda, the development of Children's Trusts and other changes in the delivery of council services.

In many local authorities there has been a move away from a more centralised structure towards geographically based management structures described as localities, sectors, wedges or hubs, and are defined geographical areas where integrated services for children, and increasingly young people (aged 0–19 years) are delivered. Locality managers are often responsible for the management of Children's Centres, Extended Schools or services and the delivery of services for children, young people and parents and carers across the 0–19 age group. This arrangement is often supported by a locality or area advisory board of stakeholders with responsibility for the range of services for children and young people being delivered in the area.

The following examples demonstrate the management structures and changes taking place within which Sure Start Children's Centres are being developed.

> **Examples: Management structures for children's and young people's services**
> • In 2006 a rural authority had an early years strategic manager responsible for the development of six Children's Centres from Phase I and the development of more than 20 Children's Centres, with a very small number of staff and a commissioned architectural company.
> In 2007 an integrated services structure has been put in place that will be fully locality based with Children's Centres developed and managed alongside extended services, childminding and other services by six integrated services managers.
>
> • A small local authority has a Children's Centre programme manager, Children's Centre assistant programme manager and a planning officer responsible for all the tasks involved in the development of five Children's Centres in Phase 2 (as described earlier) and the continuing development of 16 Phase I Children's Centres.

- A large city has a planning team and a capital team who do some of the work on the development of Children's Centres together with a Children's Centres programme manager and six delivery managers with responsibility for the continued development of 25 Children's Centres from Phase 1 and the development of 25 new Children's Centres in Phase 2. The six delivery managers are aligned with a locality structure, each responsible for the development of the Sure Start Children's Centres in their area.

Staffing structures

Different models of Children's Centre will require differing staffing structures, depending on: the phase in which they were developed, whether they are in an area of high or low level of deprivation and whether in a rural or urban area. The staffing structure will also be affected by decisions made by local authorities about how they will configure their services; for example, some local authorities are providing family support services on an authority–wide basis for all of their Children's Centres.

The examples of staffing structures below, based on Phase 3 Planning and Delivery Guidance, (DCSF, 2007), reflect services being provided directly by the Children's Centre. Childcare staffing is not included as this is dependent on the number of places and is prescribed by regulations. It is also not costed in the same way because the staffing for childcare (and also childcare overheads) is expected to be funded through fees or other income, such as for free places for three- and four-year-olds.

Example: Staffing of a centre serving the most disadvantaged communities not directly providing childcare

Post	Full-time equivalent
Children's Centre manager	1
Deputy manager	1
Head of parenting/family support	1
Outreach workers	3
Childminder network supervisor	1
Parenting and family support worker	1
Teenage pregnancy worker	0.3
Fathers' worker	0.2
Parent/child drop-in worker	1
Qualified teacher	1
Administrator/reception worker	1.5

Example: Staffing of a Centre serving an affluent community	
Post	**Full-time equivalent**
Children's Centre manager	0.5
Sessional childcare worker	1
Family support/outreach worker	1
Administrator/reception worker	0.5

Sure Start Children's Centre staff have a variety of professional backgrounds including nursery nursing, nursery education, early years, social work, health visiting and teaching. The need for highly trained and confident staff in relation to all roles is recognised. Children's Centre managers are expected to train to a high level and the NPQICL has been developed at a postgraduate level to provide Centre managers with the leadership skills they need (NCLS, 2007). The development of the early years professional (EYP) status and training is intended to provide a higher level of qualification in relation to early years (DfES, 2006a). Qualified teacher status (QTS) and the role of the teacher allocated to each Centre is intended to ensure that early learning can be developed to a high standard across the range of services provided by Children's Centres, including the role of parents and childminders in addition to staff directly and indirectly involved in the Centre.

With the development of Sure Start Children's Centre services there is a very real recruitment challenge. As more Centres are developed, the people with appropriate skills to be Centre managers are becoming increasingly difficult to recruit; a problem which is particularly acute in rural areas and in large cities. The difficulty is mirrored throughout the workforce, making the task of recruitment, retention and the development of appropriately skilled staff a serious challenge.

The contribution of Sure Start Children's Centres to the ECM agenda

The development of Sure Start Children's Centres as a universally available service, which also provides some targeted services, is a key component in the ECM agenda. Children's Centres are intended to provide services that enable and assist parents and carers to give children the best start in life and provide access to services that meet the needs of young children and so, by its very nature, contributes to all five of the ECM outcomes.

Be healthy

The Sure Start Children's Centre agenda addresses the antenatal and postnatal care of women, assisting in the provision of easily accessible services. This is particularly important in relation to recognised differences in maternal and infant mortality rates between advantaged and disadvantaged areas. There is increasing location of midwifery and health visiting services within Children's Centres and, where this is not appropriate, close links between these services are being developed. The development of this universal service offers an opportunity to assist parents in relation to the health of their children and for early identification of health issues in young children. Health promotion services are being developed jointly with health services in Children's Centres, such as healthy eating projects, breastfeeding initiatives, smoking cessation programmes, and physical activity projects for both adults and young children.

Stay safe

Children's Centres offer a unique opportunity for the prevention of child abuse and the early identification of difficulties by providing services to meet the needs of very young children and their parents and carers. There will always be some children who cannot be protected in their own homes and early identification of such children will hopefully limit their suffering and future difficulties. The ability to co-ordinate the work of midwifery, health visiting and outreach work should assist in earlier identification of this small number of babies and children, enabling better planning for their future care. Identification of family difficulties and parenting problems at an early stage should also enable agencies to provide co-ordinated and effective support to assist parents to develop better parenting skills and to provide safe care for their children.

Ensuring that young children are safe when provided with childcare through the provision of high-quality services is also a prime objective for Children's Centres.

Enjoy and achieve

Children's Centre services are providing children greater opportunities for play and development, as well as providing an integrated service that aims to give each child the optimum chance for enjoying and achieving through providing the best start possible.

Children's Centres also provide services for teenage parents, and the combination of services provided aims to give such young people an opportunity for personal and educational development and opportunities for education, training and employment.

Services provided for parents to enable them to access training, make informed choices and take up employment should also help families to avoid poverty and provide an environment within which their children have the best chance to enjoy and achieve.

Make a positive contribution to society

Children's Centres are intended to provide the best start possible for children so that they can take full advantage of subsequent educational opportunities and play an active part within society as they grow up. Many services within Children's Centres are being developed for parents to enable them to remain in employment and/or to access training opportunities so that they are not disadvantaged by their childcaring roles and can be offered opportunities to achieve their potential.

The focus on involvement and participation by parents in the development of Children's Centres and in planning services also provides an opportunity for empowerment and personal development that may well encourage people to go on to play other active roles in their communities.

Achieve economic well-being

As noted above, the opportunities for children to develop and learn within Children's Centres are intended to provide a basis for them to grow into young people who are better prepared to access opportunities for education, training, taking up employment and participation in society. The services for parents, in addition to aiding good-quality parenting, are intended to enable parents to access education and training, make informed choices and have access to employment so that they can avoid poverty resulting from a lack of skills and unemployment.

Future trends

Policy issues

The development of Children's Centres in every community will provide opportunities for the development of training and education for workers that are focused on the holistic needs of children and their families. It will be helpful for the status of children in our society if this leads to a different view of the professional status and role of those working with young children. This will strengthen the need for, and importance of, a well-educated workforce that provides a consistent and professional service to specified, regulated standards and continued improvement.

There remains a view that equates parenting difficulties with poverty and deprivation and the desire to simply target funds for parents and young children to disadvantaged areas plays to this belief. While acknowledging the much greater difficulties that parents face if they are coping with poverty and its attendant deprivation, it is important not to lose sight of the difficulties that most, if not all, parents have when facing the changes to their lives that they are likely to experience on the birth of their children. There are some particular difficulties that are faced by some middle-class and affluent families if the services they require are not accessible and particularly if they are isolated either geographically or socially. It is also not only children of parents experiencing poverty and deprivation who are abused and neglected, and universal services for young children are particularly important in providing preventative services for them and to enable early identification of such difficulties which could otherwise go unrecognised.

The current expectation that Children's Centres will provide a universal service with some targeted services to meet locally identified need is threatened by a growing view that they should provide *all* services. Conversely, there is also the view, alluded to in the previous paragraph, that Children's Centres should only be provided in areas of greatest need and that the funding for them should be targeted on areas of deprivation. These two conflicting views ignore the original purpose of ensuring that *all* young children and their families have access to good services and that through universal provision it is possible to identify children and families who require targeted and specialist services that can be provided without, or certainly with less, stigma. Within this framework families could be encouraged to choose to access the services they require to enable them to provide better parenting or to meet the needs of their children, rather than being coerced into accepting them as can be the case due to the way in which services are currently provided.

It is easy to envisage Sure Start Children's Centres being provided within fully integrated tiers of service for children and families, with the services they provide linked appropriately to those specialist services better placed to meet particular need. This becoming easier to achieve as Children's Centres become more established within relatively small communities that Centre managers will be better able to know and understand. However, achieving this in practice is less easy and requires strategic vision, coherent policies, strategies, procedures and agreements that create the framework in which this can be realised. The confusion about the role of Children's Centres as a universal service, a targeted service or 'all things to all' at a policy level will serve to make it even harder to achieve.

Multi-disciplinary and cultural issues

The role of Children's Centre staff in relation to the CAF will be developed according to the individual local authority strategy, but there is great potential for the role of lead professional to be allocated and the CAF used for the early identification of a need for additional services for children by Sure Start Children's Centre staff.

Children's Centres are intended to bring together education, social care, health, employment and other services for young children and their families, breaking down unhelpful barriers between groups of workers and working in a co-ordinated and integrated way to meet the needs of children and families. An example of what this can look like is presented in Figure 5.1.

Children's Centres that have developed from Sure Start Local Programmes will already have a cultural ethos related to those developments and may find it difficult to move to a more multi-disciplinary approach in which there is a strong

Figure 5.1: Harrow Council Wheel of partners and services

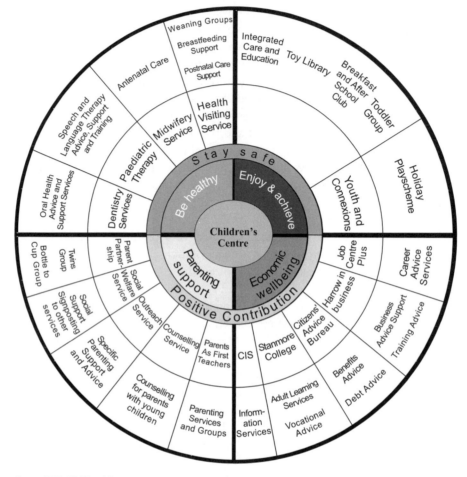

Source: TfC, 2007, p 15

emphasis on early learning and in which there is a number of perspectives, values and traditions to incorporate.

Some settings have had more of a focus on meeting the needs of children through providing services for parents and, in some cases, work for and on behalf of those parents rather than with them, through enabling and empowering them so that they have choices. Many members of existing staff are concerned by the emphasis on getting women into work in the Sure Start Children's Centre programme, especially when they may only have access to low-paid employment. It is sometimes difficult to envisage how change can happen for families in the 'poverty trap' but the emphasis on providing opportunities to reach personal potential should be valued by all staff. It would be a shame if a particular doctrine – either that of getting people into work or of not forcing women down the low-paid employment route – takes precedence and creates obstacles to the provision of services that offer opportunities for personal and educational development and optimising potential.

Children's Centres in Phase 2 are increasingly being developed within schools, in many cases under the leadership of head teachers and the governance arrangements linked with the school governing body (although it should be noted that DCSF Guidance for Phase 3 recommends that head teachers should not be Sure Start Children's Centre managers). Historically, many schools have not been successful in engaging the families and children who most need services. If Children's Centres are to be the key agency for engaging families and children that currently find it hard to access or take full advantage of services, those based within schools will possibly be working counter to the culture of that organisation, which will add to the already recognised problems in achieving this aim. On the positive side, success by Children's Centres in reaching families not currently well engaged in education will hopefully be transferred on to schools if transition arrangements are good and there is good co-ordination between services and an inclusive culture developed across services.

It is important that multi-disciplinary working within Children's Centres does not preclude good multi-disciplinary working with professions outside the Children's Centre, such as children's social work, acute health care provision and so on. It is equally important that individual professional expertise continues to be developed and recognised and that multi-disciplinary working does not lead to blurred professional boundaries. New Sure Start Children's Centres must work hard to develop their identity and to build cohesive team work, but it is equally important that this happens alongside an outward-looking focus that continues to involve parents, carers and the wider community and avoids institutionalisation. The need to maintain appropriate professional differences while working in an integrated way is crucial for ensuring high-quality service provision.

Summary

This chapter has described Sure Start Children's Centres and has tried to capture the complexities within the range of services that come under this umbrella at their current stage of development. Children's Centres are in the middle of a phased programme of development and are therefore quite difficult to describe. Additionally, the nature of Children's Centres, the fact that they are being developed by building on and developing existing services, that they are meant to be very locally based and provide services that meet local need within the context of local management arrangements makes them even more difficult to define. The nature of Sure Start Children's Centres, what they look like, what they provide, their staffing structures and management arrangements have been described. The chapter also gives information on how centres are developed and the phases through which they become designated and verified as providing the full core offer.

This chapter has described the phases of development and current government guidance on the nature of the services, their role within integrated children's services and outlined their importance in relation to the ECM agenda. It has concluded by discussing some of the policy disputes around Children's Centres and the differing views of what they are meant to achieve and for which families.

References

Barlow, J., Kirkpatrick, S., Wood, D., Ball, M., and Stewart-Brown, S. (2007) *Family and parenting support in Sure Start Local Programmes*, London: NESS

Bertram, T., Pascal, C., Bokhari, S. and Gasper, M. (2001) *Early Excellence Centre Pilot Programme First Evaluation Report 1999 – 2000*, Research Report 258, London: DfES.

Bookstart (2007) 'About Bookstart', available at www.bookstart.co.uk/Parents-and-carers/Parents-About.

DCSF (Department for Children, Schools and Families) (2007) *Sure Start Children's Centres: Phase 3 Planning and Delivery Guidance*, London: DCSF.

DfES (Department for Education and Skills) (2004) *Every Child Matters – Change for Children,* London: DfES.

DfES (2006a) *The Children's Workforce Strategy – the government 's response to the consultation,* London: DfES.

DfES (2006b) *Sure Start Children's Centres: Practice Guidance,* London: DfES.

DfES (2006c) *Sure Start Children's Centres: Planning and Performance Management Guidance,* London: DfES.

DfES (2007) *Governance Guidance for Sure Start Children's Centres and extended schools,* London: DfES.

Glass, N. (1999) 'Origins of the Sure Start Local Programmes', *Children & Society,* vol 13.

Holman, R. (1987) 'Family centres', in P. Righton and S. Morgan (eds) *Child care concerns and conflicts,* London: Hodder & Stoughton.

I CAN (2007) 'About us', available at www.ican.org.uk/home/.

London Borough of Harrow (2007) 'Harrow Council Wheel of partners and services', available at www.surestart.gov.uk/

NCLS (National College for School Leadership) (2007) *National Professional Qualification in Integrated Centre Leadership,* London: NCLS.

TfC (Together for Children) (2006) 'Together for Children', available at www.togetherforchildren.co.uk.

TfC (2007) *Toolkit for business planning,* Birmingham: TfC.

Tunstill, J. Aldgate, J. and Hughes, M. (2007) Improving Children's Services networks: Lessons from Family Centres, London: Jessica Kingsley.

Williams, F. and Churchill, H. (2006) *National evaluation summary: Empowering Parents in Sure Start Local Programmes,* London: NESS.

SIX

Nursing and Every Child Matters

Steve Campbell and Judith Hunter

Introduction

As with all attempts to describe the implications of policy developments for nurses and nursing, the diverse nature of the profession needs to be addressed. In the case of Every Child Matters, it is even clearer that any nurse working with patients has obligations that relate to ECM and the child protection legislation. Gone are the days when a nurse working solely in an adult area can claim that it is unnecessary for him/her to know about child policy and child protection. For instance, a nurse caring for a woman who has been subject to domestic violence needs to know whether or not there were children in the household. If children were present, the police need to investigate, as this triggers a newer principle of the child protection legislation to protect children being exposed to violence. This chapter therefore attempts to cover the full range of implications for nursing across the full range of nurses and nursing, including midwifery and health visiting.

Background and policy drivers

The health and well-being of children

Child health has improved greatly in the past century and children in the UK are generally healthier (Hall, 1989; Hall and Elliman, 2003). Despite this progress, there are challenges to health that unduly affect disadvantaged and marginalised children (Roberts, 2000), leading to:

- increased rates of some common childhood infections;
- high rates of accidental injury;
- rapidly increasing levels of obesity;
- low levels of physical activity;
- increasing rates of smoking among teenage girls;
- high rates of alcohol consumption;
- growing rates of sexually transmitted disease;
- increases in behaviour problems and mental health needs (DoH, 2004a).

Other factors also present risks to the health, physical and emotional development, and safety of children, including:

- **the family:** such as domestic violence, substance misuse and adult health problems;
- **the child:** such as disability;
- **economic and social circumstances:** such as poverty, poor housing, lack of education and social isolation (DoH, 2004a).

The presence of multiple risk factors increases vulnerability and access to appropriate, high-quality healthcare is more difficult for the most vulnerable. Healthcare therefore needs to be delivered to vulnerable and disadvantaged children in innovative and accessible ways (Acheson, 1998a).

Dealing with inequalities in health

There are enduring inequalities in the health of children, related to income and social class, ethnic group and geography (Roberts, 2000). Babies born to less affluent families are more likely to be premature, have higher rates of infant mortality, greater poverty, impaired development and chronic disease in later life (Solar, 2003). This leads to a vicious cycle of health inequalities in families. Acheson (1998b) concluded that the best chance of breaking this cycle of disadvantage was with children and parents, particularly present and future mothers. Within ECM and other government initiatives there are a number of policies that are being pursued:

- economic policies aimed at eliminating child poverty such as child tax credit;
- increasing the availability of nursery and day care provision;
- initiatives such as Sure Start, Connexions and the Teenage Pregnancy Strategy that aim to improve opportunities for disadvantaged children;
- child health and inequalities targets for infant mortality, smoking in pregnancy, obesity, breast feeding and teenage pregnancy (DoH, 2004a).

The National Service Framework (NSF) for Children (DoH, 2003a, 2003b; DfES/DoH, 2004) aims to ensure high-quality health and welfare provision for all children, attempting to address health inequalities, with the development of Children's Trusts and Children's Centres aimed at delivering more integrated, holistic services (Sloper, 2004).

Services for vulnerable children and families

Professional contacts and child health initiatives are not of themselves necessarily beneficial – it is the quality, appropriateness and acceptability of interventions that are crucial (Lloyd et al, 1997) . This underlines the importance of starting from the perspective of vulnerable children and families in designing services, in order to secure maximum reach and effectiveness.

A number of characteristics have been shown to contribute to the provision of more effective services including:

- services based on a local needs assessment and involving local people;
- services that combine intensive support for those who are vulnerable with action to strengthen communities and improve the environment for children and families;
- initiatives designed with the help of target groups to ensure they are acceptable culturally and educationally and work through settings that are accessible and appropriate;
- training and support for volunteers, peer educators and local networks maximising benefit from community-based initiatives;
- comprehensive services that cross professional boundaries and are coherent and easy to use, where both the structure and individual staff are flexible in their ability to respond to unexpected demands;
- staff with the time and the skill to establish relationships of respect and trust with families;
- the child is seen as a member of the family and the family as part of the community;
- projects that have enthusiastic committed leadership, clearly specified measurable aims and focus on families with high levels of need, for example people in poverty, unsupported and young people, or those with children who have special needs;
- sustained high quality and quantity of input and sufficient continuity to develop a relationship with the individual client (this implies starting a relationship in pregnancy rather than after the child is born);
- earlier, more intensive and high-quality interventions with disadvantaged children and families, to ensure a greater likelihood of long-term success;
- services that protect children incorporate systematic assessment, listening to children, effective communication with parents, explicit referrals and sharing of relevant information, good record keeping and clear accountability (DoH, 2004a).

Planning services to eliminate gaps

Services are now moving away from planning based on titles or traditional roles to services based on the needs of children and families in which their views and choices are taken into account. This planning also needs to take on board appropriate epidemiological population-based data. There is also a need to articulate the unique contributions of nursing, midwifery and health visiting within children's services – they may provide general support to children, or specialise in one area according to local health needs and circumstances.

The current position

Children are regular users of the health services and now also have greater involvement in decision making. The NSF for Children sets standards for a wide range of services and seeks to ensure consistent healthcare for children and young people wherever they may live. With the change in funding arrangements via the Primary Care Trusts (PCTs), a greater number of services are being delivered outside of the hospital environment, and different roles, teams and services are in place to deliver more integrated and accessible services. The NHS Improvement Plan (DoH, 2004b) set out priorities with an emphasis on prevention and chronic conditions which are aimed to improve the health and well-being of children.

Nurses, midwives and health visitors provide a wide range of health services for children and families in many different settings, such as the home, communities, schools and prisons, making important contributions ranging from work in primary prevention to managing chronic conditions and palliative care.

The views of children and young people

Intrinsic within ECM are key issues for children. They want:

• to be asked about themselves and their opinions;
• to be spoken to and listened to in their own right;
• to have non-judgmental, confidential, accessible services;
• information that is appropriate to their age and understanding;
• younger professionals who would understand young people;
• professionals who are kind and knowledgeable, who spend time with them and talk to them (DoH, 2004a).

Children with disabilities want to be offered information and choices about their treatment and care. For looked-after children, lack of privacy is a major issue as well as professionals tending to regard them as a collection of problems in their notes rather than as real people with potential. For asylum seeking children, the gathering of information and accessing services has been identified as a major challenge (DoH, 2004a).

Within hospitals 'friendly nurses' are seen as one of the best things. In the community children tend to seek help from general practice on a range of emotional and physical health issues. However, they are not always satisfied with general practice and refer to lack of trust and confidentiality, difficulty gaining an appointment, lack of respect, and a failure to listen (DoH, 2004a).

The views of parents

Parents from disadvantaged and marginalised groups suggest that they particularly value services that are non-judgemental and treat the individual as a person not a problem. They want nurses who listen and respond to the parental needs and do not only focus on the children's needs. They want services that offer continuity of care, and that are convenient and available when people need them (DoH, 2004a).

Challenges for the workforce

In the *Chief Nursing Officer's Review* DoH (2004a), it is suggested that the work of nurses is predicated on four concepts:

1. **Personal**: tailoring services to each individual child, family and young person.
2. **Caring**: providing competent care that makes a difference and through which people feel they are treated with dignity and respect.
3. **Partners**: sharing information and decisions with children and their families, with colleagues and with other services.
4. **Professional**: taking responsibility and accountability, acting on concerns and exercising a duty of care towards children.

Working with vulnerable children is demanding, particularly as a result of changes to professional roles and services. Nurses need to re-examine the nature of their professionalism continuously in an environment where decisions can be difficult and complex (DoH, 2004a). For instance non-NHS organisations such as the local authority, and the voluntary sector, may be employing a range of different practitioners, including nurses, and with whom NHS staff are not familiar. Particularly non-NHS employers and independent contractors (including GPs) need to understand their professional and clinical responsibilities towards this workforce. These need to include clinical supervision, CPD, professional advice and regular appraisal with a line of professional accountability to a lead nurse or midwife. Employers need to understand the regulatory framework and code of conduct for nurses and ensure that staff are appropriately registered. There are also aspects of being a professional that all nurses working with children need to embrace.

All nursing professionals working with children should embrace:
- speaking out and taking responsibility for acting on behalf of children;
- not waiting for consensus and being ready to challenge other professionals;
- communicating concerns clearly and working with doctors to develop a common language, both written and verbal;
- holding themselves accountable for achieving health outcomes for children;
- changing the nursing culture to one that promotes self-care and empowers children and families, involving them in decision making, using tools for assessing health needs such as Family Health Plans;
- understanding and exercising their responsibility for the non-registered workforce such as community mothers, peer support workers and assistant practitioners (DoH, 2004a).

Are there enough nurses, midwives and health visitors?

The planning of the nursing workforce for any organisation needs to take into account other services and local needs. The current shortages of children's and public health nurses as well as midwives need to be addressed. This must be balanced with more focused and appropriate use of the specific and rare skills of these nurses, such as CAMHS nurses. DoH (2004a) reported that there were 13,000 health visitors and around 2,500 school nurses, compared with 40,000 social workers for children and families and 440,000 teachers. Given this relative paucity, the emphasis is on the nursing professions to raise everyone's awareness of health as a key aspect of a child's life. Similarly, given the shortage of nurses for school children, PCTs, Children's Trusts and local authorities need to develop similar systems that focus their rare resources, by setting, for instance, a minimum of one full-time, qualified school nurse for each cluster or group of primary and secondary schools, taking account the health needs and school populations (DoH, 2004a).

There is now a broader range of roles in the nursing workforce, for example support workers, assistant practitioners and nurse consultants are becoming better established, and there is better recognition of the roles of nursery nurses and play staff. These new and developing roles provide a useful template for the development of a wider range of careers and roles for specialists working with vulnerable children.

Nurses, midwives and health visitors have had a history of being family-centred and from this base are well placed to respect the need for parents and children being seen as jointly responsible for health outcomes with similar respect for their knowledge and skills. With the shortage of nurses in this area and the premium on their skills it is important that there are good and effective recruitment and retention programmes in place. The DoH (2004a) suggests that particularly vulnerable areas are school nursing, child protection, neonatal nursing, health visiting, midwifery and CAMHS. There are also recruitment and retention problems in deprived communities as these are particularly challenging environments to work in. It has been suggested that there should be incentives in place to keep staff in these areas, such as flexible working, learning opportunities and rotational posts. The ageing workforce is also a factor, with PCTs and Children's Trusts needing to develop flexible retirement programmes and support for those wishing to work on past retirement age.

New roles for the nursing profession

New and expanded roles for nurses have the potential to improve health and healthcare for children. There has been an emphasis in the UK on role development to enhance the contribution of nursing and midwifery (DoH, 1999, 2002), including:

- nurse, midwife and health visitor consultant posts;
- nurses as the first point of contact in NHS Direct, walk-in centres, general practices and accident and emergency departments;
- nurses and midwives undertaking a wider range of responsibilities to speed up care, enhance responsiveness and improve quality;
- specialist roles to support key clinical and public health priorities;
- more nurses prescribing, referring and ordering investigations;
- leading improvements in care and helping to drive up standards (DoH, 2004a).

More practitioners are taking on lead roles for children, covering long-term conditions, first contact and acute care, public health and child protection. Nurses, midwives and health visitors are working across organisational and professional boundaries, in integrated Children's Centres and leading services for children. However, they still need to develop skills and knowledge to respond to the needs of children, young people, families and communities (Knott and Latter, 1999).

Training needs

There are many and varied learning needs for nurses, midwives and health visitors working with children that are generally unmet as a result of the tendency for educational establishments to concentrate on mass education. With respect to ECM this is made all the more important because of the need for post-registration education to be more integrated with other professions caring for children.

Despite a need for improved education generally there are some key priorities. Child protection training should be seen as mandatory by institutions and professionals in the same manner as fire safety. Enabling children to be active participants in healthcare decisions requires the training of these nurses in methods that fulfil this aspect of ECM. While nurses, midwives and health visitors have developed some aspects of their professional practice, there is still a need to develop advocacy skills on behalf of children, as well as other specific knowledge and skills such as ethics and information sharing between the professions.

Competencies

Work is ongoing to clarify the competencies required to work with all children. As diversity in service provision and the number of access points to the NHS increases children are bound to come into contact with nurses who are not qualified in nursing children. Other nurses working in general healthcare have responsibilities for children and need formal training and skills to be recognised. Such nurses might be working in general practice, out-of-hours services, NHS Direct, walk-in-centres and A&E. It should also be remembered that the NHS is a family service and many adults who are also parents may have health concerns, and these, particularly mental health issues, may have an impact on the child.

Competencies for working with children should include:
- awareness of normal child development and behaviour;
- child protection, identifying risk and protective factors;
- effective communication and listening to children;
- knowing who to contact when concerned about a child;
- information sharing;
- understanding the key transitions for children, such as adolescence;
- health education to promote psychological and emotional wellbeing, nutrition, safety, exercise, immunisation, smoking cessation and sexual health;
- supporting effective parenting;
- assessing and treating minor injuries and illnesses and knowing when to refer (DoH, 2004a).

Interprofessional and integrated working

Care is often fragmented between services and agencies, and there appears to be a divergence between the needs and outlook of vulnerable children and families, and the skills and knowledge of nurses, midwives and health visitors with whom they work. The DoH (2004a) called for more effective leadership and governance in areas such as child protection, general practice, interprofessional relations, communication and information sharing. Similarly, the lack of an integrated, whole workforce planning system for those working with children makes it hard to secure an adequate workforce for meeting the needs of vulnerable children.

Service integration and location

Community and school-based integrated children's services predominate within ECM. However, there remains a need to overcome the current fragmentation between hospital and primary care, and between the nursing professions. Nursing professions are starting to be placed within community and school-based integrated children's teams, such as Sure Start and Children's Centres – 'following the child' is the new principle to guide their location. Nursing professionals are now sometimes operating as the lead professional for children and families with health and development needs, and contributing to the CAF. There is a particular challenge in integrating community-based children's services such as Sure Start with general practice, with various solutions being found depending on local needs and circumstances. There are similar challenges for CAMHS, which need to be integrated better into children's services and trusts.

General practice and the new integrated children's services need to work together and communication systems need to be in place to identify and monitor vulnerable children in a joined-up manner. These systems should include a wide range of access points, such as out-of-hours services and walk-in centres. While this form of communication is important, informal day-to-day contact is also needed to promote team working and early discussion about children who are causing concern (DoH, 2004a).

Furthermore, when managers and commissioners identify general practices that find it difficult to meet the needs of vulnerable children, they can improve provision by strengthening the nursing, midwifery and health visiting input and linking to other services, such as Sure Start programmes and Children's Centres and walk-in centres.

Time honoured traditions such as the division between hospital and primary care are being dealt with by PCT lead nurses, NHS Trust nurse executive directors and directors of midwifery working together to develop integrated services. Children's nurses, midwives, health visitors and school nurses, while having much in common tend to be trained and managed separately and this exacerbates the divisions and lack of co-ordination. Children's services need to involve other specialists routinely, such as CAMHS nurses, midwives, learning disabilities nurses and children's nurses. Professional dilemmas of balancing confidentiality with information sharing and clarifying different professional responsibilities within teams need to become things of the past.

Liaison roles

Effective communication and integrated care between primary and secondary care settings is of major importance to all children. Liaison nurses therefore have an important role in assisting NHS Trusts, PCTs and so on to work together. Improved information sharing and joint learning needs to be at the heart of this co-operation.

Liaison nurses also need to be supported to work in all areas, allowing career progression established on necessary experience in both hospital and community. common assessment documentation and protocols for communication and information sharing are part of this. Discharge planning needs to take into account the child's social and emotional environment and effective communication with primary care. The new liaison posts take into account the current fragmentation of care between hospital and the community and the changes that have taken place in primary care services.

The contribution of nursing to ECM

Specialist children's nursing

Specialist nurses work in communities and hospitals and are able to provide greater continuity and more holistic care (Elston and Thornes, 2002). However, as described in ECM, a stronger community base and integration with wider children's services is needed if they are to provide better support for children (While and Dyson, 2000). The responsibility of community children's nurses for vulnerable children must be given greater emphasis and their role within integrated community and school-based children's services clarified locally. Services including specialist nurses need to be staffed by nurses who are qualified and who have the skills to work in the community. They also need to be accessible to local families and work alongside other child and family providers, which means challenging their current position within hospital settings. Specialist nurse services are often acute focused, isolated from colleagues and may not fully understand the public health issues and wider needs of children and families. These services need to be integrated with, for instance, learning disability services, and potentially managed within the community, reaching into hospitals, in keeping with the principle of following the child. A career pathway can be foreseen that would enable community children's nurses to make a greater contribution to both public health and school health.

Health visitors

The role of the health visitor has been much discussed over the past 20 years and, while their expertise is valued, there are so many competing demands on health visitors that there is a consequent thinning of their impact on specific groups such as children (Elkan et al, 2000). However, with their public health nursing and family support skills (Clark, 1973), they are central to the delivery of the aspirations of ECM. The role of the health visitor in public health (see DoH, 2001) needs to be clarified, particularly within Sure Start programmes and Children's Centres, Children's Trusts and PCTs, so that children who need them can get easy access to their skills. With the advent of ECM, PCTs are now attempting to distinguish between those health visitors with responsibility for the public health of children and those with wider public health responsibilities.

Health visitors in deprived communities and those in affluent communities are poles apart in terms of the challenges they face. As noted above, health visitors in deprived communities need to be better supported and have resources redeployed to reflect needs in their areas, focusing on identified local public health priorities (Cowley et al, 2004).

Specified health outcomes for vulnerable and disadvantaged children need to be agreed locally and nationally, so that health visitors are used appropriately and are able to focus their work systematically. This will lead to a proper focus on public health with supporting health information and leadership. In common with many other areas of clinical practice, health visitors need to develop skills in mental health, building on their listening and communication skills with children, they need to improve skills for working with fathers, as well as supporting families with children with physical and learning disabilities and leading skill-mixed teams (Kirk, 1999). There remain opportunities to increase the primary care, public health and safeguarding children orientation of pre-registration training for child branch students. This could bring benefits to children, as well as creating earlier opportunities for new junior and supporting roles for health visitors.

GP and first contact services

Given that 90% of the patient experience of the NHS is via the GP and that children are their highest users (DoH, 2004a), there are good reasons to focus on this aspect of the NHS above others when considering the health implications of ECM. There is currently a shortage of practice nurses with the skills to work with children and this may lead to lost opportunities for health promotion, during immunisation visits for example. Some GPs have been reluctant to allow practice nurses training in child protection, which is clearly linked to GPs' employment responsibilities and professional code of conduct (DoH, 2004a). However, strengthening practice nurse competencies to work with children is a clear priority of ECM.

There are various ways in which this group could be developed but the first step should include an assessment of the skills gap. It has been suggested that it would be useful to have a self-assessment tool, for instance (DoH, 2004a). Because of the contractual arrangements with GPs, the use of such a tool needs to be backed up by an undertaking from GPs to address skills gaps identified in the interests of the children that they serve. There is also a clear need for practice nurses to have access to, supervision and support from an experienced registered children's nurse, with general practice also being promoted as a career option for children's nurses.

School-aged children and young people

The size of the school nursing workforce, estimated to be between 2,000 and 2,500 (DoH, 2004a), is currently insufficient to provide the three core functions of first contact care, public health and support for people with ongoing health needs (Harris, 1995). The principle of 'following the child' will mean also considering the needs of young people absent from school or in the youth justice services. One way of dealing with the shortage is the provision of a minimum of one full-time, whole year, qualified school nurse for each set of primary and secondary schools (however defined), focusing on health needs and the school population (DeBell, 2000). However, the contribution of school nurses within integrated services remains unclear and needs to be articulated. In order to meet local health needs these nurses need to lead and work in skill-mixed teams with youth workers, teachers, social workers and others (Cotton et al, 2000; Croghan et al, 2004).

Partnership working with health visitors and others needs to be emphasised so that children are better supported during transitional periods. Immunisation programmes are of great importance to child health but make considerable demands on school nurses at the expense of fulfilling other health needs. PCTs are working with health protection colleagues and schools to explore more efficient ways of delivering these programmes, such as the creation of immunisation teams.

Hospital care

Hospital-based nurses often have the opportunity to observe children over a long and intensive period of time, but they are undermined in their ability to meet the needs of vulnerable children (Audit Commission, 1993; Robertson et al, 2002). This could be improved by increasing the work of the child protection services with nurses in the acute sector. Child advocacy requires a change in culture in hospital in some acute settings by creating a supportive and facilitative management style and greater equality between the medical and nursing professions. Nurses in acute settings need to change their range of working by increasing their ability to intervene at the primary level of prevention, through parental support, managing common behaviour problems and helping parents to understand and respond to their child's development needs. Similarly, neonatal units need to provide an environment that supports parent–child attachment and 24-hour parent–child contact (DoH, 2004a). Greater access to specialist CAMHS advice is needed and acute nurses need to improve their skills in CAMHS.

Nurses working with adults

Many adults using the NHS are parents and their children may be affected by their health, especially if they have mental health issues. Effects on children are likely to be more acute in settings such as prisons, A&E, substance misuse services, mental health and learning disability services (DoH, 2004a). Nurses need to consider the needs of a child in any family and take action if they think a child may be at risk. Nurses in A&E will need to assess the family situation and take steps if they think a child is at risk in situations such as domestic violence or aggressive behaviour. Child protection training therefore needs to be seen as a core part of nurse education, not simply within registered nurse training, but within ongoing mandatory training.

Midwifery services

Midwives have much potential for protecting and promoting the health of vulnerable children, and this is discussed in detail in the next chapter.

Child protection

The role of named or designated child protection nurses is an important one in the protection of vulnerable children. The aspirations of ECM have highlighted many areas for development of this role. The seniority of the role requires the authority to act on behalf of children with a line of accountability to the top of the organisation, or trust board. Some organisations are very large, so it will be important to ensure that roles are achievable and services are responsive and accessible. Other non-traditional organisations, such as prisons, also need child protection nursing support. In these and other settings nurses need regular support and supervision to deliver the right quality of child protection specialist services.

Practice issues for nursing, midwifery and health visiting

The needs and views of children and families provided an important starting point for nurses to reflect on their own role, and to consider ways in which their services and relationships can be changed to fit in with ECM. This reflection shows that there are gaps in services and in the ways that nursing, midwifery and health visiting services are presently organised.

Nurses working in general practice have a great deal of interaction with children in clinic settings, but are often unaware of which children are vulnerable, thereby missing opportunities for prevention and early intervention. This is partly due to their lack of training and awareness of vulnerable children and child protection. School nurses are regarded as having great potential to deal with the needs of vulnerable children of school age (Cotton et al, 2000; Croghan et al, 2004). However, the small number of school nurses is a significant barrier to effectiveness. School nurses also need more opportunities to work with families (DoH, 2004a). CAMHS and learning disabilities nurses have similar restrictions because of the manner in which they work and could benefit from more contact with other frontline nurses as well as with services for children. CAMHS nurses have a clear role with vulnerable children especially those outside the 'norm' such as asylum seekers and young offenders. There is also a role for adult mental health nurses in relation to the children of the adults in their care.

Nurses working in secondary care have great potential to improve care for vulnerable children, but this is not fully developed, including their potential advocacy role for children. Similarly, liaison nurses currently have insufficient resources, skills and knowledge to fulfil their role in the context of ECM.

Midwives have much to offer vulnerable children but being located in acute units stifles this potential. They could be integrated into community-based teams, possibly Children's Centres, where they would have potential to work more preventatively with vulnerable children as well as more closely with fathers.

Health visitors are well-equipped to deliver the aims of ECM, but there are tensions between their work with individual children and families, and with the potential for public health work with the wider population. There is a risk that health visitors will be drawn into 'medical' aspects of care at the expense of primary prevention. However, with this caveat, health visitors are able to respond holistically to a wide range of needs and this is one of their strengths. There are specific needs for:

- earlier identification of vulnerability and protective factors in the antenatal period;
- more intensive preventive health care for vulnerable families during the antenatal and early postnatal period;
- better skills in identifying and supporting vulnerable children and families across the workforce with confidence in taking steps to safeguard children at risk;
- more holistic services with improved continuity of care and a greater emphasis on CAMHS;
- a significant increase is needed in the provision of accessible healthcare for children of school age and better support for their parents;
- better child health promotion and protection in general practice;
- more action at community level to build health resources for vulnerable children and families (DoH, 2004a).

Summary

This chapter has described the wide and demanding range of roles and tasks that must be fulfilled by nurses if their contribution to the ECM agenda is to be best achieved. It has suggested that new policies and practices need to be developed to overcome the fragmentation of services, and that the nursing profession needs to develop at both pre- and post-qualifying levels to make the best contribution to working alongside and with the other children's services.

Note

The term nurse has been used to indicate any professional registered with the Nursing and Midwifery Council. The terms midwife and health visitor have been used when specifically making points which are relevant to these professionals.

References

Acheson, D. (1998a) *Public Health in England: The report of the committee of enquiry into the future development of the public health function*, London: The Stationery Office.

Acheson, D. (1998b) *Independent inquiry into inequalities in health*, London: The Stationery Office.

Audit Commission (1993) *Children first: A study of hospital services*, London: HMSO.

Clark, J. (1973) *A family visitor: A descriptive analysis of health visiting in Berkshire*, London: Royal College of Nursing.

Cotton, L., Brazier, J., Hall, D., Lindsay, G., Marsh, P., Polnay, L. and Williams, T. (2000) 'School nursing costs and potential', *Journal of Advanced Nursing*, vol 31, pp 1063-71.

Cowley, S. Mitcheson, J. and Houston A. (2004) 'Structuring health needs assessments: the medicalisation of health visiting', *Sociology of Health & Illness*, vol 25, pp 503-26.

Croghan, E., Johnson, C. andAveyard, P. (2004) 'School nurses: policies, working practices, roles and value perceptions', *Journal of Advanced Nursing*, vol 47, pp 377-85.

DeBell, D. (2000) *An assessment of change in the management and delivery of school nursing*, London: DoH.

DfES (Department for Education and Skills) (2004) *Every Child Matters: Next steps*,London: DfES.

DfES and DoH (Department of Health) (2004) *National Service Framework for Children, Young People and Maternity Services*, London: DoH.

DoH (2003a) *Getting the right start: The NSF for children, young people and maternity services – standards for hospital services*, London: DoH.

DoH (2003b) *Getting the right start: The NSF for children, young people and maternity services – emerging findings*, London: DoH.

Downie, R., Tannahill, C. and Tannahill, A. (1996) *Health promotion: Models and values*, Oxford: Oxford University Press.

Elkan, R., Kendrick, D., Hewitt, M., Robinson, J., Tolley, K. Blair, et al (2000) 'The effectiveness of domiciliary health visiting: a systematic review of international studies and a selective review of the British literature', *Health Technology Assessment*, vol 4, pp 1-339.

Elston, S. and Thornes, R. (2002) *Children's nursing workforce July 2002,* London: Royal College of Nursing & Royal College of Paediatrics and Child Health.

Hall, D. (ed) (1989) *Health for all children*, Oxford: Oxford University Press.

Hall, D., and Elliman, D. (eds) (2003) *Health for all children*, 4th edn, Oxford: Oxford University Press.

Harris, B. (1995) *The health of the school child*, Buckingham: Open University Press.

Kirk, S. (1999) 'Caring for children with specialized health care needs in the community: the challenges for primary care', *Health & Social Care in the Community*, vol 7, pp 350-7.

Knott, M. and Latter, S. (1999) 'Help or hindrance? Single, unsupported mothers' perceptions of health visiting', *Journal of Advanced Nursing*, vol 30, pp 580-8.

Lloyd, E., Hemmingway, M., Newman, T., Roberts, H. and Webster, A. (1997) *Today and tomorrow: Investing in our children*, Barkingside: Barnardo's.

Roberts, H. (2000) *What works in reducing inequalities in child health*. Barkingside: Barnardo's.

Roberts, I., Kramer, M. and Suissa, S. (1996) 'Does home visiting prevent childhood injury?', *British Medical Journal*, no 312, pp 29-33.

Robertson, L., Kawik, L., McCourt, C., Forster, M., Pask, E. and Dexter, Y. (2002) 'Do children's nurses make a difference?', *Paediatric Nursing*, vol 14, pp 30-3.

Sloper, P. (2004) 'Facilitators and barriers for co-ordinated multi-agency services', *Child: Care, Health and Development*, vol 30, pp 571-80.

SOLAR (2003) *Mind the gap: Health futures for young people in Hounslow*, Bristol: University, West of England/Hounslow Community Health Council.

While, A. and Dyson, L. (2000) 'Characteristics of paediatric home care provision: the two dominate models in England', *Child: Care, Heath and Development*, vol 26, pp 263-76.

SEVEN

Maternity care and Every Child Matters

Fiona Hutchinson

> Children and young people are important. They are the living message
> we send to a time we will not see; nothing matters more to families
> than the health, welfare and future success of their children. They
> deserve the best care because they are the life blood of the nation and
> are vital for our future economic survival and prosperity…. (Aynsley-
> Green, 2004, p 4)

The above quote succinctly summarises how important it is to invest time and
effort in caring for our younger generation. Maternity services are delivered by
a range of key professionals both in primary and secondary care. The principal
care providers are midwives, neonatal nurses, health visitors, obstetric staff,
general practitioners and the recently introduced maternity care workers. Other
professionals who may be involved are dietitians, mental health specialists and
health promotion experts (NESS, 2005). This chapter will focus on care provided
to the mother and baby before, during and immediately after birth. For this
reason, the key roles discussed will be those of the midwife, neonatal nurse and
maternity support worker (MSW). It is important to acknowledge however that
the roles of the community midwife and health visitor are inextricably linked, as
the health visitor takes on the care of the family after the midwife has fulfilled
her remit. Professionals involved in the immediate period before, during and after
birth have an important role to play in ensuring that every child receives the best
start in life and each plays a part in ensuring that the phrase 'every child matters'
is the philosophy underpinning their practice.

The first part of this chapter will provide an introduction to maternity services
in the UK and why it is the foundation of Every Child Matters (DfES, 2004).
It is the earliest healthcare intervention of all for the child and it is essential to
get it right for babies and parents. The roles of the key professionals involved in
care provision will be explained, as they may be unfamiliar to some readers. By
using case studies as examples, the chapter will then explore how each of them
contributes to addressing the key recommendations of ECM including the
Common Assessment Framework (CAF) and discusses the strategic challenges
of the children's workforce. The final part of the chapter will focus on discussing
future trends in maternity care with relation to ECM.

Background: an overview of maternity services

Women have always helped one another in childbirth, and the first formal arrangement for the control of midwives was made in 1512. All persons (male and female) seeking a licence to practise medicine were required to submit themselves for examination by the local Bishop (midwives were considered akin to surgeons at this time). By 1902 the Midwives Act provided legal recognition and protection for midwives and state registration became compulsory by law. Midwives' training was three months' long and they could not practise unless they were certified on the midwives register. The limits of their responsibility were then set by doctors (Donnison, 1977).

Until 1948 (the introduction of the NHS) women had to pay for the services of a midwife. Following the arrival of the NHS, GPs became the first point of contact for the pregnant woman and they were paid by the government for providing maternity care. Maternal and infant mortality rates were high, especially in the socially disadvantaged population.

In the early 1950s women had a 1 in 1,500 chance of dying during or after childbirth, and during the 1960s 30 out of every 1,000 babies were either still born or died soon after delivery. Thankfully, maternity care has greatly improved over the last 50 years due to better recognition of risk factors and advances in medical treatment.

The 1973 NHS Reorganisation Act allowed midwives to take on more responsibility for pregnant women, for example family planning, health education and neonatal care (that is, care of the newborn baby).

The current position

Childbirth today is a much safer event for the mother and baby and the number of women dying during or after childbirth has been reduced to 1 in 20,000 (Shribman, 2007). The disadvantage of advances in maternity care is that there has been a dramatic increase in medical intervention in childbirth, thereby turning what is usually a normal process into a medical event. The Government Statistical Service stated that during 2003/2004 a total of 23% of deliveries were by caesarean section and approximately 12% were instrumental deliveries (Government Statistical Service, 2005). In the 1950s 49% of women had their babies either at home or in a nursing home. By the 1970s 66% of women opted for a hospital delivery and the percentage of home births had fallen to about 12%. This was mainly due to changes after the publication of the Peel Report which recommended that all births should take place in hospital (Hunt and Symonds, 1995). Today only about 2-3% of women opt for home births and about 4% in a midwife birthing centre (Shribman, 2007). While some would advocate that the hospital environment is lower risk, it does not meet all women's needs, as the hospital environment lends itself to a more medical and interventionist approach to care. Over the past decade there has been a shift in policy towards a more 'woman-centred' model of care based on research suggesting that the psychological and emotional needs of women have impacts on outcomes for both the baby and the mother (Kitzinger, 1992). In the light of this shift, recent government initiatives are geared towards providing women with choice about where and how they want to have their baby with the emphasis on providing a safe service (DoH and Partnerships for Children, Families and Maternity, 2007).

The fundamental aims of ECM are to improve the health and well-being of all children; the health of the mother is of paramount importance in ensuring this, as healthy mothers are more likely to have healthy babies (DoH and Partnerships for Children, Families and Maternity, 2007). The weight of a baby at birth can be an indicator of the mother's long-standing health problems and also a predictor of the baby's mortality and future health and well-being. To illustrate the significance of this, the Office of National Statistics (ONS) reported that 64% of infant deaths in England and Wales in 2003 were babies weighing less than 2,500g which is the WHO definition of a low-birth-weight baby (Collingwood Bakeo and Clarke, 2006). A low-birth-weight baby is one who has either been born prematurely (before 37 completed weeks' gestation) or who has failed to reach the adequate weight for their gestational age. Babies may also be born with a combination of these two factors. Several follow up studies of babies have demonstrated that babies born with a low birth weight have a higher risk of developing chronic health conditions and also a reduced quality of life (Dineson and Grieson, 2001; Mayor, 2005; Dubois and Girard, 2006). In addition to this, babies who are born prematurely are also more likely to have neurological and developmental disabilities (Wood et al, 2000). These babies require specialised care at birth and immediately after to minimise the risk of any complications. Risk factors for babies being born with a low birth weight are:

- maternal age (very young or older mother);
- smoking;
- poor diet;
- substance misuse;
- socio-economic deprivation;
- lone mother;
- maternal illness;
- non-white ethnic group;
- domestic violence;
- mental health problems (Collingwood Bakeo and Clarke, 2006).

The priority for today's maternity services is to provide a choice of safe, high-quality care for all women and their partners, taking cognisance of the above risk factors. Current challenges include improving neonatal outcomes for the more vulnerable and disadvantaged families (DoH and Partnerships for Children, Families and Maternity, 2007). It is important to remember that maternity care is not just about delivering babies. It is also about striving to ensure that every baby has the opportunity to achieve their full growth and developmental potential. The role of the key professionals involved with maximising this potential will now be explored.

The maternity workforce

In today's NHS nursing and midwifery are regarded as two different occupations, although the current regulatory body for midwifery is still the Nursing and Midwifery Council (NMC).

Midwives

The role of a midwife may be summarised as someone who provides advice, care and support for women, their partners and families during the pre-conceptual, antenatal, intranatal and postnatal period. They are responsible for newborn babies until the 28th postnatal day, when care is transferred to the health visitor. Midwives are independent practitioners calling doctors only when there is a problem involving the mother's or the baby's safety. They work either in a hospital or in a community setting, and function as part of a multi-disciplinary team liaising with general practitioners, health visitors and social workers (NMC, 2000).

There are two ways of becoming a midwife – either through a three-year degree programme or, if the applicant has a nursing qualification, through a shortened 18-month programme. In the UK midwifery education programmes can only be delivered at NMC approved educational institutions. Training takes place in a University and at least half of the programme is based in clinical practice. The statutory supervision of midwives is undertaken by Local Supervising Authorities (LSAs). In England the LSAs are the Strategic Health Authorities (SHAs), in Northern Ireland the Health and Social Services Boards, in Scotland the Regional Boards and in Wales the LSA is the Health Inspectorate (NMC, 2007).

All midwives in the UK must complete an 'Intention to Practice' form on an annual basis, which demonstrates that they have maintained their midwifery skills. Some midwives are also specialised in the management of the newborn baby, taking on skills that have previously been undertaken by medical practitioners. These skills include neonatal resuscitation, stabilisation of the newborn at birth and the initial examination of the newborn (Redshaw and Harvey, 2000).

Neonatal nurses and nurse practitioners

In the 1960s hospitals began to recognise the need for continuing education for nurses who had completed their initial registration with the General Nursing Council (GNC). As a result of this, post-registration specialty courses, including ones for care of the vulnerable newborn baby, were devised by English National Board during the 1970s and 1980s (Allan, 2000). These educational programmes were considered to be the basic requirements for nurses wishing to develop clinical and theoretical expertise in neonatal care.

Neonatal nurses care for babies who are vulnerable, from being born with a low birth weight, or prematurely, or with a congenital birth defect. Nursing care of vulnerable babies has become increasingly technical as more and more babies require respiratory ventilation as a result of being born prematurely.

Neonatal nurses work within specialist neonatal units or in the community. As well as caring for babies, they have the role of supporting families and encouraging them to take an active role in the care of their baby.

Registered adult and children's nurses as well as midwives can work in this specialism. Normally after a period of about six months nurses and midwives are encouraged to undertake CPD (NHS Careers, 2007).

The role of neonatal nurse has continued to expand and now several neonatal units employ neonatal nurse practitioners (NNPs). NNPs are neonatal nurses who have undergone additional post-qualifying education (usually at masters level) and who have specialised in the provision of caring for newborn babies who require resuscitation at birth and management of babies requiring ventilation. NNPs also carry out the initial examination of the newborn (previously a task undertaken by medical staff) and undertake routine management of the newborn baby.

A baby born prematurely is dependent on expert care at birth and the immediate postnatal period. Initial studies have demonstrated that their care is equivalent to that of a medical practitioner (Yoxall and Aubrey, 2001; Chan and Hey, 2006) and that skilled neonatal nurse practitioners can deliver good-quality neonatal care without medical staff being resident on the neonatal unit (Ward Platt and Brown, 2004). An example of how the roles of the midwife and neonatal nurse practitioner function collaboratively to provide high-quality care for the mother and baby may be found in the North East of England, where the Ashington Audit Group (2004) have demonstrated in their evaluation of neonatal care that nurse practitioners built up a rapport with families who trusted them and found them approachable.

Maternity support workers

The role of the health care assistant has been around for quite some time and is one approach to managing diminished resources in health services. Thornley describes their development as 'a quiet revolution in recent years in the profile of the non-registered care-giving workforce in the NHS' (Thornley, 2000, p 451).

Assistants are now increasingly being introduced into the maternity care workforce as MSWs, and their role is considered by some to be somewhat controversial (Woodward et al, 2004). It is argued that they are an erosion of the midwives' role and simply a means of reducing staffing costs, while others believe that they enable midwives to focus on their care tasks and reduce waiting times for maternity services (DoH and Partnerships for Children, Families and

Maternity, 2007). The Royal College of Midwives (RCM) states that if MSWs are appropriately trained and managed by midwives they can make a positive contribution to maternity services (RCM, 2006).

Some of the key roles that they currently undertake are to support women breastfeeding, to assist with parent craft classes and to visit women under the supervision of the midwife in the community setting. One London hospital employs two MSWs to help with its community midwifery service; funded by Sure Start monies, the MSWs visit women at home and provide general support, for example teaching mothers how to massage their babies to calm them down in the home (NHS Employers, 2006).

One of the problems of the MSW role is that there is currently a lack of standardisation in MSW training (Mckenna et al, 2003). Previous experience of working with parents and young babies is usually required and many hospital trusts also require evidence of some study at NVQ level 2 or 3 in health and social care. When starting employment MSWs also undergo basic training on subjects such as infection control, breast-feeding support, risk management, child protection and health and safety (NHS Careers, 2007).

New roles in maternity services

In 2004 the NHS Modernisation Agency produced a document which was a guide to role redesign in neonatal services (NHS Modernisation Agency, 2004). This document was initiated by a report published by the Childcare Group Workforce Teams (CGWT), highlighting neonatal care as one of the major areas with recruitment problems. The CGWT stressed the urgent need for, amongst others, more neonatal nurse practitioners to invest in children's nursing. As a result of this, the Skills for Health Council (SfH) devised a National Workforce Competence Framework for Maternity and the Newborn to provide a high-quality service to newborn babies and their families (SfH, 2007). The SfH works in partnership with the Agenda for Change Key Skills Framework (Agenda for Change Project Team, 2004) to ensure that the different frameworks support each other. This new framework has had a major influence on how maternity care is provided as it has resulted in changes in job descriptions for all grades of professionals. Examples of newly created posts may be seen in the NHS Modernisation Agency Publication *Workforce Matters* (2004) and include nursery specialists (play therapy), Neonatal nursery assistants and family support workers. Where roles have been redesigned, the DoH emphasise the importance of ensuring that the individual is competent to undertake the sphere of practice and does not cross professional boundaries (NHS Modernisation Agency, 2004). This becomes particularly relevant when employing MSW as their role is not yet nationally regulated.

Derby Hospital NHS Foundation Trust has implemented a skill mix using MSWs to increase the effectiveness of their maternity work force.

Case study: Derby Hospital NHS Foundation Trust

Derby hospitals have recruited MSWs to assist with breast-feeding support and advice, general health promotion, undertaking blood tests and appointment booking. This has enabled midwives to reduce their 'non-midwifery tasks' by 30% and there has been a reduction of 20% in waiting times in community antenatal clinics. 18% of the home visits are undertaken by MSWs. (DOH and Partnerships for Children, Families and Maternity, 2007, p 25)

The above example demonstrates how, by redesigning the skill mix there has been an improvement for both midwives and mothers. MSWs assist the midwife with clinics such as smoking cessation, teenage pregnancy, breast-feeding and drug abuse (NHS Employers, 2006).

Interprofessional working and Children's Centres

It is a sobering thought that current estimates suggest that 30% of domestic violence cases start or escalate during pregnancy and domestic violence is associated with increases in rates of miscarriage, low birth weight, premature birth, foetal injury and foetal death (DoH and Partnerships for Children, Families and Maternity 2007). Infant mortality is highest in manual socio–economic groups, black minority ethnic populations, teenage mothers and lone parent families. One of the key contributors to bringing together services for vulnerable, disadvantaged women and their families has been the introduction of Sure Start Children's Centres.

Sure Start programmes were launched in 1998 as part of the government drive to tackle childhood poverty and social exclusion by focusing on resources and support at the start of life. In March 2006 Sure Start programmes were mainstreamed becoming Children's Centres (see Chapter Five). These are places where families should be able to access seamless health and social care services. By 2010 it is anticipated that there will be 3,500 Children's Centres – one in every community in the country (Hassan et al, 2006). Health services relating to pregnancy and childbirth provided in Children's Centres may include:

- well baby clinics;
- parent craft classes;
- healthy eating in pregnancy;
- smoking cessation for women who are pregnant;
- baby massage.

These services will contribute towards helping the Primary Care Trusts to meet public health priorities, such as reducing health inequalities, reducing adult smoking rates, halting the obesity rise in children and reducing the under-18 conception rate. An example of how this is working is provided in the box below.

Case example: Portsmouth's Maternity Outreach Programme

All families with someone who is newly pregnant living in Sure Start areas are visited early in the pregnancy at home by the maternity outreach worker. They provide information on local services and offer support with parenting education, information about 'bumps and babies' groups, infant feeding and referrals to appropriate agencies such as the smoking cessation service and infant mental health team.

Vulnerable and socially-excluded women are offered individually tailored support as agreed with the community midwife and health visitor.

All teenage parents in Portsmouth are now allocated a maternity outreach worker wherever they live (Armstrong, 2007, p 16).

The programme above is only one of many examples available. In Southampton services have been reorganised so that midwives can take care of disadvantaged women and their large refugee community. In conjunction with Sure Start Children's Centres, interpreters, social services and GPs they have organised a social model of care to ensure continuity. Their evaluation demonstrated a reduction in the incidence of low-birth-weight babies (DoH and Partnerships for Children, Families and Maternity, 2007.) During the initial phase of developing Children's Centres, some tensions arose between Sure Start staff and mainstream staff. These were mainly due to the perceived under-funding of statutory services, compared with the large influx of money provided for the Children's Centres. Edgley (2007) suggests that this will be resolved once the services are placed under the umbrella of statutory provision. She hypothesises that once the Children's Centres are established services will be drawn together in both a geographical and interprofessional working sense.

The role of the neonatal nurse is traditionally multi-factoral. Not only do they have to care for the sick baby, but also the baby's family. By utilising a family-centred care model, Henson (2000) demonstrates how families can be supported while their baby is in the neonatal unit. This support may involve co-ordinating care with the midwife, health visitor and social worker as problems may only surface during the course of the stay in the neonatal unit. Part of the planning for discharge into the community involves physical, intellectual, emotional and social assessment (Henson, 2000)

In their article discussing cross-boundary working within child health services, While et al (2006) cite the example of the sick neonate being cared for in a neonatal unit as being a baby who is very dependent on good team working both in the high-dependency setting and on discharge into the community. Neonatal nurse practitioners are ideally placed to liaise with other professionals to ensure that the care provided is seamless. Nicolson et al (2005) state that an effective neonatal care team should include a skill mix that is able to liaise with other health professionals such as midwives, health visitors, social workers and obstetricians.

The contribution of maternity services to ECM

We will now explore how maternity services can play an important role in assisting with the five aims of ECM. While all of the aims are relevant to maternity services, the two that are directly influenced by the care received before, during and after birth are 'Be healthy' and 'Stay safe'. From the perspective of maternity care, the remaining three aims are dependent on the achievement of the first two. The role of the midwife has been specifically highlighted as one of importance in helping to achieve these aims; however, all maternity staff contribute both directly and indirectly to the above aims.

Be healthy

One of the recommendations of ECM was that the Chief Nursing Officer would conduct a review of the midwifery, nursing and health visiting contributions to the care of vulnerable children and young people. At about the same time as the publication of ECM the NSF for Children, Young People and Maternity Services was published. This document provided clear standards for promoting the health and well-being of children, young people and mothers. The eleventh standard specifically addresses maternity services:

> Women [should] have easy access to supportive, high quality maternity services, designed around their individual needs and those of their babies. (DoH, 2004, p 4)

The three main visions for the future of midwifery services are:

1. Flexible individualised services with the emphasis on the needs of vulnerable and disadvantaged women.
2. Women being supported in having as normal a pregnancy and birth as possible, with medical interventions only if they are of benefit to the woman or her baby.
3. All care to be based on providing good clinical and psychological outcomes for the woman and her baby, while putting equal emphasis on helping new parents prepare for parenthood. (DoH, 2004, p 4)

A more recent report (DoH and Partnerships for Children, Families and Maternity, 2007) builds on the initial standard identified in the NSF. The report states that by the end of 2009 the government plans to guarantee four choices for women:

1. **A choice of how to access maternity care:** Women and their partners will be able to go straight to a midwife if they wish, or to their GP. Self referral to a midwife will speed up access to maternity services and is likely to be attractive to women who would otherwise hesitate to visit their doctor.

2. **A choice of the type of antenatal care:** Women will be able to choose between midwifery care or combined midwife and obstetric care. For some women combined care will be the safest option.
3. **A choice of the place of birth:** In making the decision between having their baby at home, in a local facility under care of the midwife, or in a hospital, women will need to be aware that some forms of pain relief (for example, epidural anaesthesia) will only be available in hospitals providing a 24-hour anaesthetic service.
4. **A choice of place for postnatal care:** postnatal care will be provided either at home or in a community centre such as a Sure Start Children's Centre.

It is anticipated that providing women with the choices above will also contribute to the achievement of the DoH's overall targets of reducing mortality rates and reducing health inequalities (as measured by infant mortality). Women who have control over their pregnancy and delivery are more likely to seek care.

Stay safe

Case example: Michelle and Michael

Michelle (17 years old) is the lone parent of baby Michael. Michael was born prematurely at 30 weeks gestation weighing 1200g. Neonatal nurses have expressed concern that Michelle does not appear to appreciate Michael's needs and she often acts inappropriately, for example, leaving him unwrapped and allowing him to get cold. She is currently living in a flat with friends who regularly misuse substances. Michael is nearly ready for discharge into the community and the hospital team are anxious that safe provision is made for both mother and baby.

The important issue in this case example is to ensure that Michael is cared for in a safe environment. While in the Neonatal Unit, Michael could be cared for in a comparatively safe environment: protected from hazards such as infection, cold and excessive environmental stimuli such as noise and light (Reid and Freer, 2000). The main concerns following discharge into the community in this example are: lack of parenting skills, risk of exposure to substance misuse and inadequate housing. An effective neonatal team can ensure that both Michael and his mother are in optimum physical, mental and emotional health prior to discharge into the community, and expert antenatal, intranatal and postnatal care provided by the midwife, obstetrician, neonatologist, and neonatal nursing team would minimise the risk of immediate postnatal health complications to both Michelle and Michael. It is essential, however, to ensure that Michael's continuing care is appropriate to his needs. Michelle may need guidance to ensure that Michael attends all his follow-up appointments and attends the clinic for his immunisations – especially important following his premature birth. Michelle may be receiving support from the local authority Children and Young People's Services as she is herself 'a child in need', and should have had the opportunity to attend a Sure Start Children's Centre. The Children's Centre can offer a continuing care package and provide an outreach programme if necessary. Activities available could include parenting skills, teenage parenting classes, paediatric first aid, early years child development programme, baby massage, healthy eating, sexual health and training and learning opportunities for Michelle.

Brett (2005) describes the development of a multi-agency team set up in London for teenage pregnancies providing examples of services available. Following the introduction of this service, some of the changes noted were: an increase in early access to maternity care, a fall in smoking rates among pregnant teenagers, and a reduction in the birth of low-birth-weight babies. As Michelle may need additional support to achieve the ECM outcomes, it is vital that all information regarding her circumstances is shared by health professionals. This should be achieved by the use of the CAF (DoH et al, 2000), which aims to eliminate the need for families having to repeatedly 'retell their story'.

The CAF is a voluntary assessment and the midwife or neonatal nurse is uniquely placed to identify risk factors for the mother and baby during pregnancy, birth and into childhood. An assessment may be undertaken at any time – on unborn babies, newly delivered babies or children or young people. Powell (2005) suggests that midwives are in a good position to identify vulnerability factors in relation to families. Nottingham's Children and Young People's Services have recently published a proposed integration plan for the CAF to be implemented by March 2008. Amongst the professionals required to undertake the mandatory course in utilising the CAF and taking on the role of lead professional are midwives, neonatal nurses and health visitors (Partington, 2006). The list below provides examples of how the three dimensions of the CAF could be applied to Michael's care.

- **Developmental needs:** Ensuring his immunisations are up to date, that he is receiving adequate nutrition and achieving his developmental milestones.
- **Parents and carers:** Ensuring that Michael is cared for in a safe, warm, environment. It is also important that he receives appropriate stimulation and physical contact.
- **Family and environment:** Ensuring that Michael is brought up in an environment which has basic amenities and that the wider family members do not have a negative influence on the baby. In this particular case study, one potential hazard is that Michael may be exposed to substance misuse at an early age.

The remaining three aims of ECM

- Enjoy and achieve
- Make a positive contribution
- Achieve economic well-being

While being outside the direct remit of professionals working in maternity services, the remaining three aims of ECM are strongly influenced by the care received during the antenatal, intranatal and postnatal period.

Challenges and opportunities for the future of maternity care

The future of maternity services has been described in the recently published DoH document *Maternity matters* (DoH and Partnerships for Children, Families and Maternity, 2007). It demonstrates how commissioners, providers and maternity professionals can utilise the ongoing health reform agenda to shape future provision of maternity care. Future services are being planned to address the current challenges which are primarily:

- improving outcomes for disadvantaged and vulnerable families;
- redesigning the workforce to optimise skill mix;
- providing a choice of safe, flexible care for all women.

The development of maternity services in Sure Start Children's Centres is one way of improving outcomes for disadvantaged families. Early evaluations of Sure Start initiatives have suggested that these centres are not reaching the most vulnerable women (Ormerod, 2005), although Rutter (2006) argues that evaluations of the project have been undertaken too soon to realistically be able to assist their impact. Edgley (2007), in her study examining statutory service providers' perceptions of Sure Start professionals, found that part of the problem has been the way that resources have been targeted to specific geographical areas and suggests that the reconfiguration of health services may address this by drawing services together geographically in Children's Centres. This would hopefully avoid situations as described by Elliman and Bedford (2006) whereby, among disadvantaged families using services, greater benefits were achieved for the moderately disadvantaged families than for those with severe disadvantage, thus increasing health inequalities.

As part of the Social Exclusion Action Plan a model of intensive health-led home visiting is being piloted in 2007/2008 across ten PCTs in England. This is to be undertaken in conjunction with local authorities. These sites will evaluate the impact of a parenting programme provided for the most disadvantaged families. Ensuring that midwifery and health visiting services provide tailored support for teenage parents is a step forward in addressing problems such as poor levels of nutrition, late antenatal booking, low rates of breast-feeding and smoking during pregnancy. The organisations that regulate nurses, teachers and social workers (GTC, GSCC and NMC) have recently joined forces to help promote a shared approach to improving services for children and young people. The statement of interprofessional values recently published, places much emphasis on working together more effectively in the interests of children (GSCC, 2007). This is an excellent opportunity to prevent the tragic incidents where vulnerable and 'at risk' babies and children slip through the net. It will hopefully also further enhance interprofessional communication and promote seamless care.

Amongst the national targets and local delivery plan measures described by the DoH (2006) is a requirement of local organisations to undertake a comprehensive review of their workforce capacity. With regards to the maternity workforce this also encompasses maintaining effective leadership skills to provide a supportive culture for change. This will hopefully provide the foundation for good maternity services that can fulfil the needs and expectations of women and their families. Geographical variations will also need to be taken into account as maternity services that work in an industrial town may not be appropriate for a rural area (Shribman, 2007). Changing the skill mix and redesigning the workforce has the potential to release the clinical time of midwives and doctors and improve outcomes for babies, but this must be undertaken with clear guidelines about the limits of responsibility (NHS Modernisation Agency, 2004), consistent and regulated training. Midwives must be proactive in the development of Children's Centres and ensure that all good practice developed in the Sure Start initiatives is carried forward. Midwifery is a profession already embedded in the ethos of public health and roles building on this philosophy need to be a priority of the future (Edwards, 2005). Ongoing staff development programmes are also essential to ensure that all staff caring for women during pregnancy and the post natal period have the appropriate clinical skills (DoH and Partnerships for Children, Families and Maternity, 2007).

The government's philosophy on offering a choice for women during pregnancy and birth in the future is a challenging task for future organisers of maternity care. Maternal choice must be balanced with the priority of providing a choice of safe, high-quality maternity care. Pregnancy and birth are usually normal life events supported by midwives, but it must be remembered that some disadvantaged women will need specialist care and when this is necessary it should be readily available and of the highest possible quality (DoH and Partnerships for Children, Families and Maternity 2007). Children's Centres offer a variety of help for women, but at the end of the day it is a matter of individual choice as to whether women decide to make use of the services offered. A study undertaken by Avis et al (2007) provides illustrative examples of why some women choose not to participate in Sure Start programmes and their views should be respected by health professionals.

Summary

By exploring the differing roles of professionals involved in caring for women before during and after pregnancy this chapter has described the relevance and importance of maternity services to ECM.

Being healthy starts from pre-conception, as it is then that the foundation for a healthy life starts. All babies need to be kept safe from harm; again this is within the remit of the health professionals mentioned in this chapter as they may well become the baby's advocate. In order to achieve the last three aims of ECM any vulnerable baby must receive expert care at birth in order to maximise the potential to achieve optimum growth and development. It cannot be emphasised enough how important skilled antenatal, intranatal and postnatal care is in preventing ill health in both the mother and the baby. Vulnerable groups such as pregnant teenage girls, women from minority ethnic groups and refugees may require differing maternity care and initiatives such as Children's Centres play a vital part in providing this care.

Examples of maternity practices around the UK have demonstrated how a social model of care can provide a more holistic approach encompassing the wider determinants of health. It is too early to evaluate the overall effect of these initiatives on the population – only time will tell whether there has been a reduction in neonatal mortality and morbidity due to babies being born with a low birth weight or prematurely. A final quote from the current Minister for Care Services summarises the discussion in this chapter.

> The quality of the advice, support and care provided from the early stages of pregnancy to the initial period of a baby's life is important for all families but especially those parents most at risk. Antenatal and postnatal care are crucial in ensuring parents feel adequately supported and equipped with the skills and knowledge to give their child the best possible start in life. (DoH and Partnerships for Children, Families and Maternity, 2007, p 3)

References

Agenda for Change Project Team (2004) *Agenda for change – What will it mean for you?*, London: DoH.

Allan F. (2000) in G. Boxwell (ed) *Neonatal intensive care nursing*, London: Routledge, Chapter One.

Armstrong M. (2007) *Delivering health services through Sure Start Children's Centres*, London: DoH.

Ashington Audit Group (2004) 'Evaluating a nurse-led model for providing neonatal care', *Journal of Advanced Nursing*, vol 47, no 1, p 39–48.

Avis, M., Bulman, D. and Leighton, P. (2007) 'Factors affecting participation in Sure Start programmes: a qualitative investigation of parents' views', *Health and Social Care in the Community*, vol 15, no 3, pp 203-11.

Aynsley-Green, A. (2004) Foreword, *National Service Framework for Children, Young People and Maternity Services*, London: DoH.

Brett, P. (2005) 'Addressing teenage pregnancy in Lewisham', *Midwives*, vol 8, no 9, pp 390-1.

Chan, L.C. and Hey, E. (2006) 'Can all neonatal resuscitation be managed by nurse practitioners?', *Archives of Disease in Childhood, Fetal and Neonatal Edition*, vol 91, pp F52-5.

Collingwood Bakeo, A. and Clarke, L. (2006) 'Risk factors for low birthweight based on birth registration and census information, England and Wales 1981-2000', *Health Statistics Quarterly*, vol 30, Summer, pp 15-21.

DfES (Department for Education and Skills) (2004) *Every Child Matters – Change for Children*, London: DfES.

DfES (2005) *Common Assessment Framework*, available from www.dfes.gov.uk/ ISA/framework/framework.cfm, accessed 29 July 2007.

DoH (Department of Health) (2004) *Maternity Standard, National Service Framework for Children, Young People and Maternity Services*, London: DoH.

DoH (2006) *The NHS in England: The operating framework for 2006/07*, London: DoH.

DoH/Partnerships for Children, Families and Maternity (2007) *Maternity matters*, London: DoH.

DoH, DfEE (Department for Education and Employment) and Home Office (2000) *Framework for the Assessment of Children in Need and their families*, London: DoH, available from www.doh.gov.uk/quality.htm, accessed 25 July 2007.

Dinesen, S.J. and Greisen, G. (2001) 'Quality of life in young adults with very low birthweight', *Archives of Disease in Childhood, Fetal and Neonatal Edition*, vol 85, pp F165-9.

Donnison, J. (1997) *Midwives and medical men: A history of interprofessional rivalries and womens' rights*, London: Heinemann.

Dubois, L. and Girard, M. (2006) 'Determinants of birthweight inequalities: population-based study', *Pediatrics International*, vol 48, pp 470-8.

Edgley, A. (2007) 'The perceptions of statutory service providers of a local Sure Start programme: a shared agenda?', *Health and Social Care in the Community*, vol 15, no 4, pp 379-86.

Edwards, G. (2005) 'Sure Start: public health success or expensive failure?', *British Journal of Midwifery*, vol 13, no 10, p 628.

Edwards, G. (2007) 'New roles for midwives devalue traditional skills', *British Journal of Midwifery*, vol 15, no 1, p 7.

Elliman, D.A.C. and Bedford, H. (2006) 'Health and social care service changes: the potential to increase inequalities', *Archives of Disease in Childhood*, vol 91, pp 801-2, available from adc.bmj.com, accessed on 16 July 2007.

GSCC (General Social Care Council) (2007) 'Media releases: regulatory bodies join forces to promote working together in children's services', available from: www.gscc.org.uk, accessed 31 July 2007.

Government Statistical Service (2005) *NHS Maternity Statistics, England: 2003-04*, available from: www.dh.gov.uk/en/Publicationsandstatistics/Publications/PublicationsStatistics/DH_4107060, accessed 27 July 2007.

Gustafsson, U. and Driver, S. (2005) 'Parents, power and public participation: Sure Start, an experiment in New Labour Governance', *Social Policy and Administration*, vol 39, no 5, pp 528-43.

Hassan, L., Spencer, J. and Hogard, E. (2006) 'Managing Sure start in partnership', *Community Practitioner*, vol 79, no 8, pp 247-51.

Henson, C. (2000) in G. Boxwell (ed) *Neonatal intensive care nursing*, London: Routledge, Chapter 17.

HM Government (2004) *Every Child Matters: Change for Children*, London: HM Government

Houston, A.M. (2003) 'Sure Start: the example of one approach to evaluation', *Community Practitioner*, vol 76, no 8, p p294-8.

Hunt, S. and Symonds, A. (1995) *The social meaning of midwifery*, London: Macmillan.

Kitzinger, S. (1992) in M. Enkin (ed) *A guide to effective care in pregnancy and childbirth*, Oxford: Open University Press, Chapter 3.

Mayor, S. (2005) 'Extremely low birth weight is linked to risk of chronic illness', *British Medical Journal*, no 331, p 180.

McKenna, H., Hasson, F. and Smith, M. (2003) 'Training needs of midwifery assistants', *Journal of Advanced Nursing*, vol 44, no 3, pp 308-17.

National Evaluation of Sure Start (NESS) (2005) *Maternity services provision in Sure Start local programmes*, London: DfES Publications

NHS Employers (2006) 'Midwives spend more time with women and babies thanks to new support worker role', press release, www.nhsemployers.org/aboutus/mediacentre-listing.cfm/pressrelease/90, accessed 11 July 2007.

NHS Modernisation Agency (2004) *Workforce matters: A guide to role redesign in neonatal services*, London: DoH.

NHS Careers (2007) *NHS careers in detail: Nursing and midwifery: Neonatal nursing*, available from: www.nhscareers.nhs.uk, accessed 31 July 2007.

Nicolson, P., Burr, J. and Powell, J. (2005) 'Becoming an advanced practitioner in neonatal nursing: a psycho-social study of the relationship between educational prearation and role development', *Journal of Clinical Nursing*, vol 14, pp 727-38.

NMC (Nursing and Midwifery Council) (2000) *Standards of proficiency for pre-registration midwifery education*, NMC Publications, available from www.nmc-uk.org, accessed 30 July 2007.

NMC (2007) *Local supervising authorities*, available from www.nmc-uk.org, accessed 30 July 2007.

Ormerod, P. (2005) *The impact of Sure Start,* The Political Quarterly Publishing Company Limited, pp 565-7.

Partington, A. (2006) *Common Assessment Framework Implementation Plan, January 2007-March 2008*, available from: www.nottinghamcity.gov.uk/ics_implementation_plan.doc, accessed 30 July 2007.

Powell. C. (2005) 'Every Child Matters: Change for children', *Midwives*, vol 8, no 5, pp 198-9.

RCM (2006) *Maternity care assistants: Position statement 12*, available from www.rcm.org.uk/, accessed 16 July 2007.

Redshaw, M. and Harvey, M. (2000) 'Neonatal nurse practitioners in midwifery care', *British Journal of Midwifery*, vol 8, no 3, pp 152-7.

Reid, T. and Freer, Y. (2000) in G. Boxwell (ed) *Neonatal intensive care nursing*, London: Routledge, Chapter 1.

Roberts, H. (2000) 'What is Sure Start?', *Archives of Disease in Childhood 82*, pp 435-7, available from adc.bmj.com, accessed 23 July 2007.

Rutter, M. (2006) 'Is Sure Start an effective prevention intervention?', *Child and Adult Mental Health*, vol 11, no 3, pp 135-41.

Shribman, S. (2007) *Making it better: For mother and baby*, London: DoH.

Skills for Health (2007) *Maternity and care of the newborn*, available from: www.skillsforhealth.org.uk/tools/view_framework.php?id=74, accessed 28 July 2007.

Thornley, C. (2000) 'A question of competence? Re-evaluating the roles of the nursing auxiliary and health care assistants in the NHS', *Journal of Clinical Nursing*, vol 9, pp 451-8.

Ward Platt, M.P. and Brown, K. (2004) 'Evaluation of advanced neonatal nurse practitioner: confidential enquiry into the management of sentinel cases', *Archives of Disease in Childhood, Fetal and Neonatal Edition 89*, pp F241-4, available from fn.bmj.com, accessed 2 March 2007.

While, A., Murgatroyd, B., Ullman, R. and Forbes, A. (2006) 'Nurses', midwives' and health visitors' involvement in cross-boundary working within child health services', *Child: Care, health and development*, vol 32, no 1, pp 87-99.

Wood, N.S., Marlow, N., Costeloe K., et al (2000) 'Neurologic and developmental disability after extremely preterm birth', *The New England Journal of Medicine*, vol 343, no 6, pp 378-84.

Woodward, V., Clawson, L. and Ineichen, B. (2004) 'Maternity support workers: what is their role?', *Midwives*, vol 7, no 9, pp 390-3.

Yoxall, C.W. and Aubrey, W.R. (2001) 'Evaluation of the role of the neonatal nurse practitioner in resuscitation of preterm infants', *Archives of Disease in Childhood Fetal and Neonatal Edition 85*, F96-9.

EIGHT

Playwork and Every Child Matters

Lesli Godfrey

Background: an introduction to playwork

This chapter is about playwork for school-age children and the response of playwork to Every Child Matters (ECM). In order to support the reader's understanding of this professional context, and provide a definition of playwork, the definition of children's play commonly accepted by the playwork sector is outlined first. This definition was initially embodied in the assumptions and values of playwork which underpinned the development of national occupational standards in the early 1990s, and was most recently revised in the Playwork Principles in 2004. It states that:

> Play is a process that is freely chosen, personally directed and intrinsically motivated. That is, children and young people determine and control the content and intent of their play, by following their own instincts, ideas and interests, in their own way for their own reasons. (SkillsActive, 2004)

The notion of 'freely chosen, personally directed, intrinsically motivated play' has helped to focus the role of the playworker as a play enabler: someone who provides opportunities and environments in which children and young people can engage in play unhindered; someone who can offer physical and human space and resources that can enrich children's play in a world which has become increasingly hostile to children's freedom to play naturally.

However, as Brown and Cheesman (2003) note, playwork has been heavily influenced in recent years by a powerful adult agenda: out of school childcare, increased concern for health and safety and the curriculum-based education system, resulting in the dilution and diminution of the child-centred approach taken in playwork in the 1960s and 1970s.

A recent history of playwork

Between 1880 and 1940:

> play provision was considered part of education welfare services which facilitated children's transition into work, or safeguarded them from the effects of a poor environment. The effect of city life on working-class children was thought to undermine schooling, lead to criminal activity and cause ill-health. (Cranwell, 2003, p 33)

The settlement movement of the 1860s saw the development of Saturday and weekday evening clubs for children from the most deprived areas of London, where games were played and play activities offered by volunteers. This type of provision grew until, by 1914, there were 1.5 million children accessing the clubs in the London area, and vacation 'schools' were being established to cater for children in the school holidays (Bonel and Lindon, 1996).

In parallel with this, the rise of the adventure playground movement in London saw a shift in philosophy for provision, which centred around the transformation of unused land into areas where children could build dens, light cooking fires, tend gardens and play freely under the watchful eye of a playworker. This type of provision, championed by Lady Allen of Hurtwood following the Second World War, spread across the country from the late 1950s to the 1970s, serving the wider community by offering a focus for community support and development.

Research conducted by the British Association of Settlements and Social Action Centre, led to the establishment of the National Out of School Alliance in 1981, and to promotion of the concept of after-school play provision that was accessible by all. By 1990, however, research identified that of the existing 350 after school clubs, the majority were based in the voluntary sector and struggling for funding.

Following a campaign led by the national voluntary organisation Kids Clubs Network, the Department for Employment made £45m available over three years to develop new clubs and expand the number of places offered, in order to enable parents to take up study and return to work. This funding initiative was extended by the new Labour government of 1997 to become the National Childcare Strategy, encompassing provision for pre-school children and bringing with it tax breaks for parent users, regulation by Ofsted based on the Daycare Standards and a differing approach by the playworkers, who responded to their new role as 'child carers' by considering the needs of parents for 'minders', directing children to the (adult) selection of play activities and often offering support for homework.

In addition, the emphasis on health and safety in modern society has led to many playworkers taking risk management to an extreme: putting restrictions on children's natural instinct to explore by banning tree climbing, stopping children from paddling on trips to the seaside, and locking doors to prevent children going into outside play space without an adult to accompany them.

Clearly, there is a tension between this trend and the principle of freely chosen, personally directed, intrinsically motivated play from which the theory underpinning playwork practice derives, and which is championed by those in the adventure play movement.

The current position

Because of the difficult history of play provision, we have a situation today in which current types of provision range from the 'open access' drop-in, embodied by the adventure playground and play centre, often based in areas of social and economic deprivation, to the out-of-school childcare clubs offering a facility as much for parents and carers as for the children themselves, with many variations in between. Mobile schemes, run from converted buses, can take play opportunities to rural communities; holiday play schemes can cater for children in their school vacations; parks and heaths in some areas are visited by play rangers and detached playworkers, who offer ideas and opportunities for play in the natural environment; many hospitals employ playworkers to provide opportunities for children to 'play out' their fears and familiarise themselves with treatments and therapies they will undergo. Play facilities can be privately run, based in the voluntary and community sectors, or offered by local authorities; they can be free of charge or carry a fee.

Provision of supervised play facilities is not a statutory requirement, although the child's right to play is enshrined in Article 31 of the UN Convention on the Rights of the Child.

Current trends in playwork

As mentioned earlier, playwork has seen a substantial growth in childcare facilities for school-age children over the past 15 years, shifting the emphasis of provision from adventure playgrounds and open access facilities, the numbers of which have been reducing. This reduction in 'free play' provision could be due to local authority fears of litigation and the increasing difficulties in finding funding and voluntary staff faced by not-for-profit organisations, coupled with the implementation of the national childcare strategy Meeting the childcare challenge (DfEE, 1998), which has had the effect of refocusing out-of-school provision for children to childcare. However, recent publicity regarding children's lack of physical activity, poor mental health statistics and lack of access to outdoor play, are informing moves by local authorities to plan for outdoor play through the provision of play rangers, detached playwork and an increase in fixed play areas. As David Lammy states:

> Every parent and carer knows that a child who has had enough time out playing sleeps better; eats better; is more relaxed and at ease with the world. A growing number of teachers know that they also do better at school as a result. (Lammy, 2007, p 3)

The release of £155 million through the Big Lottery Fund to local authorities, and the need to develop a local play strategy in order to access that funding, has put free play back on the local agenda in a way that has not been seen in recent years.

Furthermore, an increase in number of playwork higher education courses in the past ten years has seen a revived interest in the theoretical base of play and playwork. This has led to an exploration of the therapeutic nature of play and, in some cases, to the provision of a therapeutic approach to playwork, which at one time would have been the domain of play therapists and psychologists. Sturrock and Else (1998) claim that the playground is a therapeutic space and that playwork can provide a form of healing. In a world where children's lives are tightly scheduled and free time for playing is increasingly scarce, one can see why the concept of therapeutic play is championed in playwork.

The playwork workforce

A profile of the playwork sector

Playwork has a relatively small workforce if compared with social work or teaching: recent research (SkillsActive 2005) indicates that approximately 133,000 playworkers are employed in the UK.

According to the Playwork People 2 survey (SkillsActive, 2006a) 88% of the playwork workforce are women. However, comparisons with previous research suggest that the proportion of male workers in the sector has increased in the last few years. This research also reports that the playwork 'workforce is predominantly part-time, with 21.6 being the average number of hours worked by employees in the sector per week' (SkillsActive, 2006a, p 14). Probably as a result of this, over 28% of playworkers reported having more than one job in the sector. In addition, 16% of the workforce is voluntary and therefore unpaid, although it is acknowledged that many staff contribute in a voluntary capacity as well as being in a paid role (SkillsActive, 2005). Almost half (49%) of responding play settings described themselves as voluntary, charitable or not for profit organisations (SkillsActive, 2006a).

Playwork roles and functions

The majority of job roles in playwork are for face-to-face playworkers who provide the environment and resources to enable school-age children to engage in a variety of types of play. Tasks that playworkers undertake will vary depending on the type of setting in which they work and their level of responsibility, but will always incorporate:

- contributing to the planning, provision of resources and support for children and young people's play;
- developing and maintaining positive relationships with children, young people, parents, carers, colleagues and other professionals;
- contributing to the health, safety, security and well-being of children and young people;

- reflecting on and developing their own playwork practice.

Playworkers will be responsible for the play space, carrying out risk assessments on play opportunities as part of their role in the maintenance of health and safety, but may also provide snacks or meals for children and young people, necessitating a knowledge and understanding of nutrition, special dietary arrangements, food hygiene requirements and their application. Some playworkers might take children and young people on day trips, weekend residentials and camping holidays, which requires a variety of other skills and understandings, ranging from the recognition of signs of homesickness and an ability to deal with it, through a knowledge of legislation and guidelines relating to transport for children and young people, to the ability to light a camp fire for cooking a meal. In some settings, a playworker may work with other professionals to enable access to challenging activities such as climbing and canoeing for children and young people. In most play settings, at least one playworker will be required to administer the provision, including handling money, keeping records, writing reports to funders and managers and promoting the setting to the local community and beyond.

It follows, then, that the more adventurous play settings, offering the greater range of experiences and opportunities for play, will require staff with a wider variety of skills, knowledge and understanding to support service delivery.

Training issues and the Common Core of Skills and Knowledge

Although the majority of staff in the sector would describe themselves as playworkers, their roles may vary significantly in the percentage of time that is allocated to working face-to-face with children and young people. As a broad indicator, playworkers and assistant playworkers will spend the majority of their working day with children and comprise the majority of the workforce.

The National Daycare Standards (DfES, 2003), applied to play settings catering for children under eight years old by Ofsted in their registration and inspection role, currently require the playworker in charge (or supervisor) to have a National Qualifications Framework (NQF) level 3 qualification 'appropriate to the post' and at least 50% of assistant playworkers in a play setting to have a NQF level 2 qualification 'appropriate for the care or development of children'. It would be desirable if Ofsted accepted only playwork qualifications as 'appropriate', but the reality is that many staff have come to playwork from early years, teaching, youth work and other related professions in which they have already gained a qualification in work with children and/or young people. These are accepted by Ofsted, to enable new play settings to open and existing settings to continue operating using established staff teams. Moves are being made towards registration requiring training in the Common Core alone and this is being challenged as inappropriate for play provision.

Where unqualified temporary staff are recruited to holiday play schemes that might only operate for six weeks during the summer, induction standards at NQF levels 2 and 3 have been developed, to form the basis of endorsed training, which can be incorporated into induction programmes for holiday workers and confer a time-limited 'adequate briefing' status on temporary staff which is accepted by Ofsted.

SkillsActive (2005) identifies two other categories of staff in the playwork sector:

- Play development workers: who promote the provision of play opportunities but who do not work directly with children and young people, for example trainers and assessors, play association workers, Sure Start officers, and local authority development officers.
- Play service managers: who manage play services wholly or as part of wider service provision, for example, directors of play services, heads of play in local authorities, play managers in local authorities.

It is likely that staff working at these levels will hold a qualification at NQF level 4 or above, but this is not required by any regulatory body, nor are the qualifications held always in playwork.

At the time of writing, there is a range of nationally recognised qualifications in playwork. At NQF levels 2 and 3 there are taught playwork courses as well as NVQs, and an apprenticeship framework for those new to the sector. There is also a level 4 playwork NVQ, and a range of higher education courses from a Certificate of Higher Education up to an honours degree in Playwork offered by a small number of universities in England. At least one university also offers opportunities to engage in postgraduate studies in playwork. In recent years a Playwork Sector Endorsed Foundation Degree has been developed and run by a number of further education colleges in collaboration with universities and higher education institutions.

After extensive consultation with the playwork sector, SkillsActive (2006b) published *Quality training, quality play* – a ten-year UK strategy for playwork education and training in which professional status for the workforce is a major aim. Issues that will need to be addressed in order to reach professional status include:

- the low pay and often poor conditions of service experienced by many in the sector;
- recognition that playwork qualifications (as opposed to early years or teaching) are the most appropriate for those working in the sector;
- recognition that minimum standards are needed to encourage development of a fully qualified workforce; and
- a greater public recognition of the value of play and playwork in children's lives.

Work has begun on this and, while it is a long-term goal, there are signs that government recognition and recent local authority Lottery-driven action can be utilised to make this a reality.

Playwork and the Common Core of Skills and Knowledge

Overall, the identification of the Common Core has been welcomed by playwork in England, although there was an initial acknowledgment that all aspects of the six areas of expertise were not covered in the playwork national occupational standards (NOS). The system of registration currently being developed for application by Ofsted indicates a reliance on staff to have completed training in the Common Core, raising its profile in the children's workforce and necessitating the development of training programmes to support those staff whose qualifications do not fully encompass the Common Core. Recently, SkillsActive has undertaken work to map the Common Core into the NOS and, at the time of writing, the level 2 NOS are being revised, using a process which has fully taken account of the Common Core. The Common Core has also been identified in the recently developed level 3 induction standard.

In addition, a suite of cross sector units of assessment, based on the Common Core, has been approved for piloting by learners in the playwork sector. These units have been developed as part of a bigger project aiming to establish an Integrated Qualifications Framework (IQF) for the children's workforce, which will facilitate staff transferring across sectors as well as along a career path in one sector, and will make it easier for employers to identify appropriately qualified staff. At the time of writing, it is intended to have the IQF established by 2010.

Interprofessional working and the CAF

At time of writing, playwork is involved with a number of other government initiatives requiring multi-disciplinary working, including extended services, Children's Centres and integrated training.

In response to the extended services agenda for schools, play facilities can provide childcare as well as a range of other additional services for children, their families and the wider community. Most play settings offer a varied menu of activities which can include pursuits as diverse as go-cart building, gardening, drama production, needlecraft and cooking, all of which can enrich a child's free time. Play settings are in a good position to offer parenting support, having regular contact with parents and carers, and often offering space where ideas and practices can be shared informally as well as more formally through parenting classes. As well as enabling access to the generally therapeutic benefits of play, settings can also signpost to therapeutic play specialist services helping children come to terms with emotional issues. In the same way as a school, a play setting can become the hub for community activity and involvement, and for some, for example those who have had troubled school experiences, it will be a preferable option.

As 4Children (2004a) reported in their guide to integrated provision in Children's Centres, play facilities have been offered in some Children's Centres, alongside a range of other services, for a number of years. In Leeds the local authority decided that out-of-school play provision should be offered by all Children's Centres, to ensure that they can offer an integrated service for families. As time goes by, it is expected that more Children's Centres will encompass play provision in the services they offer.

Many people are unclear about job roles in work with children and do not understand the distinction between, for example, a nursery nurse and playworker. In order to support recruitment to these sectors, a programme called 'Making Choices in Working with Children, Young People and Families' has been developed jointly by SkillsActive and the Children's Workforce Development Council. The programme aims to help people make an informed decision about a career in playwork, early years education, childcare and foster care. In addition, transitional modules of learning have been developed for practitioners who hold a level 3 qualification in either Playwork or Early Years. The children's care, learning and development modules enable playworkers to gain the additional knowledge and skills they need in order to be effective in a setting requiring an early years qualification; similarly the playwork modules enable an early years practitioner to be qualified to work in a playwork setting. It is hoped that this approach to 'joined-up jobs' will enable staff to undertake a range of roles in Children's Centres and wrap-around care facilities, while gaining the financial benefits that combining a number of part-time jobs might bring.

Playwork's contribution to the CAF

To date there is little evidence of engagement by playworkers in the common assessment process. Staff working in out-of-school clubs and play provision offered by local authorities are more likely to have engaged in training than those from the voluntary and private sectors who often work in small settings employing only three or four members of staff. In these circumstances it is often difficult for employers to find and pay for cover to release staff to attend training. As noted above, in many cases, part-time staff have other jobs, which also makes it difficult for them to accommodate training. In addition, the completion of CAF will usually need to be done outside of work time, that is when playworkers are not working with children and therefore not counted in the service's child:adult ratio, and for small employers this raises the issue of payment for staff undertaking extra hours. If a play setting does not have access to the internet, as is the case for a significant minority, this will further impede involvement in the process. Clearly, it is important that playworkers engage in the CAF, as playworkers might become aware of a child's needs that could be used to initiate an assessment, or to complement a specialist assessment and thereby enable access to support and further services. However, it is difficult to identify an agency in the playwork arena that could take on the role of support for and promotion of the CAF.

The contribution of playwork to ECM

It would be fair to say that playworkers have not needed to change their practice in order to contribute to the ECM agenda. Rather, they have needed to consider the provision they offer in the light of the five ECM outcomes and identify their contribution. Much of the research evidence indicating the benefits of play with regard to 'be healthy' and 'enjoy and achieve' comes from sources outside the playwork sector, highlighting a need for playwork-specific evidence-based research that can demonstrate the benefits of staffed play provision and its contribution to the ECM agenda.

Be healthy

There is currently much concern about the physical and mental health of children and young people in the UK, much of it focused on a lack of physical exercise and opportunities for social interaction outside of school. According to Mackett (2004) active play uses more calories and can provide children with more exercise than many organised sports, and has been recommended by the Chief Medical Officer (DoH, 2004) as having a positive impact on physical health.

By providing challenging play opportunities, playworkers help children learn to make choices, build confidence and develop emotional well-being. Play provision will also bring children and young people together, and can serve to facilitate the development of friendship groups and social inclusion, leading to greater tolerance and acceptance of difference. In out-of-school clubs, where children may be given a meal, there are also opportunities to encourage healthy eating and to promote foods and eating habits that may not be offered at home.

Case example: Include Me Too!

In 2005, the Wolverhampton-based Include Me Too! project provided play facilities for children from the black and minority ethnic community and their families, enabling information to be provided on the health and support services available locally which had previously not been accessed via the usual routes of school, GP or hospital.

Stay safe

As the Children's Play Council has noted:

one of the main reasons children give for not playing outdoors more is that they and their parents are afraid for their safety. Fear of strangers, traffic and bullying by other children combine to keep children in their own homes. (Voce, 2006, p 20)

Staff in play settings will provide as safe an environment as possible, acknowledging that children often seek risky activity, and will provide a watchful eye to reduce unacceptable levels of danger. Good play provision, staffed by educated workers, will provide stimulating and exciting play opportunities that offer children challenge, so that they learn to appreciate and assess risks, use their initiative and find responses to deal with risk themselves:

> If we do not provide controlled opportunities for children to encounter and manage risk then they may be denied the chance to learn these skills. They may also be more likely to choose to play in uncontrolled environments where the risks are greater. (Play Safety Forum, 2002, p 2)

In addition, all playworkers must undertake training in safeguarding children from abuse, and while play settings will usually have ground rules for behaviour that have been developed and agreed by the children using the scheme, many will also have anti-bullying policies designed to support children's personal safety.

Enjoy and achieve through learning

Most children will agree that enjoyment is the essence of play. When playing, children take control, defining their goals, following their own interests and directing their own actions. This choice and control allows children a safe psychological space in which to experiment and explore, and to be absorbed in their play; to learn, grow and develop. It is unlikely that a play activity that is not being enjoyed will be pursued by the child.

Also, as Manwaring and Taylor state, 'developmental psychology ... provides a plethora of evidence-based research to demonstrate the relevance of play to aspects of development' (2006, p 17) and support for children's development will lead to their learning, whether consciously or unconsciously. In the 2005 Extended Schools report, Ofsted testified that learning through play contributes to problem solving, language and literacy skills, while the values of playwork urge staff to enable a child to 'extend her or his exploration and understanding of the wider world' leading to an increased confidence in children, and therefore a better chance of achievement of learning.

> ### Case example: Voluntary sector play project
>
> A voluntary sector play project in North Tyneside regularly received referrals from social services for children and young people who had been excluded from school. The children and young people would attend the play project and learn social skills through 1:1 time with playworkers, as well as participating in peer group activities such as camping and den-building.

When asked by Manwaring (2006) in her survey of children's views of play and playworkers what their three favourite things about coming to the play setting were, most children responded by saying: having fun, meeting or making new friends, and the playworkers.

Make a positive contribution to society

> In good supervised play provision, adults involve the children and young people in decisions about the resources and facilities that might be available to them. (Voce, 2006, p 21)

This gives children and young people the confidence and the tools to participate in decision making and can lead to involvement in school councils, peer mediation services, regional youth assemblies and parliaments. Play facilities are often active in the local community, sometimes using shared space, sometimes making links with local creative and cultural projects, which can engage children and young people in wider involvement. Furthermore, where volunteer playworkers are employed, such positive role models can encourage similar voluntary contributions from young people. It is not uncommon, in a well-established play facility, to find staff or volunteers that had attended the same facility as children.

Achieve economic well-being

The provision of good out-of-school clubs in a community enables parents of school-age children to work or attend college knowing that their children are happy and safe. This has an economic impact on the family in terms of earning potential. Added to this, the intellectual, creative and social skills that children can develop through attending a quality play setting will help cultivate thinking skills and emotional intelligence, so highly valued in today's global economy, potentially leading to better academic opportunities and improved life choices. Good play provision that offers opportunities for engagement in stimulating and exciting challenges for those who seek them, can also contribute to the prevention of anti-social behaviour on the streets, and thereby add to well-being and safety in the wider community.

While it is an easy task to identify the contribution of staffed play provision in relation to the first three outcomes of ECM and the evidence that supports this, the evidence base for playwork 'making a positive contribution' and supporting 'economic well-being' is more tenuous. Furthermore, playworkers are not always very good at articulating the benefits of play and playwork, to provide justification for their practice. To strengthen support for the sector and to provide the evidence base that can make the case for play and playwork, further long-term research is required.

Challenges, future trends and opportunities for playwork

Playwork and the four key strategic challenges in the children's workforce

1. Recruit more high-quality staff into the children's workforce

Recruitment of high-quality staff into playwork will continue to be an issue while relatively low pay, predominantly part-time and often short-term or temporary work are the norm. The most hard-to-fill-vacancies have been identified (SkillsActive, 2006a, p 39) at supervisory and playworker level and in volunteer posts, with employers citing 'not enough people interested', 'low number of applicants generally' and 'lack of qualifications required for the job' as reasons why their vacancies have been hard to fill. However, 17% of respondents reported in *Skills needs assessment for playwork* (SkillsActive, 2005) had a qualification at degree level or above, although not necessarily in playwork. Moves are also being made:

> to encourage employer adoption of recognised pay scales and conditions of service' and 'to introduce levels of pay linked to qualifications and job responsibility', which might go some way towards attracting more high quality staff into the workforce. In the longer term, the sector skills council aims to gain 'widespread recognition of the professional status of playwork. (SkillsActive, 2006b, p 16)

In order to do so the SSC will need to consider raising the qualification level required for those in supervisory roles. Plans for the promotion of vocational routes through higher education as a route to practice already appear in the *Sector Qualifications Strategy* (SkillsActive, 2007a).

2. Retain people in the workforce including by offering better development and career progression

More than ever before there are better career opportunities in playwork, allowing progression into managerial positions in Sure Start Units and Children's Centres, assessor and teacher appointments in further and higher education, and development roles within local authorities and voluntary sector organisations. However, it is still difficult to recruit enough trainers and assessors to meet the needs of further education and to service the sector's requirement for a qualified workforce. In part this may be due to the nature of playwork itself; the sector attracts people who enjoy working with children and who have a passion for play and they may be reluctant to give this up in favour of work with adults, despite the financial rewards available.

As a result, alternative routes into development and managerial work in the sector have been developed over recent years. In a move designed to increase the number of playworkers qualified in higher education, a statement of requirement and learning outcomes for a Playwork Sector Endorsed Foundation Degree have been developed. The foundation degree will provide a vocational route through higher education while enabling them to continue to work, and for those who succeed at foundation degree level, a stepping stone to honours degree study.

In addition, the sector has developed an endorsement system for training to enable employers and practitioners to identify courses that have been deemed 'fit for purpose' and have met quality guidelines set by their peers. Although these courses are currently not often available across the country, the endorsement system does make provision for other training providers to utilise endorsed provision in their offer. The development of the IQF, as mentioned earlier, should also facilitate uptake of units of learning by practitioners as a contribution to their continuous professional and personal development.

3. Strengthen inter-agency and multi-disciplinary working

Much work is being done on behalf of and for the playwork sector at a national level to strengthen integrated working:

- In March 2007, the CWDC produced a guide to developing integrated children's workforce strategies, which lists potential partners that should be involved at a local level and includes play.
- SkillsActive is leading on development of the vocational education and training aspects of the IQF.
- A programme of information dissemination is being planned to help playwork employers, playworkers and training providers understand how the IQF will support their needs.
- Briefings have been written for local authorities and schools on the contribution that playwork can make to extended services, and more briefings aimed at playworkers are planned.
- 4Children, in partnership with the National Children's Bureau, is developing a level 3 modular learning programme – Integrated Practice – which aims to support the delivery of integrated children's services.

At a regional and local level, there are many examples, some of them longstanding, of playworkers working with other professions, for example, in extended services, Children's Centres, therapeutic settings, family centres, women's refuges, children's homes and leisure centres.

For example, 'the Ace Children's Centre based in Oxfordshire has provided integrated services for children across the age group in a rural environment for many years (which includes) ... early years education, childcare and play services for children aged three months to 14 years old, all under one roof, throughout the day and in holidays... [and] ...training courses are delivered locally and tailored to meet the needs of parents, carers and playworkers' (4Children, 2004a, p 11).

In Berwick-upon-Tweed, the family centre offers play facilities for school-age children, as well as parent and toddler groups, and training for adults including parenting classes.

As multi-agency, integrated work continues to appear at regional and local level, national strategies to strengthen and further support the work need to be developed and implemented with speed.

4. Promote stronger leadership and management

Strengthening management and leadership in playwork will support recruitment and retention in the sector, by providing better support mechanisms for those working face-to-face with children in play settings and improving the quality of provision, thereby enhancing the status of playwork as a profession. There are a number of initiatives in playwork that have been designed to underpin improvements in this area. Some units from the management and leadership occupational standards have been imported to the playwork NOS at level 3 and level 4, with the aim of alerting employers to the managerial roles in those levels of playwork, in order to inform job descriptions, training needs analysis, training and qualifications. A workforce development CD-Rom has recently been produced which aims to encourage employers of any size to provide for staff development and includes a toolkit and process to help it happen. 4Children (2004b) has produced a training resource, *Making it happen*, to support the development of voluntary management committees, which was further enhanced by Playwork Partnerships' (2005) publication *Getting it right legally*. As part of the same European Social Fund project, the North East Centre for Playwork Education and Training (Armitage and Morris, 2004) produced a training resource to address a lack of understanding of and provision for staff supervision in play settings. The resource is designed to be used flexibly, either with staff from playwork, early years and youth work settings, or from a single sector.

While there is no doubt that these initiatives are useful in their own right, there has not been a coherent strategy in the sector to strengthen management and leadership. However, in 2005 SkillsActive identified a need for training in management skills in the workforce and has subsequently made a commitment 'to promote stronger and more consistent leadership and management' (SkillsActive, 2006b, p 18) and to 'co-ordinating and enhancing provision of Management and Leadership awards' (SkillsActive, 2007b).

Future trends, opportunities and challenges

Opportunities for open access are now increasing through the establishment in the past three years of new adventure playgrounds around the country and the provision of play rangers by local authorities, largely through the Play England/Big Lottery project. These new developments appear to be based on the arguments for improved access for children to physically active play which can also provide challenge and the chance for children and young people to assess and manage risk. The outcomes for children proposed by ECM offer significant justification for this type of provision, and will perhaps serve to redress the balance between childcare and open access provision.

The workforce reforms outlined in ECM may also serve to support the professionalisation of playwork in terms of the recruitment and retention of a quality workforce, the offer of improved career opportunities and the development of better leadership and management.

The issue of recognition of playwork by the government, and by the population as a whole, is noteworthy. While the government has demonstrated a heightened awareness of the benefits of playwork in recent years, there are still confusing messages coming through ECM. Sometimes playwork is included in references to childcare, and sometimes the term refers solely to early years or pre-school provision, which does not help playwork in its quest for recognition. However, playwork has gained some champions in government through work on ECM, and this foundation needs to be extended. Recognition by the public still evades playwork, but there is an opportunity, through the current local authority development of play strategies as part of the Play England/Big Lottery Fund project, to raise the profile of the sector with the population at large. The development of local play strategies combined with ECM might even make it possible to put the production of a national strategy for play on the government's agenda, with the ultimate goal of statutory provision in each local authority.

However, there are several challenges to be overcome before that vision can be realised. Playwork is a small part of the children's workforce, with a long road to travel before parity with the professions can be reached. The distinctiveness of playwork must be promoted with government and with the public, to raise its profile and secure its future as a profession. Higher level qualifications must be developed and promoted, and a professional benchmark for practice identified that is on a par with other sectors in the children's workforce to ensure that quality services, commensurate with the ECM vision, can be maintained.

Summary

Playwork has changed radically in the past 15 years due to a powerful government agenda promoting out of school childcare, increased parental and public concern for health and safety, and the curriculum-based education system. There is a tension between this trend and the principle of freely chosen, personally directed, intrinsically motivated play from which the theory underpinning playwork practice is derived. However, in the past two or three years, opportunities for open access, free play are now increasing and, with this, the varied menu of activities that provide opportunities for children to meet the ECM outcomes is becoming more widespread.

Playwork has a relatively small workforce, which is largely part-time, poorly paid and under-resourced, and often has insecure or short-term funding. In this situation, one would expect recruitment of high-quality staff to continue to be an issue. Nevertheless, the workforce reforms outlined in ECM can serve to support the professionalisation of playwork in terms of the recruitment and retention of a quality workforce, provide improved career opportunities and the development of better leadership and management to provide strategic direction and better financial support. Recognition of the value of playwork is vital in raising its profile as a profession, and further long-term research is needed to strengthen support for the sector and provide an evidence base for playwork.

Much work is being done at a national level to strengthen integrated working and prepare a place for playwork in the integrated children's workforce. It is hoped that the opportunity to further improve the quality of provision through professionalisation can be seized in order to better meet the needs of children and young people.

References

4Children (2004a) *Integration in practice: A guide to integrated provision for 0-16s through Children's Centres and Extended Schools*, London: 4Children.

4Children (2004b) *Making it happen*, London: 4Children

Armitage, M. and Morris, B. (2004) *Staff supervision: A training resource pack for people working in playwork, early years and youth work*, Newcastle: North East Centre for Playwork Education and Training.

Bonel, P. and Lindon, J. (1996) *Good practice in playwork*, Cheltenham: Stanley Thornes.

Brown, F. and Cheesman, B. (2003) 'Introduction: childhood and play', in F. Brown (ed) *Playwork theory and practice*, Buckingham: Open University Press.

Cranwell, K. (2003) 'Towards playwork', in F. Brown (ed) *Playwork theory and practice*, Buckingham: Open University Press.

CWDC (Children's Workforce Development Council) (2007) *Building the vision: Developing and implementing local integrated children's workforce strategies*, Leeds: CWDC.

DfEE (Department for Education and Employment) (1998) *Meeting the childcare challenge: A framework and consultation document*, Cm 3959, London: The Stationery Office.

DfES (Department for Education and Skills) (2003) *National standards for under 8s day care and childminding: Out of school care*, London: DfES.

DoH (Department of Health) (2004) *At least five a week: Evidence on the impact of physical activity and its relationship to health*, London: DoH.

Lammy, D. (2007) *Making space for children – the big challenge for our public realm*, London: Compass.

Mackett, R. (2004) *Making children's lives more active*, London: University College London.

Manwaring, B. (2006) *Children's views 2006: Children and young people's views on play and playworkers*, London: SkillsActive.

Manwaring, B. and Taylor, C. (2006) *The benefits of play and playwork*, London: Community and Youth Workers' Union/SkillsActive.

Ofsted (2005) *Extended Schools: A report on early developments*, London: HMI.

Play Safety Forum (2002) *Managing risk in play provision: A position statement*, London: National Children's Bureau.

Playwork Partnerships (2005) *Getting it right legally*, Cheltenham: Playwork Partnerships.

SkillsActive (2004) 'Playwork principles', available at www.skillsactive.com/playwork/principles.

SkillsActive (2005) *Skills needs assessment for playwork*, London: SkillsActive.

SkillsActive (2006a) *Playwork People 2: Research into the characteristics of the playwork workforce*, London: SkillsActive.

SkillsActive (2006b) *Quality training, quality play 2006-11: The first UK strategy for playwork education, training and qualifications*, London: SkillsActive.

SkillsActive (2007a) *Sector Qualifications Strategy*, London: SkillsActive.

SkillsActive (2007b) *Playwork Sector Qualifications Strategy annex*, London: SkillsActive.

Sturrock, G. and Else, P. (1998) *The playground as therapeutic space: Playwork as healing*, available at www.ludemos.co.uk/.

Voce, A. (ed) (2006) *Planning for play: Guidance on the development and implementation of a local play strategy*, London: National Children's Bureau/Big Lottery Fund.

NINE

Social work and Every Child Matters

Richard Barker and Sue Barker

Introduction

What is the contribution of social work and social workers to delivering the Every Child Matters agenda? Since the media publicity in relation to the death of Maria Colwell in 1973 at the hands of her stepfather (DHSS, 1974), the continuing media focus about social work with children and families has almost invariably been in relation to child protection concerns (and, often, child protection tragedies). As important as protecting children is, social work with children is much wider and more varied.

Social workers potentially deal with all sectors of the population, although there is a tendency for individual workers to specialise on work with particular types of 'client' or 'service user' groups. Increasingly social workers can be divided into those whose focus of work is with adults and those whose focus of work is with children (although of course often there is great overlap between the two). The professional qualification course for social workers is generic and seeks to cover work with all groups.

This chapter will therefore look at social work in general, and will then focus more specifically on social work with children and the ECM agenda.

There are a number of definitions of social work the most widely accepted being that of the International Federation of Social Workers (IFSW):

> The social work profession promotes social change, problem-solving in human relationships, and the empowerment and liberation of people to enhance well-being. Utilising theories of human behaviour and social systems, social work intervenes at points where people interact with their environments. Principles of human rights and social justice are fundamental to social work. (IFSW, 2007)

Broadly then, social work can be seen to consist of three areas:

1. **Social change:** changing society for the better.
2. **Problem solving:** organising services, sorting out people's problems, protecting people.

3. Empowerment: helping people achieve greater self-fulfilment and satisfaction with their lives and relationships.

However, there is not universal consensus either within the profession or within wider society about what these mean for practice, and pursuing them can therefore be fraught with difficulties.

> To take a commonplace example, at what age should children with whom social workers are working be empowered to make their 'own' decisions? What are the most effective ways of doing this? At what point does empowering children conflict with the legitimate rights of their parents or carers to make decisions about 'their' children?
>
> These questions may be simple, but the answers to them are often not straightforward and vary according to differences with regards to factors such as age, the law, and the wishes and feelings of those involved. Fox Harding's (1997) framework (see Chapter Eleven) provides a useful schema for considering some different, often conflicting, value positions in relation to children's welfare.

The range of activities in which social workers may be involved is usefully summarised on the British Association of Social Work (BASW) website as follows:

> Social workers attempt to relieve and prevent hardship and suffering. They have a responsibility to help individuals, families, groups and communities through the provision and operation of appropriate services and by contributing to social planning. They work with, on behalf of, or in the interests of people to enable them to deal with personal and social difficulties and obtain essential resources and services. Their work may include, but is not limited to, interpersonal practice, groupwork, community work, social development, social action, policy development, research, social work education and supervisory and managerial functions in these fields. (BASW, 2007)

However, it is interesting to note that children are not mentioned in this range of activities.

Background: a brief recent history

It is useful to consider the historical context that has shaped modern social work. Modern UK social work has its origins in the twin structural changes of urbanisation and industrialisation in 19th century Britain. Concerns about the poor, the ill, and women and children: partly out of sympathy on the part of some of the powerful elements in society for the needs of the poor urban classes;

partly out of the perceived need for a population healthy enough to serve the needs of industry.

Thus, during the 19th century, schemes for public sanitation, education, policing, prisons, juvenile correction, public workhouses and mental asylums accompanied legislation governing working conditions and factory inspection. Alongside this there was the development of a wide spectrum of 'social work type' voluntary activity, financed and run by philanthropic agencies, but working alongside statutory agencies such as courts, hospitals and workhouses. The origins of the current large children's charities, including the NSPCC, Action for Children (formerly NCH) and Barnardo's, can all be traced back to this period.

Having developed largely as a philanthropically motivated voluntary activity on the margins of statutory services, social work in the latter part of the 20th and 21st century has become an increasingly professional activity, either carried out directly by the state or by the voluntary sector and other non-government organisations that are often funded on the state's behalf. Between 1948 and 1971, local authority social work with children took place in specialist children's departments. Throughout the remainder of the 20th century it was found within 'family-centred' rather than 'symptom-centred' generic social services departments (in Scotland, social work departments). More recently, there has been the change to social work with children becoming part of local authority Children's Services Departments. Throughout this period social work has been incorporated steadily into regulating the relationships between the state, parents and children, and boundary disputes about the rights of children, the rights of parents, and the rights of the state, are often at the heart of the dilemmas and problems with which social workers deal.

The current position

Despite this rich history, social work is a relatively new profession. Although there have been people calling themselves, and employed as, social workers for more than a century, the title 'social worker' has only been protected by law in the UK since 1 April 2005. This law in England came from the Care Standards Act 2000 to ensure that only those who are deemed properly qualified, registered and accountable for their work describe themselves as social workers. Service users and carers can check the registration of a social worker and establish whether they meet the standards. They can also raise concerns about the conduct of a registered social worker and ask for them to be investigated. The register is termed the Social Care Register (not the Social Work Register) and there are plans to widen registration to the wider social care workforce. That being said, the relationship between social work and social care is not always clear. In general, social work is considered a specialist element of social care, while social care is a descriptor of the general occupation of those who work within the area of care for people.

There are far fewer people working as social workers than in the social care field itself; on the 1 February 2007 the GSCC announced there were 90,000 registered social workers and social work students in England (GSCC, 2007a), out of a social care workforce estimated to be approaching one million. In Scotland, where the term 'social services' has been preferred to 'social care', there are approximately 9,000 social workers in a social services workforce of 138,000; in Northern Ireland, 4,000 out of a 38,000 social care workforce; in Wales, 5,000 out of approximately 72,000 in the social care workforce (Macleod, 2007).

Challenges for the workforce

How social work and social workers should be developed and shaped as a profession has been a continuing theme of recent years – from the Seebohm Report of 1968 (HMSO, 1968), through the Barclay report (NISW, 1983) and with the 2007 consultations in the four countries of the UK, such as *Roles and tasks of social work in England* (GSCC, 2007b).

With regards to social work with children and families, recent GSCC-commissioned papers highlighted two main areas of concern:

> the dominance of a narrow model of child protection work, which has been seen by service users, policy makers and social workers alike in a very negative light [and] failures to meet the needs of children in the looked after (children in care) system. (Blewett et al, 2007, p 29)

In fact, within these two areas there have been, and still are, particular challenges to best promote children's well-being, for example, how to handle suspected cases of child sexual abuse; or how to provide good-quality residential care which enhances children in care's life chances (DfES, 2006)

To summarise briefly, the main areas of activity undertaken by social workers with children are:

1. Carrying out initial and core assessments in line with the Framework for the Assessment of Children in Need (DoH et al, 2000).
2. Developing and coordinating plans for children living at home who are in need of social work support.
3. Carrying out section 47, 1989 Children Act investigations where significant harm is suspected, and developing and coordinating the delivery of child protection plans for children living at home who need protection
4. Making arrangements for children to be looked after by the local authority where it has been assessed that children need substitute care, including planning for their return home where appropriate
5. Planning for permanent substitute care for children who cannot be returned home, including residence orders, special guardianship orders and adoption orders.

It should be remembered that social workers have limited powers, and, in many of the above, plans are dependent on court decision making: care orders, residence orders, special guardianship orders and adoption orders.

What is good social work practice?

In relation to children (and indeed adults) good practice can be the subject of considerable disagreement. For example, if a child is seen by parents to be misbehaving and out of control in the family, they may want a social worker to 'do something' quickly: not infrequently, to remove the child into care. Good social work practice in relation to such a situation would expect the social worker to use their communication skills and knowledge to gather information and assess aspects including:

- the urgency of the 'problem';
- the nature of the behaviour of the child and the parents;
- the wishes and feelings of the child;
- 'reasonableness' of the parents' views about and expectations of the child;
- previous family history;
- views of any other professionals or agencies involved with the family;
- potential effects of different interventions in the family.

Of vital importance, unless the child's needs are assessed and understood, the social worker cannot decide on an appropriate course of action.

Unless the child in the case concerned was felt to be at immediate risk of serious 'significant harm' it would be most unlikely that they would be removed from their family, and efforts would be made to support the child and parents to deal with the difficulties being experienced and thereby improve the family situation. This type of approach might be frustrating to some parents – and sometimes to other professionals and agencies – because rarely, unless it is an emergency, does practice involve the 'quick fix' of removing a child from their family. In any event, such 'quick fixes' leave the challenge of how to best plan for the long-term future of the child in the light of the ECM objectives.

The current nature of social work training and social roles

At present, the basic qualification for social work is normally achieved via a three-year undergraduate degree course which combines theoretical learning with 200 assessed days of practice in a wide range of settings. The degree is generic and requires social workers in training to work in at least two practice settings with at least two different kinds of 'user groups'. Students must also meet the required roles of the National Occupational Standards (NOS) for Social Work, which are:

1. Prepare for, and work with individuals, families, carers, groups and communities to assess their needs and circumstances.

2. Plan, carry out, review and evaluate social work practice, with individuals, families, carers, groups, communities and other professionals.
3. Support individuals to represent their needs, views and circumstances.
4. Manage risk to individuals, families, carers, groups, communities, self and colleagues.
5. Manage and be accountable, with supervision and support, for your own social work practice within your organisation.
6. Demonstrate professional competence in social work practice.

Once qualified, where will the social worker be working with children and families?

1. A primary social work setting where the majority of the professional staff are social workers or in social care

For example:
- an adoption agency (which may be a section within local authority children's services);
- a community based children's services team (either uni-disciplinary or multi-disciplinary);
- a residential home for children in care.

2. A secondary setting where a minority of staff are social workers or in social care

For example:
- a school;
- a hospital;
- a GP practice;
- a youth offending team;
- a Children's Centre.

3. Independently

For example, as:
- a social work counsellor;
- an independent expert witness court adviser.

Social work may take place on a statutory basis, where the primary function relates to using legally based powers, for example a child in care, or compulsory admission of an adult to psychiatric hospital; or a non–statutory basis, such as offering therapy to a young person who is self-harming, or providing support to a family caring for a child with a physical or mental disability.

Social work roles in relation to children and families

Social workers occupy a number of different occupational roles in different settings. Many are employed by local authorities (and a smaller number by voluntary or charitable organisations) in roles such as field social workers, team leaders and managers, child protection workers, family placement workers (that is, adoption and fostering) and juvenile or youth justice workers. Social workers are also employed as family court advisers, (giving independent advice to the courts regarding children), in Connexions and Sure Start Services and Children's Centres, or within CAMHS (some of these roles are covered in more detail in other chapters of this book).

Increasingly, social workers are working in a self-employed or independent capacity, where they may provide services to local authorities or to the voluntary or private sector. Because of a skill shortage, particularly in children's services, there are also large numbers of qualified social workers employed in a temporary or interim capacity by agencies; some coming from abroad with differing levels of understanding and experience of the UK context.

The Children's Workforce Development Council (CWDC, 2007a) has suggested that social work roles with children include:

- **Enabler**: giving access to services; giving the child a voice.
- **Protector**: through child protection practice.
- **Assessor**: reflecting, analysing and undertaking complex assessments to make recommendations.
- **Networker**: involving others in order to address the needs of the child.
- **Advocate**: making the child's case for them, for example in children's rights work.
- **Autonomous advocate for children**: with specific resources to support this role in direct work with children and families.
- **Manager**: managing one's own caseload; managing a team.
- **Commissioner**: buying in services to meet needs.
- **Co-ordinator/broker**: organising events, people or services to address the needs of a child.
- **Specialist**: providing therapeutic interventions around personal change; counselling and listening skills.
- **Expert independent resource**: for the legal profession, local authorities, family court advisers, private and voluntary childcare agencies.
- **Practice assessor**: being trainer and developer of social workers and other professions.

CWDC go on to suggest that social work tasks will include applying the public law (for example, child protection); understanding (listening to children and their carers); deploying appropriate knowledge (for example, social science, social policy, psychology and law) and expert skills and knowledge in a range of setting-specific areas; working with foster carers; working in multi-agency teams and with others to 'problem solve' and to help individuals and families achieve agreed outcomes.

It can be seen that this is a very broad list of roles and tasks. Given that much work with children will involve social workers working in partnership with other professionals and vice versa, it is key for all those involved to be clear what particular role(s) the social worker(s) involved in the case occupy, and what tasks they are seeking to achieve, so that there is maximum shared understanding and minimum confusion. It will also be important to ascertain which stage of the social work process is being undertaken, namely (1) assessment, (2) planning, (3) intervention or (4) review. It should also be noted that it is not uncommon when a social worker is exercising a statutory function, such as taking a child into care, that, despite attempts to achieve agreement among all parties involved, such agreement is not achievable, at least in the short term and sometimes never. These complexities contribute to the fact that if other professionals hear that a social worker is involved with a family there will still be the need for clarification about the nature and focus of that involvement.

The contribution of social work to the CAF and lead professional role

The CAF is still being implemented and the process of its use in different areas is variable. Most areas have a CAF co-ordinator and system for its use, in some areas the processes have been viewed as becoming overly bureaucratic. Although social workers can be involved in leading CAFs and acting as lead professionals (LPs), as the CAF is a generic assessment it is more usual that these are activities undertaken by professionals from universal services for children, and that social workers are then involved in subsequent, more specialist activity that builds on the CAF. Guidance states that:

> Over time, the CAF is likely to become the main basis for information sharing and referral for children where there are welfare concerns. This will help improve the quality of referral to social care teams. (CWDC, 2007b, p 38)

Framework for the Assessment of Children in Need

When a more detailed assessment is required either instead of or following on from a CAF, it would be frequently the case that a social worker would co-ordinate this further assessment using the assessment framework guidance for assessing children in need (DoH et al, 2000). This framework (Figure 9.1) looks at the child's needs in three different domains: the child's developmental needs, parenting capacity, and family and environmental factors. While, in principle, other professionals could lead the assessment, in practice it has tended to be social workers who

Figure 9.1: Framework for the Assessment of Children in Need

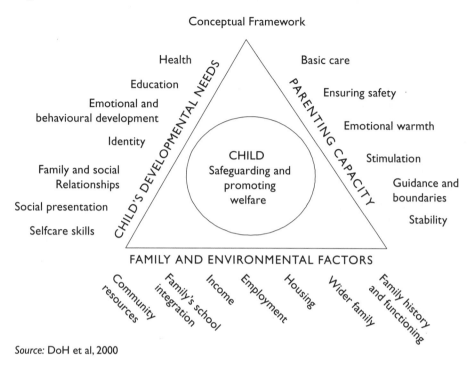

Source: DoH et al, 2000

have done this, drawing together multi-disciplinary knowledge based around the documentation and guidance.

The contribution of social work to the Every Child Matters agenda

In which ways can social work and social workers contribute to the five key objectives for children that are at the heart of the ECM agenda? It will be seen that they often involve a mixture of the NOS roles and CWDC roles as outlined earlier.

Be healthy

In relation to physical health, social work generally has a secondary role with regard to helping other agencies to support and improve the health of children. With regard to the mental health of children, social work often has a key role, sometimes as part of CAMHS (see Chapter Ten). Key areas with respect to social work, children and health include the following.

Hospital settings: There is a long history of social work in hospital settings, where the social worker often acts as the networker and link between the patient, the patient's family, the different professions involved within the hospital, and the outside world. This may often include the NOS 'supporting individuals to represent their views' role. Social work may also provide practical support to children and their families to assist in the treatment of the child, and therapeutic support and counselling to enable the child or their family to grapple with the emotional or psychological issues that ill health in children can precipitate.

Children in care: Social work has a key role with regard to the health needs of children in care. There is significant evidence that a child being in care is associated with poor mental and physical health, for example, the frequent moves that some children make because of placement breakdowns lead to medical treatment being disrupted (DoH, 2002). Local authorities are legally the 'corporate parents' of children in care and, as such, they have a clear responsibility to seek the best healthcare for these children. Each child in care should have a social worker responsible for ensuring that their health needs are met and to support children in care by representing their views and working as their advocate to ensure that the relevant health services meet these children's needs.

Community-based services: Social work has a key role to play in relation to co-ordinating community based services for children with disabilities, and in supporting children, parents and carers in their liaison with hospitals and other agencies.

> Social work involvement with children with disabilities may start from the birth of the child, or even before if problems are anticipated. As well as assessing and enabling in relation to practical support, work may involve providing the parents with opportunities, where necessary, to work on any feelings they have about having a child with disabilities. In some cases social workers may negotiate short-break care for the child, to provide the child with a wider experience and the parents/carers a break from caring for the child.
>
> In other cases, where a family prove unable or unwilling to care for the child, the social worker may arrange for the child to be taken into care, to be fostered or adopted. This would not be done lightly, however, and seeking to support the birth family in caring for the child would always be the preferred option.

Stay safe

Staying safe involves ensuring that children are not being directly or indirectly harmed. Social workers have key responsibilities in managing risk and as protectors. In the most difficult situations, this involves ensuring that children are not suffering or likely to suffer 'significant harm' or, where such harm has taken place, to prevent it continuing and ensuring that the child is safe. Current legislation gives social work the lead role in ensuring that, where necessary because of the level of risk or harm, child protection legislative orders (emergency protection orders or EPOs) are applied for to ensure that children are safe. This does not mean that social workers can of their own volition remove children from families, nor does it mean that when parents ask for their children to be taken away by social workers such removals would automatically take place.

> In the UK, legislation about protecting children, along with core social work values, is based on the principle that children tend to do best if they are raised within their own families and that the state should only intervene in families if to do so is better than not to do so. With regard to 'staying safe' this can be problematic: there are high-profile instances where it has been seen that social workers (and other professionals) should have intervened more readily to protect children, including the cases of Jasmine Beckford and Victoria Climbié. There are also high-profile cases in which it has been suggested (although these cases are often subject to differing accounts) that social workers have intervened too readily or radically to remove children from families in which they were in fact safe (for example in the Cleveland case; Butler-Sloss, 1988; Campbell, 1988).

The relationships between the state, parents and children are complex and the tensions and contradictions that exist in this arena are particularly highlighted in relation to this domain of ECM. Arrangements for keeping children safe are broadly similar across the UK. In England, each local authority area has a Local Safeguarding Children Board (LSCB), which oversees the arrangements by which different agencies work together to ensure the safety of children in their area. Prior to 1 April 2008, children who were seen to be 'suffering or likely to suffer significant harm' (HM Government, 2006, p 115) and who were in need of a child protection plan were placed on a child protection register – on 31 March 2006 there were 26,400 children on child protection registers in England (NSPCC, 2007). Since 1 April 2008, no separate register has been held; children who are the subject of a child protection plan are recorded as such on the ICS system (HM Government, 2006). In practice, this should not make substantial differences to the work undertaken with such children and their families/carers, but it does mean the use of a different form of language, as indicated by the exemplars in Table 9.1.

Table 9.1: ICS functions that replace child protection register functions

Child protection register function	ICS function
Registration of child	Child becomes subject of a child protection plan which is recorded on ICS
Enquiry to the child protection register	Child protection plan enquiry to ICS
Category of registration	Category of abuse or neglect which triggers the child protection plan
Child protection register custodian	Designated manager

Source: NSPCC website

What does this mean for work with children? There are many children who are 'in need' (as defined in section 17 of the 1989 Children Act), but in some cases there will be reasonable cause to suspect that some of these children are suffering or likely to suffer significant harm, in which case the local authority has a duty to investigate under section 47 of the 1989 Children Act. Social workers, often working with the police, are the lead agents in these section 47 investigations. Sometimes the situation will involve a mixture of making decisions about the child's welfare and investigating whether a crime has been committed. There is extensive government guidance on the processes regarding how this happens, and any worker involved should familiarise themselves with, and work to the procedures outlined in, *Working Together to Safeguard Children* (HM Government, 2006).

To summarise, if there are child protection concerns about a child (or an unborn child) a referral should be made to the local authority children's services who, if it is not already an 'open case', will decide the initial action necessary within one working day: whether there is no need for further action; whether there is a need for emergency action to protect the child (which would involve a strategy meeting between social workers and the police); or whether there is the need for a brief, initial assessment to be completed within a maximum of seven days using the framework illustrated in Figure 9.1.

> In the course of an initial assessment, [local authority] children's social care should ascertain:
>
> - is this a child in need? (s. 17 of the 1989 Children Act); and
> - is there reasonable cause to suspect that this child is suffering, or likely to suffer, significant harm? (s. 47 of the Children Act 1989).
>
> The focus of the initial assessment should be the welfare of the child. (p 112, HM Government, 2006)

After the initial assessment, the next steps will be one of the following:

1. Child in need but no suspected or actual significant harm – either ongoing support services or a core assessment under section 17 of the 1989 Children Act or no further involvement of specialist services.
2. Child in need and suspected or likely significant harm – either emergency action and/or a multi-agency strategy discussion involving children's social care, the police and other relevant services (for example, health, education).

3. Next, if decided by the strategy discussion, a core assessment led by a qualified and experienced children's social worker using the Framework for the Assessment of Children in Need (Figure 9.1) is the means by which the section 47 investigation is carried out. Health, education and other services have a statutory duty to co-operate with this.

The outcome of the section 47 inquiries will be one of the following:

1. Concerns are not substantiated – although this means the child is seen to be safe, subsequently other services may be offered as there may well be other child and family needs.
2. Concerns are substantiated but the child is not judged to be at risk of significant harm – planning to deal with the concerns will then take place on a multi-agency basis.
3. Concerns are substantiated and the child is judged to be at continuing risk of significant harm – this will lead to local authority children's care staff convening an initial child protection conference (no later than 15 days after the initial strategy meeting), to bring together and analyse in an inter-agency meeting what is deemed to be necessary to make the child safe. If the conference decides there is continuing risk of significant harm, a child protection plan and core group (usually under the leadership of a children's social worker) agree to take forward the plan. The plan will then be reviewed within three months and then at least every six months until a child protection plan is deemed not to be necessary or the child reaches 18 years of age.

At any time during a section 47 investigation or during the period that a child is subject to a child protection plan, it may be necessary to take emergency action to protect them and make them safe (which would involve a strategy meeting). It is also possible the plan can be discontinued – but this can only be decided by a child protection review.

The procedures are complex and need to be followed with care. In themselves they do not make children safe, but they do provide an agreed framework to allow professionals to carefully 'work together' – often in highly demanding and stressful situations – to try to keep children safe.

Enjoy and achieve

Social work does not have a primary role with regard to 'enjoy and achieve', although, as with health, there is a long history of social workers being placed in, or working with, educational establishments for children. Sometimes known as education welfare officers, they are generally employed by local authorities and work with children and families, liaising with other relevant agencies to deal with problems and issues that might be having an impact on school attendance or the child's achievement within school. In the past, social workers in education have been primarily involved with truancy and, indeed, they still are the focal point if support or legal action must be taken with regard to non-attendance at school. However, under the ECM agenda, the role of schools in ensuring an improvement in children's quality of life and attainment through schooling, not simply attendance, has been highlighted.

> Social workers also have a particular responsibility in relation to being enablers and advocates to ensure the barriers to children in care/looked-after children maximising their educational achievements are reduced. However, it is the role of educational services within local authority children's services, to discharge the corporate responsibility to provide appropriate educational services. There has been continuing concern that the educational achievement of children in care has been unacceptably low as compared with their peers (Harker et al, 2004), and social workers have a duty to advocate for the best services for children in care, for example, by encouraging the provision of appropriate educational services for children in care who have been excluded from school.

Make a positive contribution to society

The children with whom social workers work are often among the most marginalised by society – children in care, children from asylum-seeking families, children from the poorest families, children who have been abused or neglected, children whose behaviour may have brought them into the court systems or resulted in school exclusion. In many cases their behaviour may be making a *negative* contribution to society, so, if things can be improved for them (for example reducing their involvement with the youth justice system), it is likely to also lead to them making a positive, or at least more positive, contribution to society. Social workers often find themselves in the position of being advocates for marginalised groups – often children and young people – who, rightly or wrongly, are seen to be 'a particular problem for society'.

Achieve economic well-being

Most of the children with whom social workers are involved come from the poorer and disadvantaged sections of society. Social work is not an 'income maintenance service' but it has the important role of supporting service users, where necessary, so that they can access welfare rights services to ensure all appropriate benefits are being received. Social workers may negotiate directly with agencies to arrange the payment of service user's debts, or with charities to seek grants. However, while social work is not concerned with directly improving the economic well-being of those who use its services, social work activity may lead to an improvement in economic well-being of families and children. Where there is discord within families, this could be having an impact on the mental health of parents and affecting their ability to earn. Interventions that improve the family's functioning could then lead to adult employment being achieved and thus improving economic well-being.

> Social workers also have particular responsibilities, as enablers and advocates, for trying to ensure that children in care and children with disabilities receive the best possible help to achieve economic well-being. This is often easier to state as a principle than to achieve in practice, because of structural disadvantages for people with disabilties.

Challenges, issues and future trends

Particular challenges presented by themes

One key challenge faced by social work is that of having sufficient personnel resources to meet the demands faced. A problematic theme of social work with children over recent years has been of staff shortages and unallocated cases. At times, this has meant that if a case was an emergency it would be dealt with, and then the case would be 'closed' and only reopened if it became an emergency again. Thus, the demands of crisis intervention meant that problems that were of 'medium range' difficulty sadly would not be dealt with until the situation deteriorated, even though this would be more costly overall in terms of resources and human suffering (Barker et al, 2005).

Related to this has been the pressure to deal with child protection and safeguarding children work, resulting in a lack of time for other areas of work with and for children being possible. Thus, longer-term therapeutic work with children may be 'squeezed out' by the relentless pressure of managing risk in new, critical situations. This may be exacerbated by the cumbersome and lengthy legal processes which are often involved in childcare cases, where delays often lead to ongoing distress for children and their families, and heavier workloads for social workers.

Another challenge is in relation to knowledge and skills, and the balance between social workers requiring 'generic knowledge' to cover all types of problems and 'specific knowledge' with respect to children. There is a real challenge in social work training to provide the depth and breadth necessary to equip practitioners for the 21st century, and there has been a fear that social workers are not provided with sufficient knowledge at the basic qualifying level to work effectively with and for children. Recommendations for a social pedagogue role or specialist social work training courses as discussed elsewhere are partly related to these criticisms.

There has been some concern expressed recently that social work with children may become dominated in children's services in a way that means the distinct nature of the profession will be changed and lost. Thus, the joint president of the Association of Directors of Children's Services spoke recently of how, in his Children's Services Department, there were only 200 social workers out of a workforce of 2,000, and stated that 'social workers are a minority now and I worry that important values shouldn't be lost' (Coughlan, 2007).

Social work's contribution to the four key challenges in the children's workforce

1. Recruit more high-quality staff into the children's workforce

This appears to be on the way to being achieved for social work due to the increase in the number of students training to be social workers. This has been supported by more generous funding arrangements than previously, including (at the time of writing) bursaries, contributions towards tuition fees and travelling costs, and funding for agencies to provide practice placement opportunities for students. A number of local authorities and other social work providers have also developed salaried posts for trainees who are employed prior to and through training. This has resulted in a great increase in the popularity of social work as a subject to study at university, with an increase in the number of courses and a 33% increase in the numbers of students in qualifying training in England between 2000 and 2005 (GSCC, 2006). Respondents to the government's consultation on improving the recruitment of children's social workers cited improving pay and conditions, and a targeted advertising campaign as their main recommendations (DfES, 2005).

2. Retain people in the workforce including by offering better development and career progression

The increasing numbers of people training to be qualified social workers does not automatically mean that there will be increasing numbers in direct practice in the future. Historically, qualified, experienced social workers have often moved away from direct work with children into management roles, and there is also a view that many social workers move out of child protection work after a few years into what are perceived to be less demanding areas to avoid 'burn out'. There have also been spasmodic developments of 'career grades' to pay experienced workers more to continue working directly with clients, but experience of this is patchy.

Over the past decade a post-qualifying childcare award system for social workers has been developed, which was, in general, well received by those who undertook it in relation to both its content and the opportunities it afforded for career progression. This is now in the process of being replaced by a new post-qualifying system, which is designed to be tailored to employers' workforce needs. Whether this relatively narrow principle will lead to improvements in the new system compared to the old system is currently not clear.

3. Strengthen inter-agency and multi-disciplinary working

By its nature much social work with children involves inter-agency and multi-disciplinary working, and social workers working with children are often heavily involved in networking and as co-ordinators or brokers. Thus, children who are the subject of serious child protection concerns are usually then the subject of a multi-disciplinary planning intervention in which the social worker will usually be the key worker and team leader. Other examples of social workers who work with children in multi-disciplinary teams include hospital social workers, and social workers based in youth offending teams. Social workers should therefore be comfortable with inter-agency and multi-disciplinary work, and be well placed to take a leading role in its advancement.

4. Promote stronger leadership and management

In England in particular, the introduction of the ECM agenda has run alongside, and has partly caused, a period of great change in the leadership and management arrangements for social work services for children. Social services departments – usually managed by a qualified social worker – have become Children and Young People's Services – often managed by someone with a career background in education rather than in social work. This has raised particular challenges for leadership and management, at precisely the time of greatest difficulty. The dangers in this have been summarised by the CWDC when they suggest that:

> reforms need managers to operate in different ways, requiring different skills and, in particular, the need for them to lead the workforce through the change process. A major risk may be that managers are pre-occupied with their own role, uncertain of their future and not competent or confident to help themselves or others move forward. At worst managers at various levels may consciously or subconsciously obstruct more integrated ways of working because it cuts across organisational boundaries and undermines their traditional management role. (CWDC, 2008, p 17)

It is suggested that management development strategies, an emphasis on performance management (including the development of common principles for working across integrated services) and greater engagement of local authority elected members are needed to understand the requirements of ECM. It may be some time before these types of arrangements bear fruit, and it is likely that there will be a skill shortage of good child-centred leadership and management in the near future.

Other key themes

ECM and the Children Act 2004 assume that the greater integration of inspection mechanisms for services to children will be key to improving the quality of the services. In 2005 joint area reviews (JARs) of local children's services were implemented, to be carried out for local children's services every three years. This replaced a number of previous different inspections, with the inspection of children's social work and social care services being the responsibility of the Commission for Social Care Inspection (CSCI).

From 1 April 2007 the CSCI has merged with Ofsted and two related inspectorates to form the Office for Standards in Education, Children's Services and Skills – the new Ofsted. It is envisaged that this will lead to a closer harmony of inspections and will resolve issues related to inspection between the 'social work and social care' and 'educational' elements of children's services. This may be good news for social work and children's services, as much social work involves networking across services and greater harmonisation may reduce the problems social workers often face in relation to the 'gaps' in services.

Future trends

In 2007 there was a clear suggestion that the government is considering developing specialist, rather than generic, social work training – to have separate training and qualifications for those working with children and those working with adults, on the basis that it would allow for greater specialist knowledge to be obtained and skills to be developed in relation to the particular 'client group'. This would not be a completely new idea, the post Second World War period up to 1971 saw social work being divided into the Children's Departments, the Welfare Departments and the Mental Welfare Departments, with specialist training for each of the three areas. Critics of the current proposal for specialist awards suggest that it would lead to the fragmentation of social work and reduce the flexibility of the workforce to move between different areas of social work. More recently, it seems that for the moment at least it has been decided that social work training should remain generic, although there are plans to offer more support to children's social workers, particularly immediately following qualification, via the creation of a newly qualified social worker status (NQSW) and the development of an induction programme to help strengthen their skills, knowledge and confidence (CWDC, 2008).

There have recently been several other initiatives proposed for qualified social workers. As part of the Care Matters White Paper (DCSF, 2007) the government proposes a pilot scheme of Social Work Practices – small groups of social workers in autonomous organisations (perhaps rather like GP practices) – to see if this type of potentially less bureaucratic way of working will deliver better outcomes for children. Additionally, there is a proposal for each Government Office Area in England (of which there are nine) to have two agency-based Remodelling Social Work Delivery pilot schemes between 2008 and 2011, which will seek to deliver innovative evidence-based practice approaches within a less bureaucratic structure.

The CWDC, related to the GSCC Options for Excellence programme, is developing New Types of Worker Projects in relation to children's social work, which will aim to achieve better outcomes for the most vulnerable children and young people.

All three of these projects appear to have in common:

- a desire to increase the time qualified social workers work with children and families directly;
- a desire to reduce the administrative burden on social workers;
- a desire to make the social work with children role more attractive to current and potential social workers, to improve recruitment and retention.

How successful the projects will be, individually or collectively, with regard to these three areas is not yet clear.

In 2008, following extensive consultation, the GSCC produced its review *Social work at its best: A statement of social work roles and tasks for the 21st century* (GSCC, 2008). This adopted the IFSW definition of social work quoted at the start of this chapter, and proposed a generic statement of social work roles across work with children and families. Specific areas where it suggests a qualified, experienced social worker should be used in relation to children include:

- making judgments about whether a child is at risk and needs to be moved to a place of safety;
- being the LP for the local authority in relation to a child in care;
- working with children involved in court proceedings;
- instances where legislation or guidance stipulates that a registered social worker (for example, an independent reviewing officer for children in care) must lead a core assessment in safeguarding children cases.

While there is much of value in the review, it does straddle the worlds of adults' and children's services rather uneasily at times. One commentator suggested that this was because 'the world has moved on since 2006 [when the review was launched] and the agendas of the two departments of health and children, schools and families have diverged' (Brindle, 2008, p 2).

At a wider level than role definition or agency organisation, it is clear that the context within which children's services operate is an increasingly global as well as local context (Barker, 2007) and children's social work has a key role to play in dealing with problems related to asylum seeking or child trafficking.

A recent report about Newcastle upon Tyne (ECPAT UK/Save the Children, 2007) highlights the new types of problems which children's social work has to confront in a globalised world. It estimated that in Newcastle, between March 2005 and May 2006, sixteen children had possibly been trafficked, including seven Somali girls who had gone missing from care, who were suspected to have been brought into the UK for underage forced marriage. The report suggested that raising awareness of such possible problems among all those who work with children was necessary, as well as providing specialist services such as safe, supervised accommodation.

How the specialist nature of social work services for children will develop within Children and Young People's Services Departments, whose focus is primarily on universal services is not clear, but, if the ECM agenda is to be fulfilled for those children and families who are 'hardest to reach', the need for both universal and specialist services to prosper and work jointly is crucial.

Summary

This chapter has looked at the nature of social work with children, and the contribution of social work to the ECM agenda. It has shown that social work has changed significantly over the past two centuries. With the current challenges facing children, families, and those who work with them, it is likely that social work will, and must, continue to change as part of the process of seeking to improve the lives of children in the UK.

References

Barker, R., Reynolds, J. and Place, M. (2005) 'Action research, self esteem, and children and young people in need with "medium range" difficulties', *Journal of Social Work Practice*, vol 19, no 3.

Barker, R. (2007) 'Globalisation and child protection: towards an analytical framework', *International Journal of Child and Family Welfare*, vol 2, pp 14-27.

BASW (British Association of Social Workers) (2007) 'Role of social workers', available at www.basw.co.uk.

Blewett, J., Lewis, J. and Tunstill, J. (2007) *The changing roles and tasks of social work – A discussion paper*, London: GSCC.

Brindle, D. (2008) 'Low-key plans for social work futures', *The Guardian*, 2 April.

Butler-Sloss, E. (1988) *Child abuse in Cleveland*, London: HMSO.

Campbell, B. (1988) *Unofficial secrets: Child sexual abuse – the Cleveland case*, London: Virago.

Coughlan, J. (2007) quoted in *Community Care*, 21 June 2007, p 8.

CWDC (Children's Workforce Development Council) (2007a) *Briefing Note – Social work with children, their families and carers*, London: CWDC/GSCC, also available at www.cwdcouncil.org.uk/advice/leadershipmanagement.htm.

CWDC (2007b) *Common Assessment Framework for Children and Young People: Managers' guide*, London: CWDC/The Stationery Office.

CWDC (2008a) 'Leadership and management in integrated working', available at www.cwdcouncil.org.uk/integrated-working/leadership-and-management.

CWDC (2008b) NQSW Pilot Programme, CWDC, available at www.cwdcouncil.org.uk/nqsw/induction-pilots

DCSF (Department of Children, Schools and Families) (2007) *Care matters – Time for change*, London: DCSF.

DfES (Department for Education and Skills) (2005) *Children's workforce strategy – Analysis of responses to the consultation document*, Runcorn: DfES.

DfES (2006) *Care matters – Transforming the lives of children and young people in care*, London: DfES.

DHSS (Department of Health and Social Security) (1974) *Report of the Committee of Inquiry into the Care and Supervision Provided in Relation to Maria Colwell*, London: DHSS.

DoH (Department of Health) (2002) *Promoting the health of looked after children*, London: DoH Publications.

DoH, DfEE and the Home Office (2000) *Framework for the Assessment of Children in Need and their families*, London: DoH Publications.

ECPAT UK and Save the Children (2007) *A report on the evidence and agency responses to child trafficking*, London: ECPAT UK/Save the Children.

Fox Harding, L. (1997) *Perspectives in child care policy*, London: Longman.

GSCC (General Social Care Council) (2006) *Social work education in England – Listening, learning, shaping*, London: GSCC.

GSCC (2007a) *Social Work Education in England: delivering quality, recognising success*, London: GSCC, also available at www.gscc.org.uk.

GSCC (2007b) *Roles and tasks of social work in England*, Consultation Paper, London: GSCC.

GSCC (2008) *Social work at its best: A statement of social work roles and tasks for the 21st century*, London: GSCC.

Harker, R.M., Dobel-Ober, D., Berridge, D. and Sinclair, R. (2004) 'More than the sum of its parts? Interprofessional working in the education of looked after children', *Children & Society*, vol 18, no 3.

HM Government (2006) *Working Together to Safeguard Children – A guide to inter-agency working to safeguard and promote the welfare of children*, London: The Stationery Office.

HMSO (1968) *Report of the Committee on Local Authority and Allied Personal Social Services*, Chair Frederic Seebohm, London: HMSO.

IFSW (International Federation of Social Workers) (2007) 'International definition of social work', available at www.basw.co.uk.

Macleod, N. (2007) 'Registration of the social care workforce – a UK agenda', available at www.socialcaring.co.uk/index.php?option=com_content&task=view&id=10&Itemid=8,

NISW (National Institute of Social Work) (1983) *Barclay Report – Social workers: Their role and tasks*, London: NISW.

NSPCC (National Society for the Prevention of Cruelty to Children) (2007) 'Child protection statistics', available at www.nspcc.org.uk/Inform/OnlineResources/Statistics/ChildProtectionRegisterStatistics/.

TEN

Child and adolescent mental health services and Every Child Matters

Allan Brownrigg

Introduction

The acronym CAMHS (child and adolescent mental health services) is used to describe a range of services and personnel that offer support to children, young people, their families and carers experiencing mental health needs. It is often mistaken as only describing highly trained clinical staff specialising in childhood onset psychiatric conditions. Instead, this broad term captures all people who come into contact with children including health, education and social care professionals. This umbrella concept 'explicitly acknowledges that supporting children and young people with mental health problems is not the responsibility of specialist services alone' (ECM, 2007, p 1).

In general, CAMHS identify, assess and promote mental health for children from birth to age 18. CAMHS also operate, through multi-agency collaboration, a range of assessment and intervention services for children with psychological difficulties, psychiatric diagnosis, or where psychopathology is emerging. Services are not just geared towards children, but the child's needs are viewed in the context of their family system.

Recent epidemiological reports produced by the Office for National Statistics (ONS, 2005) indicate that one in ten children aged between 5 and 16 will have a recognisable mental disorder. Numerically this equates to over one million children within the UK who would benefit from intervention by CAMHS. These statistics are alarming and signify the importance of CAMHS within society. Statistics, however, do not capture every child and their family, so it is possible that the number of children experiencing mental ill-health could be considerably under-reported.

To understand CAMHS and their principles more fully, this chapter will highlight the context in which CAMHS are positioned. Policy drivers and professional practice dilemmas will set the scene and these will be discussed alongside the needs of children, young people their families and carers.

To bring the ECM agenda to life, in particular the aim for children to 'be healthy', the relevant outcomes will be woven throughout the text to demonstrate that these outcomes should not be viewed in isolation, but be immersed in all practice.

Background: shaping CAMHS

Over recent years CAMHS have developed against a backdrop of policy, with several reports documenting a need for improvements in how services are configured, operated and distributed (HAS, 1995; MHF, 1999; DoH, 2004). The political context for the development of these policies has been influenced by recent media and public perception of children as contributors to anti-social behaviour, members of criminal gangs, the 'hoodie' generation, binge drinkers and wild party revellers.

Nevertheless, society has also become more understanding about the negative experiences and difficulties with which many young people live, and we now expect children and young people in need to be helped, and not left to their own self-destructive activity. Acknowledging that children experience upsetting thoughts, feelings and emotions, requires prompt action; it is no longer generally acceptable to expect children to 'pull themselves together' or to simply dismiss their problems with 'what have you got to worry about'.

Changes to family life, higher divorce rates and the increase in step-families, brings attention to the impact that family systems have on childhood psychological needs. These societal developments are illuminated by research findings that highlight onset and maintenance factors contributing to mental disorder within children. Combining both sociological and psychological perspectives can help raise awareness of the emergence of childhood psychiatric difficulties and of changes to the experience of childhood. This evolution in outlook has required CAMHS to develop a repertoire of services to fulfil the needs of policy makers and the changing structure of society, as well as, importantly, to be responsive to the needs of children, young people, their families and cares.

The current position

To appreciate the depth at which CAMHS practitioners operate, an understanding of CAMHS configuration within a tiered approach to the provision of care is essential (HAS, 1995). This tiered approach attempts to create more uniform provision and enables referrers to make informed decisions regarding the appropriateness of services for each child and their family:

- **Tier 1** identifies those practitioners who have regular contact with children, and are those workers from whom children and families are likely to seek help first. They should be able to offer support and advice, respond to questions and advise families of appropriate local services. Opportunities to promote positive mental health and resilience are essential at this level.

- At **Tier 2**, workers have a specific training and skill in assessing and delivering interventions for children and their families. This training will include a specific CAMHS component. These practitioners tend to work in community-based settings and will usually work with the family alone. They are able to offer consultations to families, and deliver training to tier 1 practitioners.
- **Tier 3**, refers to specialist multi-disciplinary teams that offer a wider range of specialist services. These professionals are able to develop complex care packages for children and young people with more severe and enduring disorders. When appropriate these teams could involve several clinicians working with the same family.
- At **Tier 4**, services are provided in very specialist centres or hospitals for those who have the most serious needs.

The CAMHS workforce

Table 10.1: Examples of professionals working within a tiered approach to CAMHS

Tier 1	School teachers, family general practitioners, health visitors, social workers, school nurses, voluntary services working with children and young people
Tier 2	**Uni-disciplinary** Primary care workers, clinical psychologists, educational psychologists, practice counsellors, outreach mental health workers, youth workers, youth offending team workers.
Tier 3	**Multi-disciplinary teams** Clinical psychologists, psychiatrists, social workers, psychotherapists, family therapists, specialist group workers, nurses, occupational therapists
Tier 4	**Specialist services** Staff as in tier 3 but with specialist focus i.e. inpatient units for complex and enduring mental illness, child and adolescent forensic mental health services, services for perpetrators of sexual abuse, eating disorder units, neuro-psychiatry specialist services

It is important to note that many staff will work across the tiers in this model (Table 10.1). Additionally, other professionals who practise in CAMHS include those informed by cognitive behavioural therapy (CBT), creative therapies including art and drama, as well as those whose roots are within the psychoanalytical and psychodynamic tradition. These methodological and therapeutically different approaches, when available in CAMHS settings, have the potential to provide choice for clients. Such services also allow the client's need to be matched to a therapist who has the most relevant skills and competence to meet this need. This clearly promotes the child's opportunity to 'be healthy', by having interventions provided by the most appropriate clinician.

Significant stakeholders within this tiered approach are primary mental health workers (PMHW). They have an important role in bringing together professionals across the tiers, but with an emphasis on directing referrals to the relevant professional service, providing training to tier 1 staff, providing consultations, as well as delivering short-term interventions for children, young people and their families (Whitworth and Ball, 2004). Although primary care services have been introduced as part of the tiered approach to CAMHS, a number of significant developments warrant attention. Ford et al (2003) found that 53.1% of children with significant mental health needs did not access CAMHS services. This could indicate a need for services to be more accessible, for workers at tier 1 to have more training in recognising mental ill-health, and a need to have wider liaison with young people to determine the reasons why uptake is poor. In so doing children could be helped to 'make a positive contribution' to service development, with their involvement being used to strengthen existing provision.

CAMHS in the world of evidence-based practice

CAMHS workers routinely face complex issues that require detailed and clear assessment processors, multi-agency collaboration and a detailed knowledge of suitable interventions. At present, clinicians are also being pushed to deliver evidence-based interventions. The National Institute for Clinical Excellence (NICE) provides a detailed summary of effective interventions for a range of common mental health needs, including depression, bipolar disorder, eating disorders, obsessive compulsive disorder and post-traumatic stress disorder. Obviously these guidelines do not cover all issues as presented to CAMHS, and despite their availability the uptake and application of these to evidence-based practices is limited. Cottrell and Kraam postulate that this is because of:

> inaccessibility of some of the information, inability to interpret the evidence, unwillingness to change practice in the face of the evidence, and the lack of resources to implement some of the recommended changes. (Cottrell and Kraam, 2005, p 114)

Evidence-based practice should be based on a collection of ideas taken from expert opinion, clinical experience, service users and from contemporary research literature (Sherratt, 2005). This approach broadens the perspective held by many practitioners in CAMHS, who are guided by results from randomised controlled trials (RCTs), viewing these as the 'gold standard' for evidence-based ideas. It should be remembered that lack of evidence about a particular practice does not necessarily mean ineffectiveness, but could simply be a sign that more studies are required (DoH, 2004). Practitioners should remember that evidence generated through clinical investigations in one situation may not be as clearly transferred to another situation as authors of published RCTs sometimes suggest. It is important not to accept evidence-based interventions at face value, but rather to approach them more critically (Thompson et al, 2004).

It is argued that when evidence is not available, practitioners can be left to rely on individual ideas, experiences, sensations or hunches (Birgerstam, 2002), although, conversely, this idiosyncratic response has been cited as one component of poor practice (Shooter and Lagier, 2005). It is worth noting, however, that children and their families do not always fit neatly into diagnostic criteria, nor do they all benefit from manual-based programmes of care. CAMHS services are not just for children with 'one size fits all' needs and responses to them should be carefully considered, carefully conceptualised and thoughtful. Practitioners should remember the uniqueness of each individual, and a decision to apply a particular approach should be made in respect of its appropriateness, acceptability, risks, benefits and cost (Wolpert et al, 2006). This requires CAMHS practitioners to be aware of their strengths, while also being able to acknowledge their limitations.

Training issues

Traditional CAMHS tier 2, 3 and 4 services have developed in an era of medical dominance. These CAMHS teams tend to have a consultant psychiatrist as the lead clinician. In many instances they also act as team managers, holding responsibility for the effective running of the service. Some would argue that this responsibility takes them away from clinical practice. A challenge therefore exists in operational terms, to free up psychiatrists from management duties to deliver training, consultation to other agencies and supervision, as well as clinical interventions. Shifting from a dominance of medical management to an integrated perspective on the management of services should provide a wider depth and breadth of interprofessional issues to be captured.

Although a wide range of professionals are represented throughout the CAMHS workforce, the range of interventions offered by each clinician can be limited. Although psychiatrists and psychologists would claim to have undertaken a detailed professional training enabling them to deliver a range of high-quality interventions, the reality in practice is often different. It is more usual for CAMHS practitioners to have a general training in which different therapeutic models are explored, with practice placements being used to enable integration between theory and practice. Thereafter many choose a single therapeutic model to pursue at postgraduate level.

Evidence-based practice centres on clinical interventions, therapeutic modalities and psychopharmacology, but a question that remains unanswered is: who would be most suited to delivering psychological therapies? Given the multi-professional culture in which CAMHS are positioned, and the requirement to deliver evidence-based psychological therapy, it would be prudent to employ staff regardless of professional background, and equip them with training and skills to be competent in delivering the necessary therapy (Cottrell and Kraam, 2005). Evidence is not yet available to show that one professional group is more skilled than another at providing evidence-based psychological therapies. Despite this, core professional training and level of qualification on graduation continues to be the determining factor in deciding level of competence, perceived skill and clinical responsibility, that is to say, the higher your academic award the higher expectations are in practice.

Case example: Changing team culture

When working in CAMHS team as a lead practitioner, Allan had management responsibility for all clinical staff including psychiatrist, psychologist, nurses and social workers. The roles of the team were as follows: a psychiatrist diagnosed and took responsibility for clients with most severe needs; a psychologist provided therapy; nurses assisted the psychiatrist and psychologist in carrying out care plans and treatment interventions; social workers attended to family-based difficulties.

Allan realised that the set up of the team had developed based on an assumption about roles. What became significant was that, other than medical roles and responsibilities held by the psychiatrist, the duties expected of all team members were the same, that is, assessment, care planning and intervention. All report templates and agency policies were adhered to in the same manner, and all supervision was through a lead clinician, other than that required for professional registration purposes; a hierarchical culture existed.

When the culture was addressed the team was able to shift beliefs, and could begin to focus on common and core skills required to fulfil duties. Reaching agreement about similarities resulted in individuals developing special interests, and this proved to be an excellent resource for the team. Having a workforce committed to open communication also contributed to the team's ability to work effectively.

An ongoing issue central to working in CAMHS is deciding which specialist training should staff pursue. While CBT has the clearest evidence base, the evidence is not yet sufficient to say that this should be the core therapeutic modality within CAMHS. Workers should be enabled to pursue their own interest, but to do so within an overarching strategic overview. This will enable training to be contextualised against staff development opportunities, professional development, promotion opportunities and, most importantly, against the needs of clients. A workforce which has far reaching competencies will provide a greater level of service when compared to a workforce of staff with the same interest.

Multi-agency working

Given the complex therapeutic and professional roles adopted within CAMHS, it can be confusing for other professional groups to understand the exact duties that are considered core business within each setting (Potter et al, 2005; Salmon,

2004). It is also inevitable, as with all professional groups, that a specialist language is employed. In the case of specialist CAMHS at tiers 3 and 4, this may be in the form of medical diagnosis, clinical conceptualisations, psychotherapeutic interpretations or treatment regimes. This language dilemma is important to understand, for there is a risk that practitioners assume the message being conveyed is also being understood. Our obligation is to speak in a way that can be heard clearly and understood, which enables dialogue to occur and, through a clear professional and inter-relational approach, we should endeavour to summarise, clarify and agree what has been said. Following these principles should make it easier to develop plans that are informed by a common language, and in which there should be less potential for miscommunication.

Case example: Misunderstandings

A CAMHS practitioner attended a case conference at a local authority children's home where he provided an account of his work with Jimmy, an eight-year-old boy who had a medical diagnosis of obsessive compulsive disorder (OCD). He ploughed through interpretations and conceptualisations, offered accounts of evidence-based interventions, discussed key cognitions and disorder-specific psychological models, before concluding with a detailed intervention plan.

Within this plan he suggested that staff working with Jimmy may have been providing too much reassurance to Jimmy when his anxiety began to grow. By seeking reassurance Jimmy was learning that all anxiety had the potential to be catastrophic. In reducing the reassurance-seeking behaviour, Jimmy would be helped to increase his ability to tolerate anxiety rather than seek reassurance as soon as he felt troubled.

What the CAMHS practitioner thought to be an eloquent and clearly articulated plan was met with silence. No questions were asked and no staff member expressed concern about the plan he had put forward. The author took this as a sign of agreement. When the minutes of the meeting were produced and the amended care plan shared it stated: 'no staff member should reassure Jimmy – we have to make him as anxious as possible'. This was clearly a misunderstanding and, if acted on, could have had a significant detrimental impact on Jimmy's health. When addressing this with the manager of the home, the CAMHS practitioner discovered that the staff had not understood what he had said, but had not raised questions because they thought they were being 'stupid'.

Language is clearly significant for interprofessional working, but it is not the only dilemma facing CAMHS practitioners. It is commonly reported that professional services fail to work together (Singh et al, 2005), have different priorities (Easen et al, 2000), and do not have a clear understanding of one another's role (Salmon, 2004). To resolve these difficulties and to enable CAMHS services to flourish, several strategies could be employed. Priority could sit with a clearly developed multi-agency agreement addressing the core business of CAMHS. In addition, opportunity to outline the Common Core of Skills and Knowledge available across the service would also be of benefit. This would demonstrate the vast range of skills available and also enable the workforce to identify gaps that require training. This multi-agency vision could be shared, endorsed and used to build on existing inter-agency partnerships (Kurtz and James, 2002). This ideology would then be reviewed in the context of local policy and service development priorities, but if we remember it is the needs of children and their families that bring us together, the drive for this level of collaboration should become clearer. In devising plans that bring agencies together, communication becomes clearer and opportunities for children to 'be healthy' are achieved by a connected workforce.

Change in workforce personnel is inevitable and, as such, constant reminders in the form of multi-agency collaboration and training for other professionals should exist to ensure that the CAMHS message becomes reality not just rhetoric. It is often the case that new initiatives are promoted while they are being developed, but little attention is paid to keeping them in mind thereafter. If staff move on, their replacements may not be aware of all services available to them and to the children and families they represent. To resolve this, induction of new staff members across health, education and social care organisations could include a discussion of and representation from CAMHS to educate other professionals about the structure and philosophy of these services. This may also act as a useful introduction to multi-agency working and allow its strengths to be shared.

The contribution of CAMHS to the CAF

Salmon (2004) suggests that children will present with problems to a wide range of agencies. It is therefore crucial that these agencies have a basic awareness of children's mental health needs. However, studies have also highlighted that referrers feel unable to accurately identify those children at risk of developing mental disorders (Potter et al, 2005), which could result in problems going unrecognised (Stallard et al, 2007). CAMHS staff therefore have a clear opportunity to offer a perspective on mental health and well-being, family dynamics and systems, resilience and risk factors, psychopathology, and parenting. This perspective can be explored via direct work with families, or through other professionals bringing cases for consultation.

The strength CAMHS have in sharing these perspectives lies in their ability to offer a multi-professional analysis of the information being presented. They can also reflect on different theoretical models of communication with children and key people within their system. They are also equipped to offer a sequence of psychometric assessments which can help discover additional issues for consideration. Singh et al (2005) also suggest that assessment should focus on developmental and emotional process, this being a key area for many CAMHS practitioners. The development of clearly formulated assessment is crucial in respect of children 'being healthy' and 'staying safe'.

Case example: Balbinda

During a core group meeting regarding allegations of neglect in respect of Balbinda, aged six, a detailed assessment report had been delivered by the social worker. The report documented the child's needs and enabled the group to hear how the information had been obtained and the process of analysis that had taken place. It became apparent that the social worker was very confident in their work, assessment and interpretations. Within the report they had documented that they thought the child had an attachment disorder but when questioned by the CAMHS psychologist about what this meant, the social worker was unable to clarify.

A discussion followed, with the psychologist providing an overview of attachment disorders, their aetiology and a description of how this may manifest itself in relation to Balbinda. This resulted in a change to the assessment, as it was felt that the presentation from the psychologist allowed clarity to be reached. If the social worker had the prior opportunity to liaise with CAMHS, these issues may have been addressed. It did, however, prompt an agreement for a greater level of future collaboration, especially in cases in which issues of mental health were significant.

Specialist CAMHS could therefore have an important role in training and educating other professional groups about children's mental health needs, especially in relation to practitioners undertaking assessments as part of the CAF. Although to achieve this we must progress our thinking around multi-professional communication and joint training, as this will provide the context in which these developments can take place.

The contribution of CAMHS to ECM

A different way of working: early intervention and resilience

In 1998 the DoH provided funding for 34 projects under the banner of CAMHS innovation projects. Ten projects were awarded funding under the remit of 'promoting early intervention to reduce or prevent mental health problems'. In their evaluation of these projects Kurtz and James (2002) highlighted several important issues:

- children and young people want accessible services;
- services should be offered in non-stigmatising settings;
- assessments should be sensitively conducted;
- assessments should be conducted by staff able to engage children, young people and their families;
- interventions should be tailored to individual needs; and

- follow–up care should be organised, planned and, where appropriate, include other support services.

These proposals fit within the Common Core of Skills and Knowledge for the children's workforce and, if adhered to, will promote children's opportunity to 'be healthy'.

It is well documented that preventive programmes are effective at reducing the risk of developing mental health problems (Place et al, 2002). They are cost effective (Scott el at, 2001) and can increase a parent's ability to cope with their child's mental health needs (Kurtz and James, 2002). It is also reported that interventions which target resilience can have a positive impact on the child's self-esteem and confidence. When conducted within a context of family-based difficulties, resilience–based interventions can also help families to become more cohesive and adaptable in their functioning (Brownrigg et al, 2004).

Case example: Sam

Sam, aged ten, lived with his mum Karen, who had a diagnosis of depression. Sam often felt sad when his mum would cry; he often felt that he had done something wrong and wished he could make his mum better. Karen described herself as always low in mood, feeling unable to do nice things for Sam and worried that her illness was going to make Sam different from all the other children. Although Sam's home situation had not been brought to the attention of his teachers it was clear that when mum was poorly Sam's ability to concentrate in class was reduced. Sam would then get into trouble for not doing his homework, which he then took to be a further example of why his mum's illness was his fault. Sam's core belief was: 'She is disappointed in me'. He became more concerned about his mum's illness and worried that she would be taken into hospital again. Through a process of psycho-education about depression, Sam and Karen became aware of the impact of the illness. They were able to hear each other's perspectives, which allowed Sam to hear the illness was not his fault. Sam engaged in a resilience-based intervention, which helped boost his self-esteem, engaged him in local activity groups and developed his bonds with other people who cared for him. His energy was refocused toward friendships, as these reduced when he was worrying about his mum. By focusing on these areas, Sam's ability to bounce back from family difficulties was astonishing and his relationship with his mum changed from feeling he was to blame, to having a clearer understanding about the illness. Karen was also helped to see how Sam's resilience could be boosted, which eased the guilt she had that she should always be doing something with Sam.

Despite literature supporting resilience-informed practice, the focus for CAMHS continues to be children and young people with established disorders. This is largely due to children presenting difficulties that require intervention to prevent further deterioration. Also, witnessing a child suffer is a cause of great concern for parents and professionals. An ideal position, even if the aim is optimistic, would be the creation of widespread prevention programmes which seek to reduce the likelihood of mental health problems emerging, especially in those children and young people who are at greatest risk. Stallard et al (2007) suggests that such universal programmes could reduce the impact of mental health problems and enable children to cope better with future problems. These preventative measures may also be seen as more acceptable to children and their families (Bailey, 2005). Given the negative connotations and stigma people with mental health needs experience, opportunity to receive help before the burden of illness grips people's lives is a favourable option for future development.

Case example: FRIENDS

The FRIENDS Emotional Health Programme is a ten-session manualised intervention which combines cognitive, behavioural and physiological strategies 'to teach children practical skills to identify their anxious feelings and to learn how to relax, to identify unhelpful anxiety-increasing thoughts and to replace these with more helpful thoughts; and how to face and overcome their challenges' (Stallard et al, 2007, p 33). This programme, which is delivered by school nurses, is offered as part of the school day. Results indicate improvement in the levels of reported anxiety and improvement in self-esteem. Teachers also report that the programme facilitates a positive environment in which worries can be discussed.

The success of programmes such as FRIENDS could lie in the development of an emotionally intelligent community. By enabling discussion of mental health and promoting resilience within society, for example in schools, we are more likely to be able to express and address difficulties as they emerge, rather than hiding them and allowing problems to build up. In order to develop our positive engagement with preventative programmes we need to have confidence that their outcomes are beneficial to children, not just in the immediate but for the future. Follow-up studies are therefore required to build evidence, although the biggest shift required will be one of attitude. Concern will be raised if funding is shifted from those at risk to those only potentially at risk. However, evidence has shown that many adult-based disorders have their roots in childhood, so enhancing the availability of preventive programmes now, could result in a reduction of adult mental illnesses, and thus lead to positive outcomes for the future.

Challenges and opportunities for CAMHS

Addressing gaps in provision

A difficulty to be considered in CAMHS is the boundaries endorsed by age criteria. Teams usually operate within a clear age bracket of 0-16 but, when children reach their 16th birthdays, it can be difficult to determine which service will best respond to their needs as they enter adulthood. At these transitional times young people can fall between children's and adult services. This point is addressed in the NSF for Children, which states that:

> all children and young people from birth to their eighteenth birthday who have mental health problems and disorders [should] have access to timely integrated high quality, multidisciplinary mental health service to ensure effective assessment treatment and support. (DoH, 2004, standard 9)

At present, the structures to achieve this require attention, as each locality can interpret the guiding policy differently and difficulties in provision will therefore emerge.

Case example: Difficult transitions

In one local health authority there were three different CAMHS teams: one team worked with children aged 5-16, another 0-18, and the third 16-18 year olds. The route between services and progression to adult services was fraught with difficulty because all adult services started from age 18. In the team whose provision ended at 16, ongoing support occurred on a case-by-case basis; liaison with adult services relied on goodwill and positive professional contacts. A concern often raised was the potential for inequality across the services. It was also of note that these children deemed to be behaviourally difficult to manage were easier to be diverted away from services by virtue of age. Was it possible that an ethic of care and moral code of practice was being overlooked? Politically the management structures of these agencies felt little could be done. It was felt that this reluctance had its roots firmly set in historical responses to service development: the fact the service had always been like this prevented any opportunity for appropriate restructures.

It would be a welcome development if CAMHS services could be more flexibly operated in respect of age classification. The challenge for providers is to ensure that children's needs are met by workers who have appropriate knowledge, skills and values. In a study of young people aged between 16 and 25, and their experiences of mental health services, Smith and Leon (2001) established that many young people were disappointed with the provision they received and found that they did not easily fit into child- or adult-focused services.

Case example: Sanjay

Sanjay, aged 16, attended CAMHS for three years and had usually attended two therapeutic sessions per week. He had taken six overdoses and deliberately self-injures by cutting his arms and legs. He had the same key worker in CAMHS, but has also had involvement with other team members who have offered specific interventions. His care plan listed the role for each professional involvement, and his review notes highlighted the progress he was making towards his therapeutic goals with each worker.

On transfer to adult services he met a new psychiatrist, nurse, social worker and support worker. His care plan was reviewed in the context of adult services and was amended resulting in psychiatric reviews taking place every three months, alongside weekly support sessions with his nurse. The detailed psychological management plan developed in CAMHS was no longer in place and his identified goals had been changed by professionals and not by Sanjay.

Sanjay contacted his previous CAMHS worker to discuss this sudden change and they could not understand the reasons why in the space of a week he had gone from two therapeutic sessions in CAMHS to practical support focusing on independent living in adult services. The CAMHS worker challenged the psychiatrist only to be told "we do not have the resources" and "he's not a child anymore".

As can be seen from Sanjay's experience (which is, sadly, not uncommon) a change to age classification between child and adult services results in clients being viewed through different developmental lenses. This experience confirms the high levels of assumption-based decision making that exist within practice. Practitioners often make decisions about what they think is best and efforts are therefore needed to ensure work is client centred. In doing this, children will be better supported to 'be healthy' and 'stay safe'.

CAMHS approach to care is rooted in systemic ideas, developmental psychology, parenting interventions and behavioural management. A whole systems approach is adopted, which engages children, young people and their families, and the wider professional network. These relationships help guide the assessment and intervention process. In Sanjay's case adult services had a focus on psychopathology and its management, although their primary goal was to help improve Sanjay's ability to function. A child passing through CAMHS receiving a systemic oriented approach, combined with an individual therapy may receive very different support once they make the transition to adult services. Adult services are, of course, equipped to deal with the needs of young people making the transition to their care, but the transitional process will only be successful if workers across the services can engage more fully with one another. Rather than a referral ending the CAMHS involvement, opportunity to have a phased transfer from one service to another could resolve the problem of care plans and psychological interventions being dramatically changed on transition. It is therefore suggested that to provide the opportunity to review, support and develop this transitional process, attention should be paid to inter-agency scrutiny in each social care and health locality. There is also a need to review age parameters in order to promote seamless services.

There are also opportunities for workers to cross over their usual practice boundaries, for example adult staff could spend time in CAMHS and vice versa. This may go some way towards developing a workforce equipped to cope with the difference of approach required when working with clients who have different developmental abilities. A difficulty is that CAMHS clinicians often worry that the way they engage adults is not suitable, and on occasion can be patronising. They worry that the language used is not age appropriate. Similarly, adult team colleagues fear that their interaction with children and young people is parental and critical. Addressing these assumptions and worries through practice would improve interprofessional work, and could allow skills, ideas and values to be shared and enhanced. By updating core skills our ability to assess, engage and intervene across age ranges could be maximised.

24-hour care

A further development requiring action concerns the provision of 24-hour care. CAMHS had a national target to provide 'on call' and 24-hour specialist cover by December 2006. While this continues to be a work-in-progress in many localities, what has become clear is that the operational elements of 24-hour on-call services are fraught with difficulties. In some instances there is a shortage of staff, no access to psychiatrists, differences of opinion over what constitutes an emergency and no formal protocols to guide the process (Storey and Stratham, 2007). In order to ensure children can be seen rapidly and by suitably experienced and qualified professionals, future provision should be planned and fully resourced; for this to occur the opportunity must be grasped sooner rather than later. Existing with a skeleton service will only provide a partial solution and, unless effort is made to improve the situation, children who need help the most may be missed. With regards to ECM this will have a significant negative impact on their chances of 'being healthy' and 'staying safe'.

Accessible services

Alongside the provision of effective interventions, a further challenge for CAMHS, in particular at tiers 2 and 3 is ensuring that services are accessible, timely and resourced to suit local needs. This requires ongoing evaluation, strategic planning and insightful management structures. In addition, the experiences of children, young people and their families should be gathered in order to progress provision. It is the author's belief that the more approachable and explicit we are when evaluating services, the more able we will be to deliver services based on multiple perspectives. If we exclude the views of children and their families from service development we run the risk of developing services which are misguided. Service user involvement is therefore essential, although we must acknowledge that it is not easy. We must lower our defences if we are to accept critical commentary about what we can improve, in doing this we can shape services in which the views of our clients are of paramount importance.

Summary

CAMHS are, by their very nature, idiosyncratic. Practitioners within these teams have varied professional backgrounds, training requirements, values and ideologies. Each professional group locates its practice within a discrete professional code of conduct, and they are guided by different requirements for regulation, supervision and CPD. It is often these differences that make CAMHS a potentially fraught and politically sensitive area in which to practise. This chapter has aimed to provide an opportunity to learn more about these issues. It has also demonstrated, in the following areas, there is a need to:

- consider how to promote communication between professionals which is accurate and purposeful;
- develop role appreciation of workers across the CAMHS spectrum, to ensure an understanding is reached about who can help and under what circumstances this help can be provided;
- focus on the development of evidence-based practice in which professionals, children and families are enabled to articulate their thoughts on not just what helped, but exploration of the mechanisms that underpinned positive change.
- clarify the links between best practices, good-enough practice and evidence-based practice.
- develop a skilled workforce through advanced specialist training.

To address ECM in CAMHS requires achievement in all of the above areas. If practitioners employed to deliver services to children are unable to communicate effectively, to articulate their hopes and difficulties, challenge others, assess, plan or monitor the provision of care, it will be children whose lives are disadvantaged. Timely, accessible and clear services are essential, conducted by workers and services with complementary skills, and delivered under a shared ethos of care.

References

Bailey, S. (2005) 'The National Service Framework: children come of age', *Child and Adolescent Mental Health*, vol 10, no 3, pp 127-30.

Baruch, G. and James, C. (2003) *The National Framework for Children, Young People and Maternity Services: The mental health and psychological wellbeing of children and young people*, Report from a consultation with users of child and adolescent mental health services, London: DoH.

Birgerstam, P. (2002) 'Intuition – the way to meaningful knowledge', *Studies in Higher Education*, vol 27, no 4, pp 431-43.

Brownrigg, A., Soulsby, A. and Place, M. (2004) 'Helping vulnerable children to become more resilient', *International Journal of Child and Family Welfare*, vol 7, no 1, pp 14-24.

Cottrell, D. and Kraam, A. (2005) 'Growing up? A history of CAMHS (1987-2005)', *Child and Adolescent Mental Health*, vol 10, no 3, pp 111-7.

DoH (Department of Health) (2004) *National Service Framework for Children, Young People and Maternity Services: Change for children – every child matters*, London: DoH.

Easen, P., Atkins, M., and Dyson, A. (2000) 'Interprofessional collaboration and conceptualisations of practice', *Children & Society*, vol 14, pp 355-67.

ECM (Every Child Matters) (2007) *Child and adolescent mental health services*, available at www.everychildmatters.gov.uk/health/camhs.

Ford, T., Goodman, R. and Meltzer, H. (2003) 'Service use over 18 months among a nationally representative sample of British children with Psychiatric Disorder', *Clinical Child Psychology and Psychiatry*, vol 42, pp 1203-11.

HAS (Health Advisory Service) (1995) *Together we stand: The commissioning, role and management of child and adolescent mental health services*, London: HMSO.

HAS (2002) *Together we stand: Child and adolescent mental health services, a thematic review*, London: HMSO.

Kurtz, Z. and James, C. (2002) *What's new: Learning from the CAMHS innovation projects*, Summary, London: DoH.

MHF (Mental Health Foundation) (1999) *Bright futures: Promoting children and young people's mental health*, London: MHF.

ONS (Office for National Statistics) (2005) *Mental health of children and young people in Great Britain*, London: HMSO.

Place, M., Reynolds, J., Cousins, A. and O'Neil, S. (2002) 'Developing a resilience package for vulnerable children', *Child and Adolescent Mental Health*, vol 7, no 4, pp 162-7.

Potter, R., Langley, K. and Sakhuja, D. (2005) 'All things to all people: what referrers want from their Child and Adolescent Mental Health Service', *Psychiatric Bulletin*, vol 29, pp 262-5.

Salmon, G. (2004) 'Multi agency collaboration: the challenges for CAMHS', *Child and Adolescent Mental Health*, vol 9, no 4, pp 156-61.

Scott, S., Knapp, M., Henderson, J. and Maughan, B. (2001) 'Financial cost of social exclusion: follow up study of antisocial children into adulthood', *British Medical Journal*, no 323, pp 191-7.

Sherratt, S. (2005) 'The journal club: a method for occupational therapists to bridge the theory–practice gap', *British Journal of Occupational Therapy*, vol 68, no 7, pp 301-6.

Shooter, M. and Lagier, A. (2005) 'Child and adolescent mental health services: roles, functions and management in an era of change', in R. Williams and M. Kerfoot (eds) *Child and adolescent mental health services: Strategy, planning, delivery and evaluation*, Oxford: Oxford University Press, pp 487-500.

Singh, S.P., Evans, N., Sireling, L. and Stuart, H. (2005) 'Mind the gap: the interface between child and adult mental health services', *Psychiatric Bulletin*, vol 29, pp 292-4.

Smith, K. and Leon, L. (2001) *Turned upside down: Developing community based crisis services for 16-25 year olds experiencing a mental health crisis*, London: MHF.

Stallard, P., Simpson, N., Anderson, S., Hibbert, S. and Osborn, C. (2007) 'The FRIENDS Emotional Health Programme: initial findings from a school-based project', *Child and Adolescent Mental Health*, volume 12, no 1, pp 32-7.

Storey, P. and Stratham, J. (2007) *Meeting the target: Providing on call and 24 hour specialist cover in child and adolescent mental health services*, Final report summary, London: Thomas Coram Research Unit, University of London.

Thompson, C., Cullum, N., McCaugham, D., Sheldon, T. and Raynor, P. (2004) 'Nurses, information use, and clinical decision making – the real world potential for evidenced based decisions in nursing', *Evidence Based Nursing*, vol 7, pp 68-72.

Whitworth, D. and Ball, C. (2004) 'The impact of primary mental health workers on Referrals to CAMHS', *Child and Adolescent Mental Health*, vol 9, no 4, pp 177-9.

Wolpert, M., Fuggle, P., Cottrell, D. Fonagy, P., Philips, J., Pilling, S., Stein, S. and Target, M. (2006) *Drawing on evidence: Advice for mental health professionals working with children and adolescents*, 2nd edn, London: CAMHS Publications.

ELEVEN

Every Child Matters: current possibilities, future opportunities and challenges

Richard Barker

The agenda for improving services for children that is being progressed via the ECM programme is a challenging one, which calls on those who work with children to work effectively and creatively within their own professional areas of expertise, and alongside others from different professions and with different areas of expertise within children's services. To do this, it is important for those involved to be clear about the roles and responsibilities of different professional colleagues. The preceding chapters in this book have outlined these for key areas of children's services.

It can be seen that some areas, such as nursing, have a longer history and clearer idea of their boundaries with regard to professional expertise and regulation than others, such as playwork. It has also been seen that, as well as differences within professional groups, there are professional and ideological differences between professional groups about the nature of children and how services should be offered to them. The different professions use different terms for the children and families with whom they work, which often indicates slightly different ways of viewing the relationships between the professional and those who are the focus of intervention, be those terms 'clients'; 'patients', 'service users' or 'experts by experience'.

As suggested elsewhere in this book, agencies and individual workers may also be influenced by and mirror different perspectives on children within society, and legislation and policies about children, and it is helpful to consider this when reflecting on the contributions of the different chapters. In a classic text, Fox Harding (1997) usefully identified four perspectives that are influential with regard to children and children's services at both a policy and a practice level.

1. Laissez faire and patriarchy

This value position is characterised by a view that the role of state in child welfare should be a minimal one, and the privacy and sanctity of parent–child relationship should be respected. Underpinning this is a view that it is 'best' for society to have a 'slimline state' and 'best' for parents and children if the state 'leaves families alone' because 'parents know best' based on the special (biological) bond between parents and their children. In extreme cases, such as major child abuse, it is necessary that the state should intervene and (usually) find a new permanent home for children. It should also be noted that a 'weak' state tends to align with, and reinforce, patriarchy in families.

2. State paternalism and child protection

In contrast to the laissez faire approach, proponents of this perspective favour more extensive state intervention, not least to protect children from poor parental care. Thus, state paternalism sets higher standards for childcare than the laissez faire approach. The child's needs are seen to be paramount; children are viewed as essentially vulnerable, with need for nurturing and care rather than self-determination. The importance of parental duties towards children is highlighted, rather than parental rights over children. The state and its representatives have the duty and the capacity to judge what is best for children and, where necessary, to provide it.

3. Modern defence of the birth family and parents' rights

This perspective is founded on the belief that birth/biological families are important for children and parents, and that psychological bonds should be maintained wherever possible. To facilitate this, however, the state should not have a minimalist role. The state should support families and maintain them whenever appropriate. It is seen that class, poverty and deprivation have major impacts on parenting, so the state has a major role in providing support for families to counteract these. In the last resort, if children come into care, the state should focus on returning them if at all possible to their birth family and, in the interim, support links and contact.

4. Children's rights and child liberation

This perspective emphasises the importance of the child's own viewpoints and wishes, and is more inclined to see the child as a separate entity with rights to autonomy and freedom, rather like adults. This stresses the importance of calling into question the control of children by state or by parents – the child is a subject, rather than an object, and there is an emphasis on their competence and strength. Within this viewpoint there is some variance of opinion about the extent of children's responsibilities as well as rights; and 'liberationists' are more radical than 'protectionists' in relation to the extent of children's rights at different ages and stages.

It is useful to reflect on this typology when considering the contributions of different individuals and professions to the children's agenda – it is not unusual for differences over decision making with regard to children being as much to do with the different value positions held by the professionals involved as to do with the 'facts' of the situation.

Case studies

With the contributions of the different authors of this book in mind, how is the ECM agenda being pursued in practice? Many children will, during their lives, receive services from one or more agencies singly. However, for more complex problems and life situations there will be a need for the intervention of multiple agencies. Three case studies are provided below to illustrate how different needs present different problems and opportunities for the multi-disciplinary network of agencies.

Case Study 1: Alan

Alan is four months old and has Downs Syndrome. He is the first child of Lisa and Toby, white middle-class parents in their late 30s, who live in a detached 'executive' house in a commuter town. They had been trying unsuccessfully for several years to have children prior to Alan's birth. His condition had not been diagnosed during pregnancy; his parents are struggling to come to terms with the situation. They were very reluctant to take Alan home with them when Lisa was discharged from hospital; both have told the midwife that they do not feel a 'bond' with him, they cannot imagine bringing him up and think it would better for him and them if they didn't.

As a newly born child with disabilities Alan is 'a child in need' who will already have been the subject of contact from a range of medical professionals, including hospital consultants, neonatal nurses, a midwife and a health visitor. It is likely that he will be the focus of a CAF assessment, probably with the health visitor as lead professional. There are now indicators that he is being rejected by his parents, so a children's services social worker is likely to become involved with the family to assess the situation more fully. The social worker will arrange more specialist assessments and, at the same time, provide the parents with the opportunity to seek practical advice and, if possible, be counselled on their feelings about their unexpected position and desire to reject Alan. This social worker might be a hospital-based social worker from the hospital in which Alan was born, a community-based social worker in the community where Alan's family lives, or a combination of both. The primary focus of the interventions is likely to be on supporting Alan's upbringing within his birth family setting if possible, which may involve the provision of a range of services including early years services, Children's Centre support and/or respite care. If it is decided that Alan's safety and welfare will be best met by his entering local authority care, further reviews and planning would take place to ascertain if his needs throughout childhood could be met within his birth family, or whether alternative long-term arrangements, such as adoption, are necessary to safeguard and promote his welfare throughout childhood ('permanency planning'). To achieve any of these outcomes for Alan multi-disciplinary working and multi-agency co-operation will be vital. It will also be necessary for Alan's parents to be clear about the different roles and responsibilities of the different workers involved. Because of Alan's age he is not in a position to be an active participant with regard to decisions, but at some later point in his childhood, notwithstanding his Downs Syndrome diagnosis, it will be both appropriate and necessary to consult him about decisions that might need to be made, taking his views into account, having regard to his age and level of understanding.

Case Study 2: Rebekah

Rebekah is six years old and has been the subject of neglect by her mother, who has substance misuse problems, for several years. Recently she has been either missing a lot of school or arriving at school dirty, unhappy and with a series of minor injuries following 'accidents'. Her mother is Afro-Caribbean and dependent on state benefits, her father was Serbian but no longer lives in the UK as he was deported following drug-related offences. Rebekah has no contact with him, nor with her two older mixed-race half-siblings, who were taken into care following abuse by their father and have subsequently been adopted.

Clearly Rebekah is a 'child in need' of services as defined by the 1989 Children Act, and there is also a strong possibility that she is a child whose welfare needs safeguarding; who is in need of a detailed, comprehensive assessment. As there is a risk of significant harm in her case, she needs a level 4 assessment section 47, based on the LCSBIS procedures. Assessment of her needs will need to take into account the possibility of immediate short-term action to protect her. This will need to provisionally establish if she can remain with her birth mother and be safe or, if she needs to live elsewhere, whether there are members of her extended family who can care for her or if she will have to be admitted to local authority care. As she has older half siblings who have been adopted, it seems probable that there will not be members of her extended family who can care for her, but this is an assumption that should be tested carefully rather than being taken for granted too readily. It will be important to try to achieve the co-operation of Rebekah's mother in the assessment. Even though Rebekah is not at an age and level of understanding to make the final decision about her future, her wishes and feelings about her situation and any plans made are very important to both ascertain and consider. The assessment of Rebekah will need to have regard to her health and educational needs, so the involvement of professionals such as school nurses, teachers and possibly paediatricians and health visitors, collaborating to plan for her childhood will be crucial. It is likely that specialist substance abuse services may be currently involved with Rebekah's mother; in any event they will need to be involved and consulted to assess the family situation. Planning for Rebekah in the long term will need to consider how the five ECM outcomes can be best achieved for her. This will need to take account of the fact that she is of dual-heritage status and that she has a mother who may continue to have substance misuse problems. It will also be important for Rebekah that there is a key worker who will co-ordinate the planning and intervention process in relation to her, because the multi-agency and multi-disciplinary planning and intervention necessary to best meet her needs will be complex.

It may be that, although most children are best raised by at least one of their birth parents, in Rebekah's case another family placement, such as adoption, will better meet her needs. However, finding adoptive parents who could 'match' Rebekah's parents' heritages will be extremely difficult. If adoption was appropriate for Rebekah the adopters of her siblings would be considered as possible placements. The different value positions outlined in Fox Harding's schema are highlighted through a case such as Rebekah's, particularly in relation to the different views of the rights of the parent versus the rights of the state to take away those rights.

Case Study 3: John

John is 15 years old, and lives with his white, English, working-class mother and father in state housing on the edge of a large city. His father is long-term unemployed as a result of a series of heart problems; his mother works as a school cleaner. John's involvement for several years with a local 'gang' has resulted in several appearances in youth court; his parents were increasingly distraught about this and wanted him to be 'taken into care'. Recently, John has reported feeling unwell and has been diagnosed with leukaemia. He is refusing to have treatment; his parents state that if he will not have treatment they cannot have him living with them as it is "killing his father with the stress". John is therefore living with short-term foster parents supervised by the local authority.

Unlike the cases of Alan and Rebekah, John is of an age where he is probably able to make decisions about his own situation and have them respected to a large extent. Thus, in relation to his medical condition, it needs to be assessed whether or not he is 'Gillick competent' (*Gillick v West Norfolk and Wisbech AHA* [1985]), that is, that his level of understanding is such that he is able to make informed decisions about medical treatment and it is not simply 'up to his parents to decide'. Because of his position in care, the local authority is legally sharing parental responsibility with his birth parents. To enable John to be healthy, enjoy and achieve, and achieve economic well-being it is clearly in John's best interests to seriously consider accepting medical treatment. At the same time, he needs a stable living situation with support to be able to deal with whatever his medical condition leads to, and he needs to be able to engage effectively with the educational system so that he can maximise his educational success. His situation is a challenging one and there are likely to be a number of different professionals involved in his life: he will have a local authority children's services social worker working with him because of his family situation and care status; he may benefit from support from a CAMHS worker to help him consider the options available to him; there will be a paediatrician and specialist nurses involved; as well as a hospital based-social worker; and effective educational services need to be provided for him, regardless of whether he is at home, in a children's home, a foster home or in hospital. Thus, effective co-ordination of these services delivered to him will be essential.

These three case studies illustrate how making decisions about children is not a clear cut process, but one that needs to be done with care following reasoned debate and the sifting and evaluation of information. It also necessitates professionals considering their own, and others, value positions regarding such matters as their theories of child development, their professional values, and their views on the rights and responsibilities of parents and the state in relation to children. They all highlight that, while parents have responsibilities for and rights in relation to children, the welfare of the child should be paramount in making decisions and plans about, and delivering services to, the child in question.

What are the opportunities and challenges?

Moving on from these case studies, we will now conclude with brief discussion of some of the main current and future opportunities and challenges within the ECM arena.

Integration and co-ordination of policy at a central level

Centrally, while the development of the ECM agenda was led by the DfES, other departments were also involved, including the DoH, the DCMS and the Home Office. Paradoxically, while a key aim of ECM was to produce better 'joined-up thinking and action', there appears to have been, at times, an absence of 'joined-up thinking and action' between some of these departments, which has thus confused the ECM agenda. However, there are clear signs that the government has realised the necessity of tackling this issue. There are also clear signs of the continuing and increased priority that government is giving to the children's agenda – it was probably a symbolic statement of this that led to Gordon Brown's first public duty as new Prime Minister being a visit to a Children's Centre. Additionally, following the reorganisation of the DfES into the DCSF in the summer of 2007, the National Children's Plan discussed in Chapter One was launched in December 2007.

Management

Much of this book has been about individual and collective professional practice and, while it is not the central purpose of this book, it is important to remember the impact of management with regard to practice and change and children's services. Hartley and Allison's analysis of the role of leadership in the modernising and improvement of public services has relevance for the ECM change agenda. They suggest that the complexity and importance of inter-organisational leadership has not been sufficiently recognised in public services modernisation programmes and in the complex new situations outcomes cannot be specified in advance (Hartley and Allison, 2006). If this is correct, it might be assumed that this presents a major stumbling block for the ECM objectives to be achieved, as much of the endeavour is precisely based on achieving outcomes specified. However, Hartley and Allison go on to suggest that there is a solution: to further empower workers, not only to 'implement', but to 'enact' and enable the 'emergence' of the most appropriate outcomes. They recommend that models of leadership in the UK public sector need to be updated because:

> Innovation cannot be pre-specified, and therefore part of the role of leadership is to provide a framework and to observe, nurture, shape and reflect as well as to implement. (Hartley and Allison, 2006, p 232)

Such a solution appears to chime with a move away from rigid targets that is currently taking place across the public sector – it potentially empowers workers in the children's workforce more than in a traditional bureaucratic, hierarchical structure, but at the same time it places a greater responsibility on those workers to achieve effective change for the users of their services.

The political context

Since the autumn of 2007 it has appeared to be increasingly possible that the Labour Party might not form the next government, a general election being due no later than the summer of 2010. If this was to be the case, it is clear that there would be some subsequent changes to services to children and families, but what these would be and at what pace they would occur is, in 2008, unclear. Although it could be said that all the main UK political parties seek power via occupying the middle ground of politics, it would seem that a Conservative government (the most likely alternative to a Labour government) would seek to achieve their commitment to improving the welfare of children, and mending a 'broken society', by having measures which would differ from the current government's in that they would:

- involve a smaller public sector and a larger voluntary sector than is currently the case;
- strengthen the rights of parents and teachers;
- provide greater freedom to schools;
- increase support for two-parent families and marriage;
- make society more 'family friendly'.

In the area of children's welfare, one of the few specific pledges that the Conservatives have made is to increase the numbers of health visitors by 4,200 to provide support for families, by diverting money from Sure Start outreach services.

> Health visitors are the kind of support that parents want. Not laissez-faire: just leaving parents to get on with it. Not nanny state: some bureaucratic system telling parents what to do. Just sensible, practical, personal support that people trust. That's what the modern Conservative Party is all about. That's what I mean by making this country more family friendly. (Cameron, 2008)

Thus, the Conservative Party is suggesting that in relation to services for children – or perhaps, more correctly, services for families – they will aspire to being neither laissez-faire nor nanny state, and the details of what such a position would involve for these services remains to be seen.

The relationship between universal and specialist services

There is undoubtedly a tension in delivering the ECM agenda between providing specialist services for 'children in need' and general services for all children, as has been illustrated in discussions relating to the roles of health visitors for example. In an attempt to tackle this on a process level, the Integrated Children's System (ICS) has recently been introduced by government as an electronic case record system to record information that can then be shared and used to bridge the gap between those children and families whose needs can be met by universal services and those whose need to access more specialist services (levels 3 and 4 in the CAF). The ICS, which attempts to bring an integrated approach to assessment, planning, intervention and review, is underpinned by the electronic case record system which seeks to 'record, collate, analyse and output the information required'.

There are three elements to the system:

- a conceptual framework for assessment, planning, intervention and review – the Framework for the Assessment of Children in Need (DoH et al, 2000; as outlined in Chapter Nine).
- a set of data requirements for children's social care, based on individual children's records, intended to facilitate both holding data across agencies and using the data to plan and produce services;
- case study examples of how data can be used to produce reports.

It can thus be seen that the ICS, ContactPoint, the CAF and the assessment framework are intended to provide more effective integration of information to improve services to children. While this is a laudable aim, in the short term at least there have been implementation 'glitches' (not least the postponement of launching ContactPoint) and, anecdotally, growing concern has been expressed that servicing the system has reduced the time that social workers can spend in direct work with children. However, early results showed 'a greater focus on outcomes and objectives leading to better plans ... [better] multi-agency information sharing ... and easier access to information' (Royal Holloway, 2006).

Related to the ICS, recent guidance on the ECM website (ECM, 2007), builds on Figure 11.1 to indicate the relationship between common and specialist assessments and the ICS.

Figure 11.1: Integrating children's services

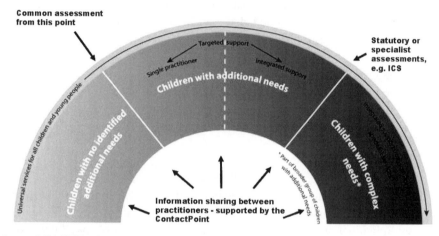

Source: ECM, 2007, p 2

In itself this tool does not provide for more integrated services, or solve information-sharing problems between professionals who may not know, let alone trust, each other, or solve the specialist–universal dilemmas that are related to professional issues, resources and strategic challenges. Despite these challenges, services for children do appear to be becoming more 'seamless' and integrated in some areas. A number of contributors to this book have noted the significance of Children's Centres as actual and potential vehicles for responding to the challenge of making all tiers of services accessible to children and families.

Evidence-based practice

The use of an EBP approach is one that has been greeted with some enthusiasm in most sectors of children's services, particularly those relating to health, although to a lesser extent in social work. EBP, developed in the 1970s in medicine, can be defined as:

> the conscientious, explicit, and judicious use of current best evidence in making decisions about the care of individual patients.... [It] means integrating individual clinical expertise with the best available clinical evidence from systematic research. (Sackett et al, 1996, p 71)

This is obviously an attractive proposition on which to base interventions – to use the best available 'facts' about dealing with a type of 'problem' as the basis for dealing with new examples of that 'problem'. However, in many of the cases facing children's services, the 'facts' may be disputed, as may the nature of the 'problem(s)' and the 'evidence'. Additionally, different professions have broadly different world views and ways of understanding; to generalise, medicine is often more positivistic, social work more interpretivist (McLaughlin, 2007). All at times need to provide the best services they can to children, based on our knowledge of 'what works', while recognising that we often do not know 'what works', and that 'what works' is indeed a value laden concept. It has been suggested that EBP itself involves four key problems:

- the problem of 'evidence';
- the problem of applying 'evidence' to 'practice';
- the relationship between 'evidence' and values;
- the relationship between providers and users of services'. (Frost, 2005, p 128)

Thus, research evidence comes from different epistemological standpoints: there are disputes over theories, methods, concepts and so on. 'Evidence' gained in one situation, for example how best to deal with truancy, often cannot be easily applied to other, individual, unique situations of truancy. 'Social problems', 'knowledge' and 'what works' are as much, if not more, value concepts as technical concepts. Finally, professional interventions should be about negotiating between providers and users rather than the slavish imposition of the 'best approach based on the evidence' regardless of the wishes of the service user (Frost, 2005).

It is also true that some forms of practice with children, such as CBT by a CAMHS professional, are more susceptible to an EBP approach than others, for example facilitating freely chosen play by a playworker. It may be that it is therefore more appropriate to talk about evidence-informed practice (EIP), as this allows more scope for subjectivity, values, negotiation and partnership, while at the same time having regard for the necessity to provide effective services to individual children and to show how 'targets' and 'outcomes' are being achieved.

Empowering patients, pupils, users and carers?

A key theme of the ECM agenda is that of empowering those who are actually or potentially in receipt of services. As mentioned earlier, across children's services different terminology is used to describe children (and family members) and, to some extent, the terminology does reflect and reinforce different social constructions of the power relationships between those who deliver services and those who are the recipients of services. Health services tend to refer to 'patients'; education services to 'pupils'; social work services to 'users' (and 'carers'). All at times can also refer to 'stakeholders'. Changing terminology, or developing a shared terminology, will not in itself increase the power of those who are the recipients of services. The ways in which more empowerment might be achieved will present challenges for different sectors of children's services and for interprofessional activity.

How might user-participation be improved and facilitated? SCIE has produced a guide for social care services which suggests that:

> Organisations need to adopt a 'whole systems' approach to participation to affect change or improvement in their services. This approach suggests that there are four parts of service development that need to be considered: culture; structure; practice; review. (Wright et al, 2006, p 6)

SCIE suggests that this approach is not an alternative to other methods of enabling children's participation, rather it unites the overarching themes from different approaches into one unified framework. It would appear that the nature and type of the organisation is likely to have an impact on improving participation – in general it is easier to bring about change in a small voluntary organisation than a large statutory organisation. However, SCIE does evidence a number of initiatives as exemplars of good practice, one of which, the RAPP project, is illustrated below.

Case example: Rights and Participation Project, Humberside

Rights and Participation Project (RAPP), funded by Social Services, and the Warren Centre, with support from Connexions Humber.

Established in 1997, RAPP offers independent advice, support and advocacy to children and young people, aged between nine and 21 years old, who are in need or at risk.

How participation has been developed

Participation and listening to young people is emphasised throughout RAPP's literature and job descriptions and is stated in the 'RAPP code' – the value base of the service. Young people have been involved in designing service information, staff recruitment and service development, by completing the 'snapshot review' questionnaire. The project works with children and young people to help them voice their views on the issues that are important to them and to influence local services. A number of young people's groups operate at the project: young trainers who run workshops for social work students and foster carers; a 'Bog Off Bullies' group that campaigns about the exclusion of young people with disabilities; a drama group for young people in care; and a peer-mentoring service. RAPP works alongside other agencies to influence local services and the council. A regular young person's newsletter keeps young people and partner agencies informed about developments and opportunities at the project. RAPP also works with social services and other local agencies to ensure that young people are involved in shaping the services that they receive and that service providers listen to their views.

Changes or improvements as a result of children and young people's participation
- Children and young people have been involved in the consultation for the appointment of an appropriate disabled young people's advocacy worker.
- RAPP has reinforced the value of involving young people with other local agencies and is regarded as a key driver in promoting a children's rights approach.

Source: Adapted from Wright et al, 2006, p 73

It is clear that it is in principle easier to bring about change in a small voluntary organisation, rather than a large statutory one, and that it is more difficult to engage with young children, children with disabilities and those who have English as a second language (or not at all). However, if the UNCRC and the principles in legislation such as the 1989 Children Act are to be realised, then engaging children more effectively in the decisions and services that shape their lives is not desirable but essential.

A new role for working with children?

In part because of the debate about universal and specialist services and in part because of the desire to improve services, during the consultation over the changes to the children's workforce there was a proposal to develop the workforce via the greater adoption of what was seen to be the potentially transformational role of the pedagogue, a role more commonly found throughout the rest of Europe:

> The pedagogue sets out to address the whole child, the child with body, mind, emotions, creativity, history and social identity. This is not the child only of emotions, the psychotherapeutical approach, nor only of the body, the medical approach, nor only of the mind, the traditional teaching approach. (Moss and Petrie, 2002, p 174)

Training for pedagogues is underpinned by the concept of the shared 'life space' between child and pedagogue, and there is emphasis on learning and working in groups, and developing expertise in practical and creative skills (Cameron, 2007). It was suggested that pedagogues, supporting children's overall development and 'upbringing', would be graduate-level qualified and would work at the key levels of practitioner, senior practitioner, service manager and strategic leader. As such they would provide an integrated, unifying approach to working with children within the wider social policy context.

The government's response on the workforce consultation noted that:

> The idea of exploring a social pedagogue role attracted relatively few responses. Generally, those who did respond welcomed the principles underpinning the role, but felt that the skills that such a role would need are in fact the same as those needed by a good social worker. There was also some resistance to, and scepticism about, the creation of new professions. (DfES, 2006, p 14)

However, while the CWDC consultation did not result in acceptance of the widespread take up of the pedagogue role in the UK, it has been suggested that:

> The strategy as a whole does indicate a movement in the direction of a more pedagogic approach to children's services, focussing on children's needs and outcomes throughout childhood. There is an understanding that those working with children will be most effective if they cooperate closely to meet children's needs; needs that may span numerous specialities. (Farook, 2007, p 27)

Recently, the government has appointed a high-level Expert Group, to advise on taking forward the National Children's Plan (DCSF, 2007). It has also funded a pilot social pedagogue project in residential children's homes, and has asked the Expert Group to advise on the merits of introducing new professional disciplines, including social pedagogy, into the children's workforce.

The pace of change

Responses to the pace of change have varied within and between different local areas, so that some have embraced and developed the ECM principles and services more readily than others. Farook (2007) has suggested that the future will be more uncertain for members of the children's workforce, and that they will need to be more adaptable to work towards what will be less easily defined goals, and become more skilful in identifying their roles as problems solvers in changing and changeable situations. It is also clear that the 'problems' that are engaged with by professionals and agencies must be viewed within the cultural, economic and political context (Parton, 2006).

In all three case studies in this chapter, multi-agency and interprofessional working is necessary to achieve successful outcomes for the children and families concerned. Such working is not always easy, and the different structures, professional and, at times, personalities involved in agencies and the local context can be highly influential. Thus, clarity about professional roles and objectives is important if there is to be positive experience of working together, which can then build trust between professionals and agencies. However, the role of team membership and team culture in influencing behaviour should not be underestimated. It has been suggested, implicitly or explicitly, by all the contributors, that progressing the ECM agenda will involve workers being able to accept change within their professions and in the ways they work with other professions. This is more difficult for individual professionals to achieve by themselves than if it is facilitated and supported by management and organisations.

It has been suggested that the professions represented within this book are all moving towards versions of practice based on EBP but, as Lawler and Bilson have noted, 'change such as implementing EBP involves challenging long held assumptions and altering established patterns of behaviour' (Lawler and Bilson, 2005, p 202).

Anning et al (2006) suggest, on the basis of their research into multi-professional teams working with children, that key factors to facilitate change include: shared procedures; clear lines of accountability; role clarity and a sense of purpose; dealing with different conditions of service, different role and career expectations, and status/hierarchy barriers; leadership vision; transparent structures for communication with partner agencies; agreed strategic objectives and shared core aims; co-location of service deliverers; acknowledging professional diversity; awareness of the impact of change on those who use the services; the need for 'specialist skill retention'; and ongoing support for professional development.

While some of these factors do not at all times or in all instances apply to the wider children's workforce progressing the ECM agenda, most of them do to a lesser or greater extent, and the size of the list illustrates the extent of the challenge.

Nevertheless, while, paradoxically, at a time of change and reorganisation for agencies and workers change can often be harder to achieve, if it is not achieved it is the children who are in need of services who will suffer the most.

At a government and social policy level there is a clear agenda about, and commitment to, improving the position of, and services to, children and families. In the last decade there have been major changes and developments that have led to improvements in the services to children.

As discussed in Chapter One, the DCSF has recently produced the first ever National Children's Plan (DCSF, 2007). Clearly this plan will be influential in seeking to bring about change at a policy level, across central and local government and at a practice level within the agencies and professions that interact with children and families. Policy interacts with and shapes practice; practice interacts with and shapes policy. The range of professions and services that work with children need to be aware of how they can best interact to work with one another to serve children and families.

It is hoped that this book will play a part in helping those who work with children, now and in the future, to understand one another's roles and responsibilities more clearly to be more flexible, skilful and effective in their vital work with each other, and with and for children.

References

Anning, A., Cottrell, D., Frost, N., Green, J. and Robinson, M. (2006) *Developing multi-professional teamwork for integrated children's services*, Maidenhead: Oxford University Press.

Cameron, C. (2007) 'Social pedagogy and the children's workforce', *Community Care*, 9 August 2007, pp 24–5.

Cameron, D. (2008) 'Yes, we can get the change we really want', Speech to Conservative Party spring forum, 15 March.

DfES (Department for Education and Skills) (2006) *Government's response to the consultation on the children's workforce strategy*, London, DfES.

DCSF (Department for Children, Schools and Families) (2007) 'What is the Children's Plan about?', available at www.dfes.gov.uk/popularquestions/

DCSF (2008) *Building brighter futures: Next steps for the children's workforce*, London: DCSF.

DoH (Department of Health)/DfEE (Department for Education and Employment)/Home Office (2000) *Framework for the Assessment of Children in Need and their families*, London: DoH.

ECM (Every Child Matters) (2007) *ICS, CAF and ContactPoint – an overview*, available at www.everychildmatters.gov.uk/_files/ICS%20CAF%20and%20ContactPoint%20overview%20Nov%202007.pdf

Farook, F. (2007) *Future generations – The children's workforce 2007*, London: Demos/CWDC.

Fox Harding, L. (1997) *Perspectives in child care policy*, London: Longman.

Gillick v West Norfolk and Wisbech AHA [1985] 3 All ER 402.

Frost, N. (2005) 'A problematic relationship? Evidence and practice in the workplace', in A. Bilson (ed) *Evidence-based practice in social work*, London: Whiting & Birch.

Hartley, J. and Allison, M. (2006) 'The role of leadership in the modernization and improvement of public services' in D. Mayle (ed) *Managing innovation and change*, 3rd edn, London: Sage Publications.

Lawler, J. and Bilson, A. (2005) 'Towards a more reflexive research aware practice', in A. Bilson (ed) *Evidence-based practice in social work*, London: Whiting & Birch.

Moss, P. and Petrie, P. (2002) *From children's services to children's spaces*, London: Routledge.

Parton, N. (2006) *Safeguarding children: Early intervention and surveillance in a late modern society*, London: Palgrave Macmillan.

Royal Holloway, University of London (2006) 'Integrated children's systems, early findings 2006', Presentation, London: Royal Holloway, University of London, available at www.everychildmatters.gov.uk/socialcare/integratedchildrenssystem/presentations/.

Sackett, D.L., Rosenberg, W., Gray, J., Haynes, R. and Richardson, W., (1996) 'Evidence based medicine – what it is and what it isn't, *British Medical Journal*, no 312, pp 71-2.

Wright, P., Turner, C., Clay, D. and Mills, M. (2006) *The participation of children and young people in developing social care*, London: SCIE.

Index

A

Abbott, L. 67
accountability 9
Ace Children's Centre, Oxfordshire 142
Acheson, D. 96
achievement *see* enjoyment and achievement
adventure playground movement 130
advisory boards and Sure Start Children's
    Centres 80, 84, 85, 86
after-school play provision 130
age and rights of children 8
Agenda for Change Key Skills Framework 116
Allen of Hurtwood, Lady 130
Allison, M. 192-3
Anning, A. 31, 67, 68, 200
annual performance assessments (APAs) 17
Area Child Protection Committees (ACPCs)
    21
Ashcroft, J. 31
Ashington Audit Group 115
asylum seekers and social work 165
'authentic' leadership approach 69
Avis, M. 123
Aynsley-Green, A. 16, 111

B

Barlow, J. 80
Beckford, Jasmine 8, 157
Bedford, H. 122
Bilson, A. 200
Birth to Three Matters Framework 63, 69
birth/biological families perspective 188
birthweight and future health 113
Blewett, J. 150
Bowlby, J. 59
Brett, P. 121
Brindle, D. 165
British Association of Settlements and Social
    Action Centre 130
British Association of Social Work (BASW)
    148
Broadhead, P. 50, 53
Bronfenbrenner, Urie 35-6
Brown, F. 129
Brown, Gordon 192

C

Cabinet Office: New Relationship with
    Schools 46
CAMHS *see* child and adolescent mental
    health services

care *see* children in care
Care Matters (Green Paper) 19-20
Care Matters (White Paper) 164
Care Standards Act (2000) 149
carers *see* support for families and carers
Cheesman, B. 129
child and adolescent mental health services
    (CAMHS) 22, 169-83
  CAMHS nurses 100, 103, 106, 107
  challenges and opportunities 179-83
    accessibility and evaluation of services
      182-3
    gap in provision at transition age 179-82
    provision of 24-hour care 182
  context 170
  early intervention and resilience projects
    177-8
  and ECM aims 169-70, 177-9, 182, 183
  language and misunderstanding 175
  prevention programmes 178-9
  and social work 155
  tiered approach 170-3
  workforce 171-7
    and evidence-based practice 172-4, 196
    and multi-agency working 169, 171, 174-6,
      177, 181-2
    training issues 173-4
child health and well-being as ECM aim 5
  and CAMHS 171, 176, 178, 182
  and early years services 72-3
  and education 54
  inequalities in child health 96
  and maternity services 119-20
  and National Children's Plan 24
  nursing and policy 95-6
  and playwork 137
  and social work 155-6
  and Sure Start Children's Centres 82, 83,
    88-9
Child Health Promotion Programme 83
child poverty 6, 23, 24
child protection
  'children in need' assessment 31, 150, 154-5,
    159, 189-92, 194
  definition 21
  and ECM aims 156-9
  focus on 147, 150, 161
  government recommendations 9
  and need for interprofessional working 29
  and nursing
    designated child protection nurses 107
    need for nurse training in 101, 105, 106
  official responses to child abuse 8

child protection register 157
child trafficking and social work 165
childbirth
  medicalisation 112
  see also maternity care; midwives
childcare
  availability and affordability 63
  and Extended Schools 48
  historical context and demand for childcare
    59–60
  quality of services 63–5, 89
    recruitment and retention of workforce 65
    training and qualifications of workforce 64
  and reduction in 'free play' provision 131
  and Sure Start initiative 79–80, 83, 89
  Ten Year Childcare Strategy 12–13, 61
Childcare Act (2006) 51, 61, 63
Childcare Bill (2005) 51
Childcare Group Workforce Teams (CGWTs)
  116
Childcare Sufficiency Assessment 63
childminding 60, 64, 79, 82, 83
children: legal definition of child 8
Children Act (1946) 8
Children Act (1989) 7–8, 51, 67, 158, 198
Children Act (2004) 5, 7, 47, 61
  database of children 16–17
  and information sharing 30
  inspection mechanisms 17–18, 163–4
  and safeguarding children 21
Children and Young People's Plans (CYPPs)
  19–20
children and young people's services 45, 163,
  166
children in care 19–20, 150, 156, 160, 191–2
'children in need' *see* child protection
children with disabilities 156, 189–90
Children, Young People and Families
  Workforce Development Council
  (CWDC) 6, 10–11
  see also Children's Workforce Development
  Council
Children's Centres *see* Sure Start Children's
  Centres
Children's Commissioner for England 15–16,
  30
Children's Departments 8
Children's Information Service 63
Children's Minister 23
Children's Plan *see* National Children's Plan
Children's Play Council 137–8
Children's Services Departments 149
children's services
  inspection frameworks 17–18, 163–4
  see also child protection; social work
Children's Trusts 20, 24

children's workforce
  change and flexibility 199–200
  'climbing frame' of qualifications 6
  development of 10–11, 102
  early years workforce 65–9
  education workforce 52–4
  key policy challenges 65–9
    and playwork workforce 140–3
  maternity workforce 114–16, 123
  nursing and challenges for workforce 99–101
  pedagogue role 198–9
  and playwork 132–5, 140–3
  recruitment programme 136
  and Sure Start Children's Centres 87–8
  valuing staff as recommendation 9
  see also interprofessional/multi-agency
    working; training and qualifications for
    children's workforce
children's workforce action plan 24
Children's Workforce Development Council
  (CWDC) 6, 10–11, 136, 141, 153–4, 163,
  164, 199
Children's Workforce Network 10
Children's Workforce Strategy 6, 11
Churchill, H. 80
Climbié, Victoria 8–9, 21, 157
clubs for children 130
collaboration *see* interprofessional working
co-location and collaboration 31–2
Colwell, Maria 8
Commission for Social Care Inspection
  (CSCI) 17, 164
Common Area Assessments (CAAs) 17
Common Assessment Framework (CAF) 6,
  13–15, 194
  and CAMHS workforce 176–7
  and interprofessional working 30, 31, 32, 39
  case study 189–90
  early years services 68
  and maternity care 121
  in schools 45, 53–4
  and Sure Start Children's Centres 91
  and playworkers 136–7
  and social work 154–5
Common Core Curriculum 11, 38
Common Core of Skills and Knowledge 11,
  12, 66
  and CAMHS 178
  and playwork 133, 135
community-based services and social work
  156
Conservative policy and ECM 193
ContactPoint database 16–17, 194
Cottrell, D. 172
Coughlan, J. 161–2
courts and children 7

Cranwell, K. 130
curriculum 54
  National Curriculum limitations 46
  and personalisation 49-51, 55

D

database of children 16-17
Dearing, Lord Ron 45
Department for Children, Schools and
    Families (DCSF)
  Care Matters 164
  Children's Workforce Unit 5-6, 13, 47
  integrated working study 32
  National Children's Plan 13, 23-4, 23-5, 74,
    192, 199, 200
  Sure Start, Extended Schools and Childcare
    group 80-1
Department for Education and Skills (DfES)
    68, 192, 199
  Every Child Matters – Change for children 5
  Every Child Matters – Next steps 5, 9
Department of Health (DoH)
  CAMHS innovation projects 177-8
  *Framework for the Assessment of Children in
    Need and their Families* 31, 150, 154-5, 159,
    194
  Maternity matters 122
  and maternity services 115-16, 117, 119-20,
    122, 123, 124
  and National Service Framework for
    Children 22
  NHS Improvement Plan 23, 98
  planning for nursing workforce 100-1
  positive impact of play 137
Derby Hospital NHS Foundation Trust 116-
    17
detached playwork 131
devolution and children's services 9-10
Directors of Children's Services (DCSs) 18-19
disabled children *see* children with disabilities
domestic violence and maternity services 117
Dyson, A. 49

E

Early Childhood Studies degrees 66
Early Excellence Centres 48, 79
Early Years Development and Childcare
    Partnerships (EYDCPs) 48, 67-8, 79
Early Years foundation degrees 66
early years foundation stage (EYFS) 46, 51, 63,
    64, 65, 69-70
  danger of targets 73-4
  themes and 'principled approach' 70-1
early years professionals (EYPs) 64, 66, 69, 74,
    88

early years services 59-74
  historical context 59-60
  issues and dilemmas 73-4
  and multi-agency working 51, 67-8, 74
  policy developments 62
  quality of services and outcomes 60-1, 63-5
    and management 68-9
  and Sure Start Children's Centres 83
  workforce contribution to ECM 69-73
  and ECM aims 71-3
  see also childcare; playwork; Sure Start
    Children's Centres
ECM *see* Every Child Matters (ECM) agenda
economic well-being as ECM aim 5
  and playwork 139-40
  role of schools 56
  and social work 160-1
  and Sure Start Children's Centres 90
ECPAT UK 165
Edgley, A. 118, 122
education 45-56
  and ECM agenda 54-6
  learning through play 138
  role of social worker 159-60
  standards and testing agenda 45-6, 56
  transition reforms 24
  workforce 52-4
  quality of staff in early years settings 64
Education and Inspection Act (2006) 18
Education Reform Act (1988) 45, 51
education welfare officers 159
educational attainment and National
    Children's Plan 24
Effective Provision of Preschool Education
    (EPPE) 60-1
Elliman, D.A.C. 122
Else, P. 132
emergency protection orders (EPOs) 156-7
emotional intelligence and mental health 179
employment *see* Jobcentre Plus
empowerment 196-8
enjoyment and achievement as ECM aim 5
  and early years setting 73
  and playwork 138-9
  and role of schools 47, 55
  and social work 159-60
  and Sure Start Children's Centres 89-90
Every Child Matters (ECM) agenda 5-25,
    187-200
  case studies 189-92
  ECM as government approach 5-6
  historical background 8-10
  key trends 10-11
  perspectives 187-8
  policy opportunities and challenges 192-200
  political context 193-4

see also child health and well-being; economic well-being; enjoyment and achievement; positive contribution; safeguarding children
Every Child Matters (Green Paper) 5, 9
evidence-based practice (EBP) 195-6, 200
and CAMHS 172-4, 196
problems of 196
evidence-informed practice (EIP) 196
exercise *see* physical activity
Extended Schools and services 22, 47-9, 50, 51
and playwork 135
Sure Start Children's Centres in schools 93

F

family centres 79
'family friendly' policies 61
family structure
and demand for childcare 59
and mental health needs 170
family support *see* support for families and carers
family support workers 116
family–state relationship and intervention 187-8, 191
Farook, F. 199
flexibility 61, 199-200
Ford, T. 172
4Children 136, 141, 142
Fox Harding, L. 148, 187-8, 191
Framework for the Assessment of Children in Need (DoH) 31, 150, 154-5, 159, 194
'free play' 131, 143-4
FRIENDS Emotional Health Programme 179
Frost, N. 196

G

General Nursing Council (GNC) 114
General Social Care Council (GSCC) 150
Options for Excellence programme 164
Social work at its best 165
geographical location and collaboration 31-2
'Gillick competency' 8, 191
governance and multi-agency working 20
Government Statistical Service 112
GPs and ECM agenda 105
Graduate Leader Fund 64
Graduate Teacher Programme 52

H

Hartley, J. 192-3
health *see* child health and well-being; health services
health care assistants 115

health and safety and playwork 130
health services
and NSF for Children 23
and Sure Start Children's Centres 82, 83, 88-9
see also child and adolescent mental health services; maternity care; nursing
health visitors 34-5, 100, 101, 104-5, 108, 111
case study 189
Conservative pledge 193-4
and vulnerable groups 122-3
Henson, C. 118
Hevey, D. 67
hospitals
hospital care and nursing 106, 107
and social workers 155-6
Hudson, M. 61
Huxham, C. 31

I

immunisation programmes 106
individual learning plans (ILPs) 49-50
inequalities in children's health 96
information sharing 15
and early years services 67
and interprofessional working 29-31
ContactPoint database 16-17, 194
Integrated Children's System 30, 31, 157, 194-5
Information Sharing Index 30, 31
inspection frameworks 17-18, 163-4
integrated centres and services 195
and early years services 60-1
and nurses 102-3, 106
and play facilities 136, 141-2
see also interprofessional/multi-agency working; Sure Start Children's Centres
Integrated Children's System (ICS) 30, 31, 157, 194-5
Integrated Qualifications Framework (IQF) 11-12, 66, 135, 141
'Intention to Practice' form for midwives 114
interprofessional/multi-agency working 5, 6, 13, 29-41, 199-200
and CAMHS 169, 171, 174-6, 177
language and misunderstanding 175
case studies 189-92
and children's trusts 20
collaboration 30, 31-2, 67
in practice 38-40
definition 32-6
and early years services 51, 67-8, 74
and information sharing 29-31
interprofessional learning 29, 36-8
and maternity care 117-18, 121, 122-3
and nursing 102-4

and playwork 135-7, 141-2
in schools 53-4, 55
and social work 154, 162-3
and Sure Start Children's Centres 91-3, 103, 104
terminology of 33, 187, 196-7
International Federation of Social Workers (IFSW) 147, 165

J

James, P. 177-8
Jobcentre Plus and Sure Start Children's Centres 63, 81, 82, 84
joined-up government working 13, 192
joint area reviews (JARs) 17, 163-4
joint working *see* interprofessional/multi-agency working
Jowett, S. 60

K

Kids Clubs Network 130
Kirk, G. 50, 53
Kraam, A. 172
Kurtz, Z. 177-8

L

Labour Party 193
laissez faire perspective 187-8, 194
Laming, H. 9
Lammy, David 131
language
  and misunderstanding 175
  terminology differences 33, 187, 196-7
Lawler, J. 200
lead professional role 15, 91, 189
  and nurses 101, 103
  and schools 45, 53-4
  and social workers 154, 165
leadership 192-3
  and early years provision 68-9
  and playwork 142
  and social work 163
  see also management
learning mentors 49-50, 53, 54
Leon, L. 180
liaison nurses 103-4, 107
'liberationist' approach to rights of children 188
local authorities
  and Common Assessment Framework 31
  and director of children's services role 18-19
  early years services and childcare 60, 61, 63, 74
    multi-agency working 67-8

recruitment of staff 65-6
  training of managers 69
  and education 45, 51
  local play strategies 131, 143
  and social work 149
    child protection assessment procedures 158-9
  and Sure Start Children's Centres 81, 86-7
local needs and Every Child Matters 9-10
local play strategies 131, 143
Local Safeguarding Children Boards (LSCBs) 21, 157, 190
low-birth-weight babies 113, 120-1

M

MacBeath, J. 48-9
Machin, A.I. 34-5
Mackett, R. 137
Making Choices in Working with Children, Young People and Families programme 136
management 192-3
  and CAMHS 173, 174
  and early years services 68-9
  and playwork 142
  poor management 9
  and social work 163
  and Sure Start Children's Centres 86-7
Manni, L. 68-9
Manwaring, B. 138, 139
maternity care 111-24
  and choice 113, 119-20, 123
  current position 112-14
  and ECM aims 119-22, 124
  future challenges and opportunities 122-3
  historical background 112
  interprofessional working 117-18, 121, 122-3
  workforce 114-16, 123
    new roles 116-17
maternity support workers (MSWs) 111, 115-16
  case study 116-17
Me Too! Project in Wolverhampton 137
Meads, G. 31
mental health *see* child and adolescent mental health services
midwives 100, 101, 107, 108, 111, 114
  future policy on 119, 122-3
  historical background 112
  and Sure Start Children's Centres 123
  and vulnerability factors 121, 122-3
Milbank, J.E. 60
Moss, P. 45, 51, 64, 198
multi-agency working *see* interprofessional/ multi-agency working

N

National Childcare Strategy 61, 130
National Children's Bureau 141
National Children's Plan 13, 23-5, 74, 192, 199
National Curriculum 46
National Daycare Standards 133
National Evaluation of Sure Start (NESS) 80
National Foundation for Educational Research (NFER) 19
National Institute for Clinical Excellence (NICE) 172
National Occupational Standards (NOS) 135, 151-2
National Out of School Alliance 130
National Professional Qualification in Integrated Centre Leadership (NPQICL) 69, 88
National Service Framework (NSF) for Children 22-3, 96, 98
National Service Framework (NSF) for Children, Young People and Maternity Services 119, 180
National Standards for Under 8's Daycare and Childminding 63
National Workforce Competence Framework for Maternity and the Newborn 116
neonatal nurse practitioners (NNPs) 115, 116
neonatal nursery assistants 116
neonatal nurses 111, 114-15, 118, 120-1
New Relationship with Schools (NRwS) strategy 46
New Types of Workers Projects 164
newly qualified social worker (NQSW) status 164
NHS Improvement Plan 23, 98
NHS Modernisation Agency 116
Nicolson, P. 118-19
North East Centre for Playwork Education and Training 142
Nottingham's Children and Young People's Services 121
nursery schools 60, 61
nursery specialists (Play Therapy) 116
nursing 95-108
  challenges for workforce 99-101
  contribution to ECM 104-7
  and interprofessional working 102-4
  neonatal nurses 111, 114-15, 118
  and policy 95-8
    planning services 97-8
    planning of workforce 100-1
    vulnerable children and families 96-7
  and training 101-2
  and views of children and young people 98
  and views of parents 99
  see also health services; health visitors; midwives
Nursing and Midwifery Council (NMC) 114

O

Office for National Statistics (ONS) 113, 169
Office for Standards in Education, Children's Services and Skills *see* Ofsted
Office for Standards in Teacher Education *see* Ofsted
Ofsted 17, 18
  and early years education 60, 65
  and educational value of play 138
  and playworker qualifications 133-4
  and social work 164
O'Neill brothers 8
Osborn, A.F. 60
outreach and Sure Start Children's Centres 82, 83, 118

P

parenting advisers 23
parenting programmes 122-3
parents
  family–state relationship and intervention 187-8, 191
  health services and views of parents 99
  parental responsibility 7
  rights of parents 17, 188
  Sure Start and parental involvement 83, 90
  see also support for families and carers
participation *see* user participation
partnership working 7
  see also interprofessional/multi-agency working
paternalistic intervention 188, 194
patriarchy perspective 187-8
pedagogue role in children's workforce 198-9
Peel Report 112
personalisation of education 49-51, 55
Petrie, P. 198
philanthropy and social work 149
physical activity 54, 131, 137
Play England/Big Lottery project 143
play and playwork 129-44
  current trends 131-2
    diversity of provision 131
    emphasis on childcare provision 131
    and therapeutic effects of play 131, 132
  definition of play 129
  and ECM aims 137-40, 143
  and interprofessional working 135-7
  national play strategy 24
  and personalised learning 50
  playground renewal 24, 131

recent history of playwork 129-30
workforce 132-5
  and key strategic challenges 140-3
  nature of workforce 132, 140, 144
  roles and functions 132-3, 136
  training issues 133-5, 140-1
play rangers 131, 143
Play Safety Forum 138
playground renewal 24, 131
playgroups 60, 66
Playwork Partnerships 142
Playwork People 2 survey 132
Playwork Principles 129
political context of ECM 193-4
Portsmouth's Maternity Outreach Programme
  118
positive contribution as ECM aim 5
  and CAMHS 172
  and early years services 71-2
  and education 55
  and playwork 139, 140
  and social work 160
  and Sure Start Children's Centres 90
Postgraduate Certificate in Education (PGCE)
  52
poverty
  child poverty 6, 23, 24
  and Sure Start Children's Centres 90-1, 92,
  122
Powell, C. 121
power relations 196-8
Pre-School Playgroups Association 60
primary mental health workers (PMHWs) 172
private, voluntary and independent (PVI)
  sectors
  early years and childcare provision 59, 60, 64
  and social work 149
  voluntary after school play provision 130,
  139

Q

qualifications *see* training and qualifications for
  children's workforce
Qualifications and Curriculum Authority
  (QCA) 54
qualified teacher status (QTS) 52, 64, 74, 88

R

recruitment and retention 65-6, 136, 162
Registered Teacher Programme 52
Remodelling Social Work Delivery schemes
  164
resilience-based CAMHS interventions 178
responsibility: parental responsibility 7
rights

of children 188
  contradictory nature 8
  and rights and responsibilities of parents
  7, 17
  UN Convention 7, 8, 47, 131
  of parents 7, 17, 188
Rights and Participation Project (RAPP),
  Humberside 197-8
Rodd, J. 68
Royal College of Midwives (RCM) 116
Royal Holloway 195
Rumbold Report 64
rural Children's Centre model 85
Rutter, M. 122

S

Sackett, D.L. 195
'safeguarding children' as ECM aim 5
  and CAMHS 176, 182
  definition 21
  and early years services 72
  and interprofessional working 40
  and maternity services 120-1
  and playwork 137-8
  role of teachers 55
  and social work 156-9
  and Sure Start Children's Centres 89
  see also Local Safeguarding Children Boards
Salmon, G. 176
Sammons, P. 61
SATs (Standard Assessment Tasks) 46
Save the Children 165
Schagen, I. 50
School Curriculum and Assessment Authority
  (SCAA) 63
school nurses 105-6, 107
school-centred initial teacher training
  (SCITT) 52
school-leaving age 8, 24
schools *see* education; Extended Schools and
  services
Secretary of State for Children, Schools and
  Families 45, 47
Sector Skills Councils (SSCs) 10, 140
sharing information *see* information sharing
Singh, S.P. 176
Skills for Health Council (SfH) 116
SkillsActive 136, 141, 142
  Playwork People 2 survey 132
  Playwork Principles 129
  Quality Training, Quality Play 134-5
  Skills Needs Assessment for Playwork 140
Smith, K. 180
social care and social work 149-50

Social Care, Children and Young People's
  Sector Skills Council 6
Social Care Institute for Excellence (SCIE)
  197
Social Care Register 149
Social Exclusion Action Plan 122
social pedagogue role 199
social work 147-66
  definition and areas of social work 147-8
  and ECM aims 147, 155-61, 166
  focus on child protection 147, 150, 161
  future challenges 161-4, 165
  future trends 164-6
  historical background 148-9
  inspection mechanisms 163-4
  and interprofessional working 154, 162-3
  and social care 149-50
  training issues 151-4, 161
    specialist training proposal 164
  workforce
    challenges 150-1, 161-2
    good practice 151
    inadequate resources and quality of service
      161-2
    numbers 150
    recruitment initiatives 162
  see also child protection; children's services
Social Work Practices 164
Special Education Needs children and
  National Children's Plan 24
specialist children's nurses 104
specialist versus universal services 90-1, 122,
  194-5
staff *see* children's workforce
Stallard, P. 179
state funded nursery education 60
state–family relationship and intervention
  187-8, 191
Sturrock, G. 132
support for families and carers
  and Extended Schools 48, 50
  as government recommendation 9, 23
  and neonatal nursing 118
  and play settings 135
  and Sure Start Children's Centres 80, 82,
    83, 89
    maternity outreach services 118
  teenage parents 118, 122-3
Sure Start 21-2, 48, 60, 194
  Children's Centres *see* Sure Start Children's
    Centres
  and integrated services 103
  National Evaluation of Sure Start 80
Sure Start Children's Centres 22, 23-4, 38-40,
  63, 65, 79-94
  current developments 80-1

  and ECM aims 88-90, 121
  and interprofessional working 91-3, 103, 104
    and maternity care 117-18, 122
  levels of service provision 81-4
  local authority management structures 86-7
  physical models 84-5
  play facilities 136
  policy issues 90-1
  and schools 48, 50
  universal service debate 90-1, 122
Sure Start Local Programmes (SSLPs) 79-80,
  91-2
Sylva, K. 60-1, 68

T

target-setting and early years settings 73-4
Taylor, C. 138
Teach First scheme 52
teachers
  interprofessional working 53-4
  level of qualification 24, 52-3, 74
  need for continuing professional
    development 50, 55
teaching assistants 53
teamwork 199-200
  see also interprofessional working
teenage parents 118, 122-3
Ten Year Childcare Strategy 12-13, 61
Thornley, C. 115
Together for Children (TfC) 81
training and qualifications for children's
    workforce 6, 10-11
  and CAMHS workforce 173-4
  early years services
    managers 68-9
    workforce 64, 66, 74
  interprofessional learning 36-8
  maternity support workers 116
  midwives 114
  and National Children's Plan 24
  neonatal nurses 114-15
  nurses 101-2, 105, 106
  and playwork 132, 133-5, 136, 140-1
  social work 151-2, 161, 162, 164
  Sure Start Children's Centre staff 88
  teaching qualifications and entry
    requirements 24, 52-3, 74
  see also Integrated Qualifications
    Framework
Treasury Child Poverty Review 23
truancy and education 46, 50
Tunstill, J. 79

U

UK Skills for Care and Development Sector
    Skills Council 10-11
United Nations Convention on the Rights of
    the Child (1989) 7, 8, 47, 131, 198
universal versus specialist services 90-1, 122,
    194-5
user participation
    involving children and young people 197-8
    parents and Sure Start 83, 90

V

Voce, A. 138, 139
voluntary sector *see* private, voluntary and
    independent (PVI) sectors
vulnerable children and families
    and maternity care 117-18, 119-20, 121,
        122-3, 124
    and nursing 96-7, 104, 105, 107
    see also child protection; social work

W

'what works' *see* evidence-based practice
While, A. 118
Williams, F. 80
Wolverhampton Include Me Too! project 137
women: employment and demand for
    childcare 59
workforce *see* children's workforce
Wright, P. 197-8

Y

young offenders and National Children's Plan
    24